HILGARD, Josephine R. (Josephine Rohrs). Hypnotherapy of pain in children with cancer, by Josephine R. Hilgard and Samuel Lebaron. William Kaufmann, 1984. 250p ill bibl index 84-17160. 18.95 ISBN 0-86576-074-8. CIP
Recognizing a dearth of literature on hypnosis in children, these two well-known practitioners share their innovative clinical study of hypnotherapy for children in pain from cancer. They study children in pain during bone marrow aspirations and lumbar puncture procedures. Their therapy is hypnosis. Careful detail is given to the limitations and techniques utilized. Several scales used to assess the degree of readiness for hypnosis are discussed. The authors conclude that a child's development of imagination and fantasy facilitates the acceptance and ease of hypnosis. Their findings are critically compared with the results of others in the field of study. Included also are the theoretical concepts basic to the understanding and use of hypnosis. An extensive list of references adds credence to the work. In conclusion the authors identify areas needing further research to explore the many possibilities of hypnosis as an approach to control pain. Recommended for libraries serving health professionals.—*A.M. Putt, University of Arizona*

D0002722

Hypnotherapy of Pain
in Children with Cancer

Hypnotherapy of Pain in Children with Cancer

JOSEPHINE R. HILGARD,   M.D., Ph.D.

SAMUEL LEBARON,   Ph.D.

FOREWORD BY
FRED H. FRANKEL, M.B., Ch.B, D.P.M.

WILLIAM KAUFMANN, INC.   *Los Altos, California*

The cover art for this book is based on an original design by Galen Rohrs Hilgard.

The following authors and publishers have generously given permission to use quoted material from copyrighted works: From *Clinical Hypnosis: Principles and Applications*, H. B. Crasilneck and J. A. Hall. Copyright 1975 by Grune and Stratton. From *Life with Picasso*, Françoise Gilot and Carlton Lake. Copyright 1964 by McGraw-Hill. Excerpt from *Hypnos*, May/June, 1982. Hypnos Press: Institute of Applied Natural Science, Inc. From The Stanford Hypnotic Clinical Scale for Children, A. H. Morgan and J. R. Hilgard (1978/79) *American Journal of Clinical Hypnosis*, 21:148–169. From *The Youngest Science* by Lewis Thomas. Copyright 1983 by Lewis Thomas, Viking Penguin, Inc. From The Creative Imagination Scale as a Measure of Hypnotic Responsiveness: Applications to Experimental and Clinical Hypnosis, S. C. Wilson and T. X. Barber (1978) *American Journal of Clinical Hypnosis*, 20:235–249.

The research for this book was made possible by a grant from the National Cancer Institute, Department of Health, Education, and Welfare.

Library of Congress Cataloging in Publication Data

Hilgard, Josephine Rohrs.
   Hypnotherapy of pain in children with cancer.

   Bibliography: p.
   Includes index.
   1. Tumors in children—Palliative treatment.
2. Pain—Treatment.   3. Hypnosis—Therapeutic use.
4. Sick children—Psychology.   I. Le Baron, Samuel,
1943–   . II. Title.   [DNLM: 1. Hypnosis—in infancy &
childhood.   2. Neoplasms—in infancy & childhood.
3. Neoplasms—psychology.   4. Palliative Treatment—in
infancy & childhood.   QZ 200 H644h]
RC281.C4H55   1984   618.92′994   84-17160
ISBN 0-86576-074-8

Printed in the United States of America

Contents

Foreword

In their extensive examination of the use of hypnosis to relieve pain and anxiety in children with cancer, the authors have prepared more than a scientific report of a group of youngsters and their families affected by the disease. This comprehensive work will be a sensitive and valuable tool to both parents and professionals involved with the treatment of children suffering from cancer.

The reader shares in some of the many questions and answers that have evolved over a quarter-of-a-century in the Stanford Laboratory, a "think-tank" for people seriously interested in the study of hypnosis.

Distinguished by its rich clinical content, this book bridges the gap between skills and scientific issues in the clinical use of hypnosis, and is a logical extension of the highly regarded work and long-standing concern of its author, Dr. Josephine Hilgard. The work also reflects the enthusiasm, promise, and keen clinical intelligence of her young colleague, Dr. Samuel LeBaron.

Early chapters examine an introduction to the subject of hypnosis, its use to alleviate pain, and the confirmation of pain relief through hypnosis in a study of 24 children and adolescents with cancer. The authors then explore the subjective reports and behavior of a number of individual children in the study, comparing their experiences in an attempt to understand their differences.

A moving chapter that illuminates the psychological roles of parents and professional staff follows, and concluding chapters focus on practice and theory, emphasizing the development of hypnotic talent from earliest childhood.

The book conveys more than a comfortable balance between clinical skills and investigative interests; it develops their mutual importance and strong influence on each other. The authors demonstrate as much care and attention in their clinical observations as they do in their research methodology. The result is a series of cautious yet valuable explanations that enhance and confirm our understanding of hypnotherapy in the treatment of children with cancer.

A focus on the sensitive patient-staff dialogue captures the spirit of the clinical observations of the late nineteenth century, and the authors' conclusions emphasize the value of scientific logic in the interpretation of events. The work is an insightful illustration of the relevance of the methods, findings, and lessons of the laboratory to the study of a clinical population.

The book offers a significant assessment of the separation of therapy-with-hypnosis from the therapeutic influences of the clinical situation and appraises both the difference between the absorbing imaginative fantasy of hypnosis—as opposed to the nonhypnotic memory of pleasant past events—and the difference between perceived pain and anticipatory anxiety. The authors examine the developmental precursors of hypnotic talent, comparing what they describe as "protohypnosis" with the more mature model.

Concluding chapters emphasize the conceptual and developmental aspects, and the authors review their work in the context of prevailing theoretical perspectives. Their investigative findings and clinical observations strongly support the notion of dissociation, and they demonstrate how the study of hypnosis helps to increase our understanding of human development as well as human experience. They traverse the area in a deft and illuminating manner, taking care as few less well-schooled authors do, both to stress the need for further studies and to indicate the areas in which those studies should be pursued. Parents as well as professional staff are deeply indebted to them for an exemplary model of how to encompass clinical compassion, scientific rigor, and theoretical wisdom.

Fred H. Frankel, M.B., Ch.B., D.P.M.
Professor, Department of Psychiatry,
Harvard Medical School;
Past President, International Society
of Hypnosis

Preface

While this book appears as the work of two investigators, recognition belongs to many others.

Foremost among our collaborators are the young patients who wished to try hypnotherapy as a method of relieving pain and anxiety, and who willingly described their experiences of what hypnotherapy was like. Their observations formed the foundation of our clinical studies which, in turn, led to interpretations of the nature of clinical hypnosis in childhood. To maintain confidentiality, this group remains anonymous, with all names changed and with clearly identifying material deleted. We also express our appreciation to the many dedicated parents who played major roles in advancing the quality of life for the patients.

It was Dr. Jordan R. Wilbur's willingness to welcome our scientific team to the Oncology Unit at the Children's Hospital at Stanford that enabled us to start our work in 1975. Dr. Wilbur, director of pediatric oncology, with a master's degree in psychology at Stanford prior to embarking on his medical studies, recognized the potential value of investigating additional psychological aid to children and adolescents with cancer. Ten years ago, when we applied for a grant to support a controlled study of hypnotherapy in the relief of pain in children, this type of research was in its infancy. We continued to enjoy Dr. Wilbur's support when he became Director of the Pediatric Oncology Unit at Presbyterian Hospital in San Francisco. We are indeed in Dr. Wilbur's debt.

Joy N. Dutcher, M.S.W., who was Dr. Wilbur's able associate at Children's Hospital became a valuable consulting link between hospital personnel and our research team.

During the pilot phase of our investigation, in addition to the senior author, the team consisted of Arlene H. Morgan, Ph.D., who was a research associate in the Stanford Laboratory of Hypnosis Research, and David Gettinger, an assistant in psychology. As soon as it was apparent that a short clinical scale to test the hypnotic ability of children was needed (rather than the longer scales already in laboratory use), Dr. Morgan embarked on field studies at several schools to test a population of children 4 to 16 years of age and thus complete the standardization of such an instrument. This scale subsequently became one of the essential foundations of the pain research. During the preliminary study, Dr. Morgan's skills contributed to the treatment of many children.

On the Oncology Unit at Children's Hospital at Stanford, other members of the professional staff facilitated our work. We must be content to mention three: Dr. Thomas F. Long, associate director of the unit with Dr. Wilbur; Dr. Joseph Simon who followed Dr. Wilbur as director; and Joan Berkman-Walsh, R.N., nurse-coordinator of the Oncology Clinic.

The project profited from early conferences with experts in hypnotherapy with children. Among those who generously shared their talents, were Karen Olness, M.D., a member of the Department of Pediatrics at the University of Minnesota, also associated with Minneapolis Children's Health Center; and G. Gail Gardner, Ph.D., a member of the Department of Pediatrics and Psychology at the University of Colorado.

In writing this book we received many valuable suggestions and critical comments from Lonnie Zeltzer, M.D., a member of the Department of Pediatrics at the University of Texas Health Science Center, San Antonio, and Head of the Division of Adolescent Medicine. At hospitals in the San Antonio area, Donna Merin, R.N., Janine Primomo, R.N., Karen Richmond, R.N., and Anne Shea-Smith, M.A., supplied helpful suggestions. At the Children's Hospital at Stanford, Judy Henning, R.N., Discharge Coordinator of the Oncology Clinic, kept us advised of new procedural developments when patients were discharged from the hospital to home care.

The research program described in this book was part of the Laboratory of Hypnosis Research under the direction of Ernest R. Hilgard, Ph.D., Department of Psychology at Stanford University. Under his guidance, this long-established research organization promoted scientific understanding of many aspects of hypnotic phenomena that were basic both to hypnosis and to its use in the relief of pain. As principal investigator, he initiated the grant from the National Cancer Institute[1] to undertake a clinical study of pain relief based at the Children's Hospital at Stanford. Although he did not participate in any of the clinical interventions, he was available for consultation as needed.[2] We wish to express our gratitude to him for the numerous contributions he made to the successful completion of the research project and of this book.

---

1. GRANT CA 18325, National Cancer Institute, Department of Health, Education, and Welfare.

2. Because we refer frequently to two Hilgard names in the text, it seemed advisable to give each one a distinguishing initial, i.e., E. Hilgard and J. Hilgard.

1 Hypnosis, Cancer, and Pain

In 1794, a 9-year-old boy was operated upon for the removal of a tumor. Long before the use of chemical anesthetics, the boy was distracted during the procedure by being told a story so interesting that he later insisted he had felt no pain whatsoever. Eighteen years later the story "Snow White" was submitted to a publisher by Jacob Grimm, that same boy who would become one of the world's most famous authors of fairy tales (*Hypnos,* 1982, May/June, p. 1).

Many years ago the Swiss psychologist Karl Groos described the phenomenon at work for the young Grimm:

> The child who listens absorbedly to a fairy story, the boy for whom the entire external world sinks and vanishes while he is lost in a tale of adventure, or the adult who follows with breathless attention the development of a captivating romance; all allow the authors' creations to get possession of their consciousness to the exclusion of reality, and yet not as an actual substitute for it. . . . It may often be observed that the child's eyes lose their convergence as their interest is absorbed—a means of detachment from surrounding reality. Even in half-grown children the power of detachment is much greater than in adults (Groos, 1901, p. 134).

If the reality that Groos speaks of is physical and mental distress, then stories such as those told to little Jacob Grimm are capable of excluding distress from consciousness and temporarily substituting for it. Many patients have found relief from anxiety and pain through experiences not too different from that of Jacob Grimm, whose mother told fairy tales to him almost two centuries ago. Some patients like fairy tales, some prefer stories of adventure, such as Groos describes, and still others pay

1

rapt attention to closely-related, suggested events that take place in hypnotherapy.

Many children and adolescents in treatment for cancer must undergo painful procedures and are desperately in need of relief from the pain. These patients provided an opportunity to explore ways in which hypnotherapy might serve a humane role in relieving some of their distress. After studying methods of hypnotic pain control over a number of years with a college student population, we undertook to apply our knowledge of hypnosis to patients in treatment for cancer on the pediatric oncology units at the Children's Hospital at Stanford and at the Presbyterian Hospital in San Francisco. We felt that we could offer a genuine service to young patients while at the same time conducting much-needed research. In the ensuing investigation which we shall refer to as the Stanford study, children and adolescents who were required to undergo a repeated and painful diagnostic procedure, namely the bone marrow aspiration, were given the option of electing hypnotherapy as a possible method of obtaining relief from the pain. Both quantitative measures of pain and descriptions of the therapeutic interventions form the substance for clinical data and their interpretation.

That hypnosis can relieve pain associated with burns, dentistry, surgery, and various other trauma—including pain related to cancer and to hemophilia—has been established by clinical studies in adults and to a lesser extent in children. However, many questions remain: Is hypnosis as effective in treating children and adolescents as it is in treating adults? If so, is hypnosis the same for young children as for adolescents and adults? How does hypnosis produce relief from suffering? Can all patients benefit from hypnosis to the same extent? In the course of our work, answers to these questions became clearer as further knowledge about the nature and development of hypnosis during the early years emerged.

In this chapter we shall present an orientation to hypnosis, to distress in cancer particularly as it relates to the bone marrow aspiration, and to the hypnotherapy of pain.

The Nature of Hypnosis

It is not surprising that the public is confused and uneasy about the use of hypnosis as a therapeutic tool when movies, television programs, and occasional nightclub performers continue to present it in a highly dramatized and inaccurate way. Scientific studies of hypnosis during the last quarter of a century have greatly extended our knowledge of hypnosis, and it seems wise, therefore, to begin with a clear explanation and discussion.

Hypnosis has long been identified with suggestion. When the hypnotist says, "Your eyes are closing by themselves," responsive subjects feel their eyes closing "automatically" despite efforts to keep them open. Usually these suggestions of the hypnotist call for active participation by a subject, such as imagining that the eyelids are heavy. Other hypnotic suggestions seek to activate the imagination even more, by guiding the subject's regression into childhood. The difference between the fantasies entertained in hypnosis and those associated with ordinary daydreaming is that, in hypnosis, the imagined events are experienced as real: the eyelids *do* feel heavy, and the person actually *does* reexperience childhood events. One way of describing this condition is to call it "believed-in-imagination." The hypnotic experience can easily be terminated by the hypnotist, or, after a little experience and training, by the hypnotized person. Contrary to misconceptions that result from movies and nightclub performances, hypnosis does not involve the casting of a "spell" whereby the hypnotist, through some special power, controls the subject's mind. Rather, hypnosis requires a mutual agreement between hypnotist and subject, and the quality of the hypnotic experience depends on the subject's own abilities.

To explain the nature of responses to suggestions, the French investigator, Pierre Janet (1889), introduced the concept of *dissociation*—that is, a division of consciousness. An example of dissociation is when the subject, whose eyes are about to close, wonders in some part of the mind whether they will, in fact, close. Similarly, when the person is a child again in regression, part of the mind is ready for the suggestion to come back to the present. In other words, dissociation refers to a splitting off from each other of certain parts of the mind that normally interact. The significance of dissociation in hypnosis has been recognized and updated by E. Hilgard (1977). Although dissociation was introduced by Janet in connection with hypnosis, mild dissociations occur in everyday life; accordingly, some distinctions need to be made to account for the more extensive dissociations characteristically achieved through hypnosis.

Dissociation in Everyday Life. Mild dissociations are familiar events of everyday life. They occur whenever we engage in two activities at once. For example, we eat dinner automatically while we pay close attention to a television program. We drive a car and talk politics with our passenger without giving much thought to the mechanics involved in controlling the automobile. A skilled pianist can play a well-rehearsed concerto while carrying on a spirited conversation with a colleague. Experienced typists can continue to produce accurate copy while answering questions addressed to them. In each of these activities, attention to the task recedes as the skill is mastered and becomes essentially automatic. Once it has been automatized, attention is free to be directed elsewhere, to the television screen or to conversation. Of course if trouble develops—a pit is discovered in the cherry pie, the traffic becomes snarled, or the typewriter keys stick—

attention is redirected immediately. In other words, it is appropriate to describe activities as *dissociated* when one of them goes on automatically, with little conscious effort, as the other is carried out with attention focused on it.

Nighttime dreams represent another form of dissociation in that dreams arise spontaneously, often to our surprise, despite the fact that we produce our own dreams. The experience is one of dissociation because the planning of the dream has proceeded unconsciously, whereas the dream itself, to the extent that it can be recalled as a "happening," is a conscious product.

An altered state of consciousness is characterized by a shift in subjective experience or in psychological functioning that one perceives as distinctively different from the usual alert, waking consciousness. It is not possible to draw a fine line between a minor dissociation and an altered state of consciousness because they often shade gradually from one to the other, much like the transition periods of such ambiguous states as dusk and dawn. In reverie, or "wool-gathering," ideas and images flow automatically as we attend to other things, but normal contact with the environment is easily regained. Other states that provide for transitions are the drowsy states between waking and sleep, or the gradual shifts from a loosening of the tongue to intoxication that may follow the drinking of alcoholic beverages.

Degrees of Dissociation in Hypnosis. A distinctive characteristic of hypnotic dissociations is that they are more readily enhanced and maintained than those occurring in everyday experience. Those who do not confuse imagination with reality under ordinary conditions may, under hypnosis, convert an imagined object to a hallucinated object which, in the extreme, is perceived as if real. With a suggestion from the hypnotist, for example, a hypnotized person may see someone sitting in a chair that is actually vacant. He or she may converse with the hallucination, hear its voice, see it as a person, and accept its remarks as if another person is actually talking.

It is this distortion of normal mental functioning in hypnosis that has led to the concept of hypnosis as a *trance* or an *altered state of consciousness.* It would perhaps be simpler to adopt the term "hypnotic state" as many contemporary hypnotic practitioners do to describe hypnotic involvement. Unfortunately, the simplicity of this terminology is misleading because there are many degrees of response to hypnotic suggestion. Therefore, we prefer to speak more precisely of *degrees of dissociation* produced by hypnotic suggestion. If dissociations are extensive and profound, and the changes are pervasive, we would agree that the hypnotic condition can be described as an altered state of consciousness or trance. For the most part, however, the dissociations produced by hypnotic suggestion leave unaffected major fractions of the person's cognitive functioning. These partial dissociations are very valuable in hypnotherapy.

There are several ways of characterizing a person's degree of hypnotic involvement. Because hypnosis was formerly described as analogous to sleep, it became common—and is still prevalent—to use the metaphor of depth of hypnosis corresponding to depth of sleep. Even though hypnosis is no longer considered a form of sleep, the metaphor is familiar and easily understood. A related concept is that of degree of involvement in the experiences suggested by the hypnotist. For example, if a new identity has been suggested, a profoundly involved subject may act and feel as if he or she were indeed the suggested person. This ability is sometimes referred to as *role involvement.* What these different characterizations have in common is that they all attempt to explain differences in the extent to which the hypnotic suggestions have been effective. The dissociative interpretation of hypnosis points to divisions of consciousness on a continuum between the limited ones and those that are widespread. Some illustrations will clarify how these degrees of dissociation apply.

Suppose the hypnotist tells 8-year-old Roy: "Now please hold your right arm and your fingers straight out." Compliance with such a request involves no hypnosis, for if Roy is socially cooperative, he will simply comply. But suppose that the hypnotist suggests the use of imagination: "*Think* of making your arm very stiff and straight, very, very stiff. Think about it as though you are a tree and your arm is a strong branch of a tree, very straight and very strong, like the branch of a tree . . . so stiff that you can't bend it . . . Now see how stiff your arm is . . . try to bend it. Try." Roy may now find that he has temporarily lost his normal capacity to control his arm. When he tries to bend it, the muscles tighten and the arm becomes even stiffer. Voluntary control of the arm is said to be dissociated, because his own plan of action does not produce the intended movements. When the hypnotist cancels the suggestion, Roy's normal voluntary control returns. The disturbance in Roy's voluntary control represents a limited dissociation.

Such a limited dissociation often proves to be very effective in hypnotic treatment. One of our Children's Hospital patients, Charlotte, who was about to receive an injection that had previously been quite painful, was able to achieve numbness in the arm that was to receive the injection. After hypnotizing her, the therapist suggested that the arm would be numb and would not feel the injection. Next, following the standard practice of implanting a posthypnotic suggestion, he suggested that the arm would remain numb after she had been aroused from hypnosis. After arousal, when asked how she felt, she said that everything was as it had been before she was hypnotized. Her conversation was normal in every way, with no signs of altered consciousness, although her arm remained as numb as if she had received a local anesthetic. Charlotte talked in a spirited way with the physician during the subsequent injection procedure and showed no signs of discomfort. It is appropriate to say that the conscious awareness of her arm was dissociated; no discernible change occurred in her total consciousness, nor was there any sudden change in her orientation after the feeling in her arm was restored through suggestion. In the midst of the hypnotic session, prior to the posthypnotic suggestion, her dissociation had been extensive. After her arousal from hypnosis, the activated posthypnotic suggestion restricted the dissociation to the numb arm.

Posthypnotic suggestion is also used to increase the rapidity of dissociation. One illustration is the use of a brief signal to reinstate what previously had required a longer induction. Doris, a child of 10, was sitting in a relaxed state with her eyes closed while she was hypnotized. She was told that after awakening and becoming alert, she would go back into hypnosis when she heard the hypnotist's hands clap together. A few minutes after arousal from hypnosis, the signal was given and the automatic reaction took place promptly. At one moment Doris was talking in an animated fashion but, in the next moment, when she heard the clapping, she suddenly slumped, her eyes closed, and she became limp. For Doris, the dissociation through the posthypnotic suggestion was profound, while for Charlotte it had been limited.

The alterations a person can undergo in a suggested age regression often exhibit the changes associated with a more extensive dissociation. A lawyer who had been referred to one of us for hypnotic treatment of low back pain was tested initially for his responsivity to hypnosis before deciding on the preferred course of treatment. His reaction to age regression illustrates how the reliving of childhood episodes can be dissociated from the adult experience. Following the induction of hypnosis, age regression was induced as follows:

> Something very interesting is about to happen. In a little while you are going back to a happy day in elementary school . . . to the third grade . . . ONE, you are going back into the past. It is no longer 1980, or 1975, or 1970, but much earlier . . . TWO, you are becoming much younger and smaller . . . In a moment you will be back in the third grade, on a very nice day. THREE, getting younger and younger, smaller and smaller all the time. Soon you will feel an experience exactly as you did once before on a nice day. FOUR, soon you will be right back there. FIVE, you are a small boy in school.

When asked what was happening, he talked freely about what he was doing and what he saw:

"I'm playing marbles in the schoolyard with my friends. Some older guys are playing baseball over there in the corner of the yard ... Recess is about over and my teacher is ready to call us. . . ."

After he was brought out of hypnosis, he said his experience as a 9-year-old boy had been very real to him. He felt as though he had, in fact, been small. This complete change in his awareness of himself was sufficient for it to be classified as an altered state of consciousness. In some instances, the hypnotized person has a double experience during age regression—that of an observing adult and that of an experiencing child—and both experiences are perceived as genuine.

The Process of Hypnosis

With the nature of the hypnotic experience in mind, let us now consider the practices used in inducing hypnosis and in measuring the differences that are found in the degree of hypnotizability from one person to another.

Inducing Hypnosis. In the ongoing experiences of everyday life, we are involved mostly in the realities around us, whereas in hypnosis we set most of these reality demands aside and concentrate on a restricted set of experiences. Induction procedures are designed to provide a gradual transition from our usual generalized reality orientation to the limited orientation characteristic of hypnosis.

Two common procedures for inducing hypnotic dissociation are referred to as *eye fixation* and *arm levitation*. Both techniques typically make use of relaxation, a familiar technique used in conventional hypnotic practices. Although relaxation is not essential to an induction (Banyai and E. Hilgard, 1976), it is helpful in enabling subjects to set aside their ties to ordinary activities and problems so that they can devote full attention to the hypnotist's suggestions. Relaxation is furthered by having the subject sit in a comfortable position in an easy chair before giving specific suggestions to relax the arms, the legs, and other parts of the body, in turn. In eye fixation, the subject is asked to focus attention on a "target," perhaps a thumbtack on the wall or a thumbnail on the hand. The hypnotist will suggest sensations of drowsiness that become strong enough for the subject's eyes which were open and staring at the target, to become fatigued and to close "by themselves." With eye closure, the subject begins to experience the feeling of dissociation that is implicit in the difference between the voluntary effort of keeping the eyes open and their involuntary closing as a consequence of the hypnotist's suggestions.

In arm levitation, the subject is first asked to pay attention to a hand that is in the lap or on the side of the chair, then is given a suggestion that the hand feels light and is about to rise by itself from its resting position. The suggestion is reinforced with various verbal images, such as "becoming light as a feather," or "tied to a balloon." As the subject's hand rises, suggestions of general relaxation continue. The hypnotist indicates that when the hand touches the face, the subject will know that the hypnotic condition has been established and the hand will return to the lap. This method has the advantage of showing the hypnotist how responsive the subject is; in fact, the levitation response can be used as one of the measures of a person's hypnotizability (E. Hilgard, Crawford, and Wert, 1979).

There are other induction techniques besides eye fixation and arm levitation. In many instances, the hypnotist simply arouses vivid imagery in the subject. Hypnosis with children usually concentrates on evoking vivid images and fantasies, which are so accessible during this period of life.

Induction in Self-Hypnosis.   Hypnosis does not depend only on the presence of a clinician who is trained in hypnosis; one can also hypnotize oneself, assuming the two roles of hypnotist and hypnotized person. Many of us are familiar with the experiences of talking to ourselves and obeying our own instructions. For example, when thoughts interfere with sleep, we say, "I must get to sleep," and then adopt some kind of sleep-inducing technique—counting sheep—to do so.

Even in heterohypnosis (i.e., when the hypnotic experience is directed by a hypnotist), the potential for self-hypnosis is present in the form of a small but active fraction of consciousness that continually monitors the hypnotic interaction. Immediately after the conclusion of a successful hypnotic session, a subject will often estimate the fraction of him/herself that was monitoring ongoing events. This splitting of consciousness into a participating part and a monitoring part permits the subject to regain control whenever desired. Once having been hypnotized, the subject can reconstitute the condition on another occasion, repeating the words and imitating the approach used by the hypnotist. Many subjects hypnotized by another have told us that they tended to repeat the hypnotist's suggestion to themselves.

Some people prefer self-hypnosis; others, feeling that the split role in self-hypnosis prevents deep involvement, prefer heterohypnosis. In terms of achieving therapeutic goals, both may be quite successful. In dealing with recurrent problems, such as insomnia or migraine headaches, the ability to use self-hypnosis on the spot has proved valuable. Self-hypnosis as an aid to a musician in overcoming stage fright illustrates its helpfulness.

Henry was in his early 30s when he sought hypnotherapy as a way of dealing with his uneasiness when playing the piano in the presence of other people. As he described it, whenever he played alone and could hear himself playing well, he relaxed, but when he attempted to play in the presence of his family, friends or his music teacher, he felt tension build up between his shoulders and down both arms to his fingers, which became almost rigid and caused him to make many mistakes. He had tried taking tranquilizing drugs before each recital, but they did little good. He thought his problem had to do with a fear of not performing well before others; however, all efforts to forget about the presence of an audience had failed repeatedly.

When tested on a standard scale of hypnotizability, Henry proved to be highly hypnotizable. In hypnosis, the therapist suggested the possibility of his separating the music he was playing from the environment around him by telling himself: "Tune in the music, tune out the teacher, audience, and family." A further suggestion was to visualize himself at the piano, repeating these phrases, paying attention only to the beauty of the music and feeling more and more relaxed, more confident and successful. The final suggestion was that he would find these ideas returning automatically whenever he sat down at the piano, whether other people were present or not. Aroused from hypnosis, he reported that the suggestions were reassuring and that he liked them.

He proved to be adept at self-hypnosis, and was thus able to do these things for himself. Two weeks later, Henry reported that the program really worked. Except for the times his teacher spoke to him, he now focused only on listening to the music he was producing. Before the next recital several months later, he took no tranquilizers. "Before sitting at the piano, I told myself I would enjoy playing, I would be relaxed and listen to myself play. After I sat down I told myself, *Tune into the music.* It worked like a charm." These four words acted like a posthypnotic suggestion, automatically reinstating the direction he wished to take.

Playing the piano *and* knowing that people were present had belonged together as a natural unit in Henry's experience. Through hypnosis he effectively isolated one from the other so that his concentration now centered only on playing and listening to music. He had dissociated the emotional reactions that had interfered with the musical performance. One need not assume that he was in a hypnotic state throughout the recital; a limited dissociation had sufficed to reduce the conflict between his musical performance and his stage fright.

Hypnotic Induction in Children.   In the Stanford study, we used two methods of induction, both of which young children found congenial. In the first method we asked them to focus on a visual target, such as a "funny face" drawn with a red felt-tip pen on a thumbnail, while relaxing body and mind and concentrating on what we said. In the second method we directly encouraged involvement in fantasied play. The choice of which method to use was made on the basis of the patient's capabilities and interests, as well as the purpose for which the hypnosis was needed. One method emphasized relaxation and concentration, and the other emphasized fantasy. We found that most of these young patients enjoyed the induction "ceremonies" that marked the separation from a world filled with the usual thoughts and activities into a world of mental adventures that held the promise of relieving anxiety and pain. Children and adolescents settled down for their therapy session with a visible air of anticipation, ready to concentrate on whatever experiences the hypnotherapist suggested. The induction continued until the first evidence of involuntary action occurred. At this point hypnotic dissociation had started. For example, while the hypnotist repeated instructions for relaxation, 12-year-old Jennie, who had been holding a Lucite ball on a small chain as her target object, let the ball slip quietly out of her hand and into her lap. An involuntary response of *"letting things happen"* had started, and the usual reality orientation of *"making things happen"* had begun to recede into the background. The induction phase had ended.

Differences in Hypnotizability: Hypnosis as a Measurable Ability. It has long been known that people differ greatly in their talent for experiencing hypnosis. More accurate information on this topic became available after tests of hypnotizability had been standardized on young adults of college age (Weitzenhoffer and E. Hilgard, 1959; E. Hilgard, 1965). The tests, administered when the subject had been hypnotized by a standardized induction procedure, consist of suggestions, each of which leads to appropriate responses characteristic of hypnotizable persons. Each suggestion, called an "item" on the scale, is scored as passed or failed. The total score is determined by the number of items passed. The distribution of hypnotic ability scores shows a bell-shaped curve, much like the curve for intelligence tests. In other words, a few people at the high end are very talented in their hypnotic skills and are able to pass the most difficult items with ease. At the other end, some people have little or no capacity for being hypnotized and fail even the easiest items. Most people possess a moderate degree of ability or talent, passing some items and not others.

Research followed on the existence of this ability among individuals of different ages (Morgan and E. Hilgard, 1973). From the test data on children, it was clear that hypnotic talent developed slowly during the preschool years, accelerated markedly after the age of 5, and reached its peak between the ages of 9 and 12 years. When these data were compared with those on adults, it was further evident that many more children than adults were in the highly hypnotizable category. On a later, shortened scale (7 items) designed for children, the Stanford Hypnotic Clinical Scale for Children, SHCS:Child (Morgan and J. Hilgard, 1978/79), average scores showed children to be more hypnotizable than adults who had been tested on similarly constructed scales.

Follow-up studies of subjects first tested as college students and again tested ten years later demonstrated a remarkable stability of hypnotic talent over time. Scores at retest were within a few points of earlier scores, yielding a correlation of .60 (Morgan, Johnson, and E. Hilgard, 1974). These facts point to a *capacity for hypnotizability* that resides within the individual. Those who are hypnotizable may resist hypnosis at first because of fear of loss of control, but as they become more comfortable with the procedure and the hypnotist, they will gradually reach their characteristic level. Once that characteristic level of hypnotic ability has been reached, however, it does not change much. A stage hypnotist gives a false impression of having great power over all subjects, but the critical observer can easily note how few of the people who come to the stage are retained for demonstration purposes. The stage hypnotist quietly uses a few tests of talent to weed out those who are unlikely to respond to all suggestions.

Is there a hereditary component to hypnotic talent? Members of families containing twins and other children were separately hypnotized to compare hypnotizability between identical twins, fraternal twins, nontwin pairs of children, and the parents. The results were similar to comparable studies designed to ascertain the inheritance of other psychological traits; that is, a greater resemblance was found between identical twins than fraternal twins or nontwin pairs, findings that suggest the distinct possibility of a hereditary component (Morgan, E. Hilgard, and Davert, 1970; Morgan, 1973).

Although inheritance qualifies as one factor in the development of hypnotic capacity, a systematic study identified the presence of a capacity for *imaginative involvement* as a major contributor to hypnotic capability. It appears that both hereditary potential and the capacity for imaginative involvement influence one's hypnotizability.

The Role of Imaginative Involvement.   In a study of college students, it was found that the ability to experience hypnosis was signaled by a person's readiness to become involved in such areas as the aesthetic appreciation of nature, listening to music, reading a novel, watching a play, enjoying the adventurous pursuits of skin diving or mountain climbing (J. Hilgard, 1970/79). Excerpts from interviews with two highly hypnotizable subjects will serve to illustrate the relationship between what we mean by imaginative involvement in everyday life and the capacity for hypnotic involvement.

An 18-year-old college student was hypnotized for the first time. Asked afterward whether hypnosis was like anything she had experienced previously, she replied, "Hypnosis was like reading a good book . . . *It's stronger in a way than reading.* When I get really involved in reading, I'm not aware of what is going on around me. I concentrate on the people in the book or in the movie and react the way they react. The intense concentration is the same in a book, in a movie, or in imagination as it is in hypnosis. Reading a book can hypnotize you."

The second illustration shows the free-wheeling imagination of a child. At age 9, Joe tested at the top of a scale of hypnotic talent. Among his imaginative involvements, he reported his left and right hands as his two imaginary companions, "Peachy and Poshy." They came to life like puppets. Joe would spin long stories, talk out loud, and go back and forth from one to the other. Peachy and Poshy came into being when Joe was 3 years old and, though his interest in them was now receding, he still entertained himself occasionally with these playful characters.

Hypnosis of children depends largely on their capacity for imagination, which, although generally high in childhood, is not shared equally by all children. Throughout this book we will report the imaginative experiences of many children and adolescents in the context of hypnotic treatment to illustrate how such imaginative experiences form a major basis for dissociations in hypnosis.

When and how does the imaginative involvement essential to hypnosis originate? Pretend play, or make-believe play as it is also called, initiates a complex sequence in the development of imagination. Before the age of 2 1/2, pretend play is concerned primarily with imitation and contains hardly any novelty that would mark it as creative. A shift to *sociodramatic play,* however, enters the picture at about this age and develops rapidly up to the age of 5.

The following incident illustrates the difference between a typical 3 1/2-year-old and a typical 2 year old in this respect. Julie, age 3 1/2 years, dressed in her mother's long skirt and clearly in the role of her mother, prepared to leave the room where her playmate, 2-year-old Stephanie, remained. She turned toward Stephanie with this admonition, "Now be good, Stephanie. I'm playing bridge. *Wish me luck."* Stephanie simply stared at Julie and continued to do so despite Julie's efforts to draw her into pretend play.

Children's ability to immerse themselves in the acting roles of pretend play is a precursor to their hypnotizability. An indication of the similarity between hypnosis in children and pretend play is the desire of most younger children to keep their eyes open, even when suggestions are made to close them. For the induction of hypnosis, most children prefer an imagined sequence similar to pretend play over suggested relaxation. (Whoever heard of closing one's eyes and relaxing during make-believe or pretend play?) The kind of hypnosis involved at these early ages in the form of pretend play and sociodramatic play, can be termed *protohypnosis*. Although it shares some of the characteristics of hypnosis induced at later ages, it is not identical to it. As children begin to grow up, their imaginative development reaches a more mature level; specifically, they become capable of free fantasy—the *internal elaboration* of rich and diverse images. This transition is marked by their willingness to close their eyes during hypnosis and to follow suggestions to relax. Internalized imagery with eyes closed is compatible with relaxation in a way that pretend play is not. By the age of 6 years, overlap between hypnosis based on active pretend play and hypnosis based on the exercise of internal imagination accompanied by relaxation is usually well underway.

Does the addition of a hypnotic condition accomplish more than is possible with everyday forms of imaginative involvement? For some patients, yes. Quite illuminating was the contrast described by one of our patients, 20-year-old Richard, who suffered continuing pain from the presence of an abdominal tumor (further comments on this patient are in Chapter 5). Before hypnosis he had obtained no pain relief through his own fantasied images such as those of soaring birds. Subsequently, when he imagined them in hypnosis, he did obtain relief. By his own report, hypnosis had enabled him to enter into the fantasies more deeply and become a part of them. It is this enhanced sense of participation that makes hypnosis more effective. Hypnosis adds to the fantasy until the fantasy takes on a new reality.

The fantasies we are talking about in hypnosis are quite different from the long-enduring autistic fantasies of the mentally ill. Autistic fantasies are deeply rooted in an individual's conflicts and problems in living; in an extreme form they revolve around continuing grandiose ideas or suspicions of other people. On the other hand, the constructive fantasies useful in hypnosis are characteristic of normal development from the earliest years of childhood into the adult years. They are time-limited fantasies under the control of the individual. Whether produced by stimulation (books, drama) or by woolgathering about past experiences and future hopes, they serve their purpose and are then terminated. For the children we treated in our project, their involvement in fantasy alternated with their attention to the realistic demands of living; they did not become engulfed in dream worlds. Imaginative activity and good reality orientation can and do exist comfortably side by side.

Distress in Childhood Cancer

To understand the use of hypnosis in the Stanford study calls for a description of cancer in young patients, its impact on them and on the family members who sustain them during the illness. Only then will we be ready to consider the specific type of pain that is the focus of investigation and the hypnotherapeutic practices that we used in dealing with it.

Childhood Cancer.   In our research study most of the patients whom we treated with hypnotherapy for pain during bone marrow aspirations (the procedure on which we focused) had leukemia. Of the cancers that affect children, the leukemias are the most common, accounting for approximately 40 percent (Altman and Schwartz, 1978).

Leukemia is a cancer of the leukocytes or white blood cells normally present in the blood as a defense against infections and other diseases. Instead of the normal development of immature to mature forms of leukocytes in the bone marrow, spleen, and liver, in leukemia early immature forms called "blasts" multiply in a rapid and uncontrolled way. With too few red blood cells, anemia results; with too few platelets, the blood cannot clot; and with too few normal white cells, defenses against disease are weakened. Thus the leukemic child may present symptoms of weakness and pallor, abnormal bleeding into the tissues, or continuing infections.

Non-Hodgkin's lymphoma, a cancer of the lymph glands, is a second type of cancer in which the bone marrow aspiration must be used repeatedly. It is found in 6 percent of childhood cancers and was present in our sample.

Beyond the scope of our research study, we also treated patients with solid tumors who asked for hypnotic treatment to help them overcome various troublesome problems. Solid tumors, arising in almost any tissue of the body, involve an uncontrollable growth of cancerous cells that may spread to other sites of the body. One of the patients who requested hypnotherapy had entered the hospital with a malignant melanoma, a neoplasm of a pigmented mole on the skin; another, with leiomyosarcoma, a malignant tumor of smooth muscle in the gastrointestinal tract; and others had malignancies of the bone, some with Ewing's sarcoma and some with osteosarcoma.

With the development of multiple-drug chemotherapy, megavoltage radiation, and improved surgery, the prospect of longer survival and cure became greatly enhanced. Oncologists are justly proud of the advances that have been made in the last twenty years. Following termination of treatment in childhood leukemia, for example, more than half will remain disease-free and are considered cured of a disease that was formerly fatal. In Hodgkin's disease, also once a universally fatal cancerous condition of the lymph nodes and lymph system, over 500 of the adult patients treated and cured in the Stanford program attended a celebration held at the Stanford University Medical Center on May 8, 1982. They were living testimony of the normal lives they were able to live, free of disease. The statistics showed that, of the total treated, 80 percent had survived for at least five years and 75 percent were considered to be permanently cured. The results were even more dramatic for children than for adults, with 96 percent surviving for at least eleven years and 93 percent experiencing no relapse (Andreopoulos, 1982). Ewing's sarcoma and, to a lesser extent, osteogenic sarcoma have also shown dramatic advances.

Pervasive Anxiety. Because cancer is a life-threatening disease, fears and anxieties arise in patient, parents, and siblings when the diagnosis of cancer becomes a reality. Those involved have been transported into a new and uncharted world, with the natural reaction of severe shock, often panic, to be expected in the face of a sudden and unexpected crisis. A mother and father put into words the way their daily life had changed:

> When the doctor explained that our child had cancer, it was frightening. We were shocked. We could hardly believe it. It made a difference in all the plans we had for him and ourselves.

The required treatments, accompanied by diagnostic procedures to monitor the course of the disease, often extend over a protracted period of time. They can be painful and stressful in ways which test the stamina of young patients and their parents. The life styles of all members of the family change to accommodate the presence of a chronically ill child. New adaptations, with schedules for hospital visits, schooling, and home, can be working well when an intercurrent emergency may happen again to upset the balance. The parents whom we have just quoted described this further experience:

> We found that it was difficult to make plans too far in advance because many times the plans didn't work out, which meant disappointment. Therefore we learned to live in the present, and get all the satisfaction that was possible out of each day.

While the initial, acute anxiety subsides in the course of a few months as patient and parents learn to cope with this new reality in their lives, a residual anxiety, a sense of unfinished business, continues, not far beneath the surface. When investigators conduct research on a specific problem of pain during procedures in cancer patients, they are dealing not only with the pain and anxiety engendered by the specified procedure, but also, to a greater or lesser degree, with an invisible undercurrent of general anxiety due to the presence of a possibly fatal disease. This background factor is far different, for example, from that faced by well children whose dentists impose discomfort or pain when inserting tight bands to straighten teeth.

We observed that this hidden anxiety could still surface briefly when children and adolescents returned for periodic checkups after treatment had been successfully concluded. The pervasive anxiety and the multitude of problems which these patients and their families have faced, are well described by Koocher and O'Malley in *The Damocles Syndrome* (1981).

The Bone Marrow Aspiration. Intensive multiple-drug chemotherapy and radiotherapy, continuing over an extended period of time, constitutes the treatment program in childhood leukemia. Periodic bone marrow aspirations produce samples of the bone marrow for microscopic examination in order to assess changes during therapy.

As a result of therapy, remission is achieved when no leukemic cells are seen in the bone marrow or spinal fluid, and radiographs are negative. However, because the possibility remains that leukemia cells still are present, the child is maintained on drug therapy. Even in remission, therefore, it is essential to subject the child to the stress of bone marrow aspirations in order to assess the status of the disease. If the disease becomes active again, reinduction treatment is initiated with a different set of drugs. Depending on the type of leukemia, maintenance therapy will continue for a period of two to three years.

In a bone marrow aspiration, a large needle is pushed into the hipbone (iliac crest) in order to withdraw a sample of marrow for diagnostic purposes. There are three sources of discomfort reported by most patients: first, a sharp, stinging pain as the needle penetrates the skin; then pain and heavy pressure as the needle penetrates the periosteum, or covering of the bone; and finally an intense, excruciating pain as the sample of bone marrow is sucked into the needle. This "suction pain" may be brief and localized, but it is reported by some patients to remain in their entire upper leg for 30 seconds or more. Although local anesthesia can alter the degree of pain felt when the large bone marrow needle penetrates sensitive outer tissues and possibly the periosteum, no local anesthesia can relieve the sharp pain that accompanies the actual aspiration. Inevitably, anxiety over the possibility of pain becomes an integral part of the experience.

The Supporting Environment.   The frontline team, working together in a concerted treatment program, consists of patient, parents, and medical staff. Under the leadership of Dr. Jordan Wilbur, initially at the Pediatric Oncology Unit of the Children's Hospital at Stanford, and later at the Presbyterian Hospital in San Francisco, the medical staff recognized patients and parents as integral members of the treatment team (Wilbur and Dutcher, 1972). Young patients were encouraged to retain as much initiative and control as was possible in the treatment process. For example, during a bone marrow aspiration—that inevitable part of the leukemia patient's life—we saw patients cooperate with a sense of dignity when they could say "now" to indicate that they were ready for the needle insertion. They explained that while only a physician knew enough to make the medical decision as to how often a bone marrow aspiration had to take place, *they* were the ones who knew when they were prepared. Patients resented relinquishing all responsibility to others who did things *to* them. They welcomed a status as team members.

Parents who are with a child in the hospital are deeply troubled themselves over their child's illness, but they must gather strength to become a major support for the ailing child. Physicians and nurses aid in this process through their readiness to share knowledge and answer the questions that arise from time to time throughout the illness. Naturally the information shared with young patients needs to be commensurate with their age and developmental level.

When the patient returns home but continues treatment through regular appointments at the clinic, there are new stresses. The former activities of daily life may now be affected by reduced strength or changes in appearance. A wig that replaces hair loss (due to medication) may result in teasing. Alterations in weight or a bloated appearance—also due to medication—modify both the self-image and the image projected to peers. Such problems, well handled in the hospital setting where other patients may be similarly affected, are aggravated when the child returns to an environment where he looks different. Increasingly, as the extent of the reentry-to-school problem has been recognized, professional workers including teachers, are trying to devise ways that will insure a welcoming and understanding atmosphere.

We may distinguish between the problems of the patient at home who is able to go to school and play on the playground, but is troubled by change in appearance as described above, and the child who is confined at home because of the severity of distress connected with the illness. For such a child, the same type of time-filling activities that were provided in the hospital need to be available at home. This is no easy assignment for parents. In a later chapter we shall discuss these issues and possible solutions to them.

The Nature of Pain

There are many kinds of responses to pain. These responses include pain as it is presently felt, pain remembered from the past, and the anticipation of pain in the future. In other words, pain is not simply a sensory product resulting from stimulation of pain receptors—it is also a psychological response that includes both an anxiety and a sensory component.

When the pain is debilitating, long-lasting, or recurrent, depression may also be present.

The anxiety component of pain may be aroused by remembered and anticipated pain experiences. When the pain is evoked repeatedly in procedures, as is the case in the bone marrow aspiration, a patient's anxiety can be aroused simply by entering the treatment room, seeing a needle, other objects, or persons associated with the painful experience. For some, even the sight of the hospital has been found to induce fear, trembling, and nausea.

The home environment affects the way in which a child experiences and expresses feelings of pain. As a part of this personal history, there are differences among cultural groups, some of which express pain much more freely than others. The attitudes, expectations, and resourcefulness of the adults who provide support during a painful episode exert a significant impact on the patient. One parent and child may be close on a basis of mutual clinging, while another parent and child may be close on a basis of independent but empathic understanding. Because of past experiences in their own backgrounds, a few parents find any contact with a child in pain too distressing to permit them to be present at all. Other parents participate actively in problem-solving, suggesting ways of coping with discomfort.

The understanding, caring, and attentiveness of clinical staff members exert an important influence on patient responses. Young patients in our investigation spontaneously spoke of how much they valued these characteristics as well as skill on the part of the physician and nurse during a painful procedure.

Self-Assessment of the Pain During a Bone Marrow Aspiration. From a very young age, children are able to describe the pain they have experienced. After interviewing 994 children ages 5 to 12 about various types of pain that required medical attention, such as headaches, stomachaches, earaches, joint problems, and leukemia, Ross and Ross (1984) concluded that a substantial number of children were capable of providing excellent descriptions of pain, providing as much information as was typically elicited from adults. A child's developmental level does, of course, affect the actual words and concepts used—children between the ages of 4 and 6, for example, preferred words like "hurt," "owie," and "ouch" rather than "pain" (Eland and Anderson, 1977)—however, even a 4-year-old boy gave an immediately recognizable description of phantom limb pain.

In the Stanford study we included the child's estimation of the pain experienced during the bone marrow aspiration. To assist children as young as 6 years old in estimating the intensity of the pain, we arranged a series of faces showing expressions from relaxed comfort to severe grimacing. Even a child of kindergarten age was able to point to the face that best expressed how the pain felt. A numerical scale from 0 to 10 accompanied the pictures and, for the older children, this scale could be used without accompanying illustrations.

Our 10-point scale for measuring children's self-report of pain is supported by a study utilizing a similar approach (Abu-Saad and Holzemer, 1981). Children ages 9 to 15 indicated the degree of their pain experience by marking a 10-centimeter scale that ranged from "I have no pain" to "I have very severe pain." The children's responses as measured by this scale correlated sufficiently well with other measures for evaluating pain (physiological manifestations, overt movements, and word descriptions) to support the validity of the self-report pain scale as an indicator of distress level. In a recent study (LeBaron and Zeltzer, in press), children and adolescents rated their pain during bone marrow aspirations on a 5-point self-report numerical scale accompanied by a series of faces. This study provides further evidence that self assessments of pain yield valid estimates.

Hypnotherapy in Pain Relief

A review of the literature from both experimental and clinical studies shows how widespread have been the applications of hypnosis for pain relief (E. Hilgard and J. Hilgard, 1975/83). In some instances, hypnosis has been found to be more effective than other methods that are frequently used to relieve pain.

Hypnotherapy Compared with Other Pain-Relieving Therapies.
Three studies have addressed the problem of the relative effectiveness of hypnotic relief of pain compared with other types of pain relief. One of these was a laboratory study with nonpatient adults, the second a clinical study with adult patients, the third a clinical investigation with child patients.

In the first study, the effectiveness of hypnosis was compared with two other types of pain relief: acupuncture and the chemical agents morphine, aspirin, and diazepam, a tranquilizing drug with the trade name Valium (Stern, Brown, Ulett, and Sletten, 1977). Following the preferred practices in such studies, placebos were used as controls for both the treatment groups. For the acupuncture treatment, the placebo consisted of inserting needles in the skin near to but removed from the accepted acupuncture spots, i.e., the areas where needles were expected to be effective. For the drug placebo, patients were given a capsule which was similar in appearance to that containing the medication but it did not contain an active agent. Severe pain was artificially produced by one of two methods: (1) immersing the hand and forearm in circulating ice water, or (2) exercising an arm and hand after the blood supply had been curtailed by a tourniquet to the upper arm. The findings revealed that for both experimental pain conditions, hypnosis ranked first in relieving pain, and morphine second. Acupuncture proved effective only for the pain induced by ice water immersion and, even then, it was less effective than hypnosis or morphine. Aspirin, Valium, and the placebos were ineffective in both pain conditions.

For various reasons, what happens in laboratory studies is not always transferable to clinical investigations. Many patients come to the hospital with a long experience of pain, for example, and often have anxieties and expectations based in part on past failures to achieve permanent relief. In a second study, this time with clinical patients rather than with laboratory subjects, the pain reduction obtained through hypnosis was again compared with other types of treatment: biofeedback, psychotherapy, placebo, and a nontreatment control (Elton, Burrows, and Stanley, 1979).[1] Patients in this investigation were suffering from abdominal pain, "phantom limb" pain (the pain felt in a bodily member that has been surgically removed), and other pains associated with tension headaches, migraine headaches, and arthritis. The average patient had suffered pain for 14 years, during which time he or she had made numerous attempts to secure relief through various combinations of surgery, acupuncture, medication, and physiotherapy—none with any lasting success. After an initial session to evaluate the patient's pain prior to the beginning of treatment (baseline data), the assigned treatment was carried out in 12 weekly sessions lasting half-an-hour each. Those treated by hypnosis were trained in specific hypnotic techniques described in later chapters. In the biofeedback procedure, the patient cooperated by learning how to relax, guided by a visual display of electrical activity recorded by electrodes placed on the forehead muscles. Patients in the psychotherapy group discussed their personal problems, methods of handling them, and coping strategies for dealing with pain. The placebo group received a nonspecific tablet that was represented as a new pain-relieving medication. Members of the control group were included in the initial baseline assessment, and then placed on a waiting list to be invited back after 12 weeks when any change in pain could be assessed. As in the laboratory investigation reported above, the results were again favorable to hypnosis, although hypnosis was only marginally more successful than biofeedback. The psychotherapy group showed a positive but lesser effect, well below hypnosis and biofeedback, whereas neither the placebo nor the nontreatment group showed any improvement. These findings were corroborated further by recalling the unsuccessful placebo and nontreatment patients, and treating them by either hypnosis or biofeedback, at which point they, too, improved. Follow-up three years later indicated that the results were lasting for the majority of patients. The authors concluded that hypnosis, which not only yielded excellent results but eliminated the need for apparatus, was the preferred method.

The relative contribution of hypnotic and nonhypnotic factors in pain relief was investigated by Zeltzer and LeBaron (1982). In their study, cancer patients aged 6 to 17 years were receiving bone marrow aspirations, lumbar punctures, or both. Patients were matched for age and divided into a hypnosis and a nonhypnosis group. Those in the nonhypnosis group were treated by an approach which involved supportive counseling, deep breathing, distraction, and encouragement of self-control behaviors for pain relief. The use of imagery or fantasy was deliberately avoided. Patients in the hypnosis group received the same treatment as the nonhypnosis group, except that these patients were helped to become increasingly involved in interesting and pleasant images and fantasies. Imagery and self-initiated fantasies were interwoven throughout all aspects of the treatment.

The 14 children who received bone marrow aspirations in the nonhypnosis group reported a modest but significant reduction from the baseline pain level of 4.6 on a scale of 1–5 to 3.9, a reduction of 0.7 scale points. For the 13 patients in the hypnosis group, there was a significant reduction from 4.4 to 2.9, a reduction of 1.5 scale points. An analysis of variance confirmed statistically that the reduction of pain through hypnotic treatment was greater than that achieved through nonhypnotic support.

A corresponding comparison of two patient groups receiving lumbar punctures, 11 patients in each group, also showed the hypnosis procedures to be more effective: Using the 5-point scale, pain was reduced by the nonhypnosis group from 3.5 to 3.2, a nonsignificant change of 0.3 scale points, and by the hypnosis group from 3.9 to 2.2, a significant reduction of 1.7 scale points.

The Hypnotherapy of Pain in Young Patients. Studies of the hypnotherapy of young patients with pain are not confined to cancer and the procedures necessary in its treatment. For example, in dentistry, hypnosis has been used to relieve the pain and anxiety of dental work such as orthodontic banding, drilling, and tooth extraction (Bernick, 1972; Gardner and Olness, 1981). Dentists have found that hypnosis can reduce unpleasant initial reactions to the injection of local analgesics and can alleviate excessive reactions to needles (needle phobias) if they should develop.

Another illustration concerns the successful use of hypnotherapy in treating the pain of severely burned children (Bernstein 1963, 1965; LaBaw, 1973). A systematic investigation of its use in relieving pain during recurring procedures, such as changes of dressings, was reported by Schafer (1975). In Schafer's study, adjunctive hypnotic analgesia in a burn unit was given to 20 patients, of whom six were children or adolescents. The results clearly indicated that the capacity to produce analgesia during these painful changes of dressings was related to the hypnotic ability of the patient, as tested on the Orne and O'Connell scale (1967).

Wakeman and Kaplan (1978) conducted a controlled study comparing burned patients treated either by a combination of hypnotherapy and medication or by a combination of emotional support and medication. Analgesic medication was available to these patients on demand, and data were collected on the amount of medication the patients in each group requested. They compared the successes of three age groups: 7 to 18, 19 to 30, and 31 to 70. Some patients' burns covered 0–30 percent of the body and others 31–60 percent of the body. Patients were randomly assigned by age and extent of the burned area to the hypnotic treatment group or to the equal-time support group.

For both the 0–30 percent and 31–60 percent burn groups, differences at the .01 level of confidence favored the hypnosis group. A lower mean percentage of medication, significant at the .05 level, was requested by the 7- to 18-year-olds than by the two other age groups. What marks this study as a significant scientific contribution is its concentration on one problem (the presence of pain), its provision of an adequate control group, its assessment of the extent of burn damage, and its measurement of the amount as well as the frequency of requested medication. Missing, however, are tests of relative hypnotizability among patients.

Hypnotically induced pain control has also been reported in two adolescents with sickle cell anemia (Zeltzer, Dash, and Holland, 1979). For both cases, pain reports from a 12-month period prior to hypnotherapy were compared with those covering a 12-month period after hypnotherapeutic treatment. With hypnotherapy, patients showed a marked decrease in the use of analgesics, emergency room visits, hospital admissions, and total number of hospital days. In addition, they reported fewer and less severe pain crises and were able to increase their normal activities.

Reports of individual patients with cancer. Pain associated with cancer has much in common with pain unrelated to cancer and, as one might expect, comparable results with hypnotherapy are found.

One of the youngest cases reported was that of a 4-year-old child with an inoperable brain tumor who was referred for hypnosis to control his discomfort (Crasilneck and Hall, 1975). Their account of the hypnotic procedure follows:

> . . . When first seen he was lying in bed crying and holding his head. When he learned another doctor was to see him he literally became hysterical with fright. But when left alone with the therapist for about 10 minutes his crying stopped. He then tearfully asked if he were going to get "medicine or a shot." The therapist assured

him that he would not get a shot and asked if he knew what hypnosis meant. The child was completely puzzled and knew nothing of the concept. He was then asked to stare at a cigarette lighter and within 15 minutes was in a state of somnambulism. Then he was given the suggestion that he would have much less pain, would eat better, would sleep well, and would enjoy television and magazines. Soon it was possible to reduce narcotic injections from five or six daily to only a minimal amount of Demerol. He ate consistently better, was able to take naps mornings and afternoons, enjoyed watching certain television programs, would look at pictures with interest, and was much more cooperative. He was seen daily the first month, three times a week the second month.

His last appointment for hypnosis came at 7 A.M. during the first week of the third month after hypnotic treatment began. He smiled when the therapist entered the room. When asked how he felt, he replied, "Pretty good, but I have a headache." Under hypnotic suggestion most of the pain was removed and the patient responded well. After his lunch that day, he took a nap and sometime during this period he expired. He died peacefully, not addicted, not in constant pain. (Crasilneck and Hall, 1975, pp. 199–200.)

A second case reported by Crasilneck and Hall (1975) involved an 8-year-old child who had been ill with leukemia since the age of 6. At the time of referral he was not only quite ill physically but he was frightened and depressed. He was refusing to cooperate during required therapeutic procedures, such as bone marrow aspirations and frequent injections. After inducing hypnosis, the hypnotherapist initiated suggestions for ameliorating his symptoms and an immediate improvement in attitude was noted. This patient was able to learn and to use self-hypnosis with excellent results.

The success of hypnotherapy used in a broader context than symptom removal was recorded by Gardner in the case of David (Gardner, 1976; Gardner and Olness, 1981). Although 11-year-old David first needed hypnosis in order to control nausea and vomiting, he soon found that he could use it for the control of pain. He asked to learn self-hypnosis so that he could meet problems as they arose at home. Equally important was the therapist's decision to teach David steps for enhancing positive experiences such as comfort and joy. Building on David's interests in outdoor life, the therapist encouraged him to develop a pleasant hypnotic dream that appealed to him, a dream of being an eagle who enjoyed flying from one safe and peaceful place to another even safer and happier place, and to recall it whenever the need arose. This fantasy, the therapist assured David, could produce total relief from unpleasant and unwished-for feelings. The close relationship maintained by the hypnotherapist with David and with his family throughout the ultimately fatal illness provided continuing understanding and support.

Hypnotherapy was used successfully by an adolescent girl with chronic myelogenous leukemia during the last four months of her life when she suffered from multiple symptoms (Ellenberg, Dash, Kellerman, Higgins, and Zeltzer, 1980). Of particular interest was the marked reduction effected in the chronic pain of headaches and backaches, as well as the substantial decrease in self-reported pain and anxiety during bone marrow aspirations. Again, although the researchers took careful baseline ratings of the patient's pain and anxiety in advance of hypnotic treatment, they did not measure her hypnotic ability.

Zeltzer (1980) reported a case in which hypnosis relieved nausea and vomiting related to chemotherapy, and severe pain from pulmonary metastases in a 16-year-old adolescent. This patient had been prescribed pain medications which did not help. Through hypnosis, he was assisted in having some intense fantasies of mountain climbing which were personally meaningful to him. During a five-month period, he was mostly free from pain.

Studies based on numerous patients with cancer. Even though systematic research controls are not included, clinical reports based on a number of patients serve as valuable indicators of how effective hypnotic practices can be. Such studies have the scientific advantage that generalizations reflect a larger data base. Single dramatic cures, while informative, tell us little about the range of results to be expected from patients with similar diagnoses and treated under similar circumstances.

LaBaw and his colleagues (1975) employed hypnotherapy with 27 pediatric cancer patients between the ages of 4 and 20, of whom 8 were age 10 or below. They reported in detail on their clinical procedures and results with 12 of the 27 cases said to be representative. Patient responses to hypnotherapy in these 12 cases were reclassified by Gardner and Olness (1981) as good (6), moderate (3), and poor (3). The symptoms treated were nosebleeds and vomiting connected with chemotherapy, as well as pain. Because the responses were not differentiated according to symptoms, no generalizations could be made about the relative efficacy of hypnotic treatment for specific types of problems. There was no assessment of hypnotic talent to which the success of hypnotherapy might be related.

Olness (1981) studied 21 young patients who were treated by an imagery technique for producing self-hypnosis. The four cases described below are illustrative of her general procedures. An 8-year-old girl was treated after her first bone marrow experience had been unpleasant. She learned to control the pain of intravenous injections by the "switch-off method" (see Chapter 4 for discussion of the "switch-off method") and she used it to control pain in her next bone marrow aspiration. In the second case, a 5-year-old boy, treated by hypnotherapy a year earlier, had relapsed and become increasingly anxious. Imagery exercises were reinstated and he used them successfully by himself, although no descriptive details were given other than that he appeared to be more comfortable, even on the night he died. The third case was that of a child of 5 who, taught to relax through the vehicle of her doll, reportedly then was able to tolerate most procedures. In the fourth case, that of a 13-year-old boy, success in pain control was estimated on the basis of the reductions in his requests for pain medication following hypnotic treatment. For the whole sample, Olness reported a 90 percent success rate. The success rate as defined by Olness did not necessarily mean that pain had undergone a marked reduction. Instead, success was estimated according to the patient's ability to make a satisfactory adjustment to the problems brought about by the illness or the pain. Because of the variety of symptoms that were included in Olness' study and the absence of any estimate of degree of improvement, it is difficult to interpret the quantitative statement of success or to generalize her findings to other settings.

In another investigation, hypnotic intervention was found to reduce pain and anxiety significantly below baseline in a variety of medical procedures, including nine bone marrow aspirations, two lumbar punctures, and seven intramuscular injections (Kellerman, Zeltzer, Ellenberg, and Dash, 1983). Again, the analysis did not distinguish among the three procedures, and the patients' hypnotic responsiveness was not assessed.

The General Plan

Throughout our exposition of the Stanford study, we shall rely upon descriptions of the course of hypnotherapy with individual patients in order to indicate the variety of hypnotic practices and the types of responses to them. The children and adolescents who elected hypnotherapy had suffered substantial pain and welcomed the possibility of relieving it through hypnosis. We studied this group in detail to see how effective hypnosis would be in relieving pain, and why it might have succeeded or failed for each patient. A number of those who did not elect hypnosis felt no need for it, because they were already using their own resources to cope with pain and felt little or no distress. How they accomplished this, as we shall see, proved very informative.

Our experiences with young patients went beyond the more restricted planned research of the Stanford study that was focused on the bone marrow aspiration. We adapted hypnotherapy to the individual needs of patients who asked for help with persistent pain, phantom limb pain, needle phobias, worry over the recurrence of cancer, and dysphagia for pills. The experiences of these patients illustrate ways in which hypnosis can serve children who face a variety of problems.

We saw patients, parents, nurses, and physicians collaborating in a team approach that promoted the psychological well-being of the patients at the same time as the goals of medical treatment were met. Attitudes and activities capable of aiding patient-comfort will be examined.

The primary focus, of course, is on patients suffering from pain and anxiety related to cancer and their hypnotherapeutic treatment. There is, however, much more to be said about the topics which have been introduced in a general way in this chapter. A persistent theme will be the differences in response between the younger and older patients. We shall draw upon many experiences which led to an understanding of the normal development of abilities essential to hypnosis and to the hypnotherapy of pain.

Notes

1. A brief account of acupuncture, behavior therapy, and biofeedback as methods for coping with pain is given in Appendix B.

2 Hypnotherapy as Experienced by Older and Younger Patients

Before turning to details of the Stanford study, we wish to call attention to differences in the hypnotherapy of older and younger patients during the years that hypnosis is developing. Through understanding the ways in which patients draw upon their own resources, significant steps that take place in the process of becoming hypnotically involved will become apparent. We have chosen to present initially three patients, two older and one younger, who illustrate concretely the sequence of hypnotic procedures and the responses to them. Toward the end of the chapter, the discussion turns to the role of the hypnotherapist and some of the qualities needed for interacting with children.

Hypnotherapy with Older Children and Adolescents

After a child is old enough to follow typical hypnotic suggestions, the usual hypnotic procedures are feasible. What is "old enough" cannot be tied to chronological age because children differ widely in their maturity. Nevertheless, an acceptable lower limit for adult-like capacity for hypnosis is commonly set at about age 6, although some children may be ready earlier and some not until age 8. To illustrate hypnotic practices with older children, we have selected a young adolescent girl, age 12.

How Jennie Was Helped to Overcome an Eating Problem Accompanying Radiation Treatment. Jennie had trouble eating after she started radiation treatment for cancer. Two months earlier a brain tumor had been removed from this 12-year-old girl and for the past month she had been receiving radiation treatment to that area. At first she became nauseated and her stomach hurt each time she ate, but soon the very sight of food provoked these reactions; her discomfort extended throughout the day. Medication had not helped, and because she refused almost all food, her weight was falling. Although her physician had expected some gastric distress, he felt that Jennie's progressive weight loss was excessive and that if it continued, this would interfere with the required course of radiation therapy. At this point he referred her for hypnotherapy.

In an interview with the parents prior to starting treatment, they discussed Jennie's eating behavior. If someone could coax Jennie to eat, frequently she could keep the food down. This information indicated that if she could be helped to enjoy food again, she might overcome her difficulty in eating. After the parents' questions about hypnosis had been fully answered, it was apparent that they wanted Jennie to try it.

What a patient like Jennie, who is initially depressed, wishes to know is that the therapist grasps the fact that "things are tough." Once that salient idea has been understood, a spirit of collaboration enters the picture. When hypnosis was discussed, she was asked, "Would you be willing to see if hypnosis could help you to eat the way you used to?" Her reply, "That would be O.K." lacked a feeling of conviction because her recent experiences had been so discouraging. In order to adapt hypnosis to Jennie's interests, some time was spent in exploring the activities she enjoyed most. She placed horseback riding at the top of the list, followed by outings at the beach and in the mountains with her family and friends. Swimming and surfing had been among her favorite sports. She also talked about specific television programs and mystery stories that had appealed to her. Through this discussion, Jennie saw the therapist as genuinely interested in knowing her as a person with an extended range of capabilities and not just as an individual with an illness. The two participants were prepared to work together in a positive way.

Jennie prescribed the induction procedure herself by asking if she could be hypnotized by looking at a swinging pendulum, the way she had seen it done on TV. A Lucite ball on a chain served as a pendulum. First the therapist let the Lucite ball swing until it stopped while Jennie watched. Then Jennie was given the chain to hold, the pendulum was made to swing, and she was told to hold her hand still, always watching the ball until it stopped swinging: "Now watch it carefully . . . if it moves a little, you'll be able to watch it, too . . . As you watch it you'll find yourself getting more and more relaxed . . . feeling good . . . feeling better and better . . . very relaxed . . . No matter how relaxed you are you will be able to hear my voice and pay attention to it . . . You'll find yourself paying attention to my voice . . . No other sounds need bother you or concern you . . . Your eyelids are apt to become very tired and you will probably feel like closing your eyes . . . If you do feel this way, just let it happen. You can close your eyes anytime . . . When your eyes close, just let your hand and the pendulum move toward your lap . . . Very, very relaxed and feeling better." The themes of these ideas were repeated until Jennie became very relaxed, her eyes closed, and her hand with the Lucite ball slipped into her lap.

Jennie was asked if she could imagine herself with a horse. As she thought about this, a beautiful silver-white horse named Silver appeared next to her. Jennie became involved in images of this horse. Part of the time she drove Silver while sitting in a cart, and part of the time she rode him through the countryside. Her face became happy and relaxed. When it was suggested that Silver was probably hungry and would like to eat, Jennie fed him crushed oats, hay, a little molasses and an apple. Asked if she could see herself at a picnic with Silver, she unpacked her own lunch basket which contained peanut butter sandwiches, an orange, and oatmeal cookies. She ate these enthusiastically as Silver continued to munch.

After a time, the therapist told Jennie it was time to leave, but that they could have more fun the next day with Silver or with other friends. Could she see herself saying goodbye to Silver? She nodded. It was suggested that hypnosis would end and that when she heard the therapist count backward from 10 to 1, she would become more and more alert; at the count of 5, she would open her eyes and at the count of 1, she would feel wide awake. She was told that as she became more alert, she would continue to feel relaxed and cheerful, she would be able to remember all the fun things that had happened—how good it was to feel hungry and eat and to look forward to reading books and seeing television programs.

As soon as the session was over, Jennie asked for something to eat. She specifically asked her mother for a peanut butter sandwich, an orange, and oatmeal cookies. Later, at dinner she ate moderately. The next morning at breakfast she announced, "My stomach hurts a little," but instead of refusing food she continued, "I think my stomach must be empty," whereupon she ate. There had been no nausea.

The next day, using the same procedure, hypnosis was induced more quickly. Because Jennie had mentioned that some day she would like to have a horse named Black Beauty, it was suggested that she look to see if Black Beauty was already with her. With eyes closed, she immediately saw him, said she was the owner, and then described him in vivid detail. Her jockey was riding him in a very important race, and she and the therapist sat nearby in the grandstand. She became intensely involved. An amusing incident illustrates the extent of that involvement. At the start of the race, she said suddenly, "Wait. I lost my field glasses. We'll have to look for them." So she searched under her "seat" and directed the therapist where to search under adjacent "seats." Since Jennie and the therapist were sitting in adjacent chairs during hypnosis, it was possible to incorporate the hallucinated grandstand seats. Both made actual searching movements under their chairs. Jennie located her hallucinated glasses, repositioned herself happily in her chair and, according to her report, a very exciting race took place:

> Black Beauty's in the middle. There's only one horse ahead of him . . . This is a race for 2-year-olds. It wouldn't matter if he came in second. ("Is that what he's doing?") Oh! He's in a dangerous spot. He's on the heels of the other horse . . . they're at the hurdles . . . he jumps, he's ahead. The last hurdle he has to jump is going up hill. It's very hard. I think he's over it, the bars aren't down. He *wins*!

To a question about the prize, Jennie replied, "It's a flat silver plate with a blue ribbon."

After a brief pause as she watched intently, she announced:

> I'm going into the circle . . . I get it . . . But what's another silver plate to a horse like that? I've got plenty of them . . . It's starting to blur a little. I'm trying to get him into the trailer, a big green trailer with a blue top, white-walled tires, it's a Cadillac . . . Black Beauty also won a new halter. He won it at a steeple-chase show; his name's on it. He has three medals. The next show will be at the Washington National Horse Show with a seven foot jump. Horses hardly ever do that. Six foot usually. If he wins that, maybe he'll be the National Champion.

After she had continued a little longer, Jennie was asked what she was eating as she watched. She answered promptly, "A hamburger . . . a coke . . . an ice cream bar." The therapist ordered the same selection and they talked together about how good it all tasted. She was told that after hypnosis was over, things would go just the way they had the day before. She would continue to be so full of the same good feelings that there would be no place for anything unpleasant. Just the *good* feelings would keep on being there. After counting from 10 to 1 to end hypnosis, Jennie said she felt sleepy and wanted to nap a little while. Detecting that she was not fully aroused, the therapist told her that there would be another count from 10 to 1, and when that was completed, she would find it easier, much easier to wake up, to feel alert, to talk about how much fun she had just been having, and to continue to feel happy. This second time, Jennie appeared alert and, soon after, announced that she was hungry. What she wanted to eat came as no surprise—at the head of the list was a hamburger.

By the end of two more sessions during the next week, Black Beauty had won the Grand National. Jennie reported details of that great race, of her trip to the winner's circle to receive the first-place blue ribbon, the silver cup, and the prize money . . . of her interview with the top newspaper and television people, of the pictures taken of her and Black Beauty to the accompaniment of flashbulbs, and of the headlines in the newspapers. Jennie's imagination of these events seemed inexhaustible.

During this same period of time, even though radiation treatment continued, Jennie was cheerful and enjoyed reading and watching television. programs. Though she occasionally commented that her stomach hurt, her appetite remained at an acceptable level. The stated goals of greater comfort and an improved quality of life through hypnosis were achieved.

When tested, Jennie received a top score on hypnotic responsiveness. With this illustration of the procedure with one child, we can summarize steps in a common core of hypnotic practices used with older children.

Steps in the Hypnotic Treatment of the Hypnotizable Older Child or Adolescent. The usual steps involved in beginning hypnotherapy with an older child were taken with Jennie: a preliminary interview, an induction leading to the established hypnotic condition within which therapy proceeded, and a termination procedure. Circumstances made it inconvenient to give a test for defining her hypnotic potential in advance, but subsequently such a test provided a more accurate index of her hypnotizability compared with that of other children.

1. The preliminary interview. Those who are clinically trained understand how essential it is to devote the first session to getting acquainted with patients and parents. Much of the usual case history is obtained from the parents. With the patient, the therapist explores the patient's motivations for hypnotherapy in relation to the disease process and the medical treatments. What the patient already knows about hypnosis may influence readiness for the next steps; it is important to discuss attitudes and correct any misconceptions about hypnosis. Because the preferred hypnotherapy is not routine and alike for all children, a prominent part of the interview consists of discovering the interests and activities that can be useful in therapy.

2. The measurement of hypnotic potential. Testing for the degree of talent for hypnosis was a regular part of our research program, but as a onetime measure, it could be introduced at any appropriate time. Ordinarily it was planned as an interesting introduction to hypnosis and therefore prior to hypnotic treatment. If the psychological condition of the child made testing unadvisable in an initial session, it was postponed until a later session, as in the case of Jennie.

3. Induction. Of the two methods discussed in Chapter 1, we used the eye-closure method combined with relaxation.

At the beginning of the induction, the focus of attention is narrowed by asking the patient to watch a target. The target was often a "funny face" on a thumbnail described in Chapter 1. Most children enjoy this playful approach and quickly stop looking at objects around the room. While visual attention is directed to this one object, the hypnotherapist suggests that the patient's auditory attention be focused *only* on his or her voice. Thus seeing and hearing, two of the most important sensory channels for making contact with a variety of experiences in the environment, begin to narrow the focus. The voice keeps suggesting comfort and contentment, as well as mental and physical relaxation to the point where the eyelids become tired and may feel like closing. When the eyes close, a major device for orientation toward outer reality disappears and the transition to the hypnotic condition is occurring.

Ordinarily the eye-closure induction requires 5 minutes or so, but the time required shows marked differences from one individual to another. Sometimes this stage can be greatly abbreviated for patients who move easily and quickly into a fantasy world. A leisurely approach may be desirable for a patient who needs to relax at an unhurried pace. After the initial session, subsequent inductions usually require less time: a "signal" such as looking briefly at a thumbnail or simply counting mentally from 1 to 10 may suffice.

4. *The hypnotic condition.* Even though the transition has been made, the kind of suggestion used in induction continues, in order to increase the hypnotic involvement. Hypnotizable older adolescents interviewed after an experience of hypnosis report that they become aware only of this "voice," not of the hypnotist as a person, and not of other sounds.

The "voice" continues to concentrate on suggestions that promote muscular, mental, and emotional relaxation. Muscular tonus, like vision, is an orienting device, and marked relaxation of muscles can cause various parts of the body to be disregarded or distorted in space—for example, the position of hands and feet. Mental relaxation ("Your mind is so relaxed—no problems to solve") reduces interest in planning and control so that patients feel less and less need to call on their own memories, their own critical thinking, or their own independent resources. Thus another orienting device, mental control, is being relinquished. Suggestions of emotional relaxation ("no troubles or worries to bother you—feeling calm, easy") are interspersed with other suggestions of physical and mental relaxation. This general relaxation and withdrawal from external stimulation other than the voice of the hypnotist produces responses that have much in common with the more extreme experiences reported in sensory deprivation; for example, Barabasz suggests, "sensory restriction forces the organism to focus, perhaps as seldom before, on internally generated imaginal activity" (1982).

Once a satisfactory condition has been established, there is a readiness to respond to therapeutic suggestions appropriate to the goal of therapy in the light of the patient's problems, interests, and capabilities. Despite the withdrawal of the hypnotized person into the world of fantasy, and the heightened responsiveness to the suggestions of the hypnotist, the ability to communicate in words with the hypnotist is not lost. Jennie continued to talk about her experiences throughout the sessions, and this is a general characteristic of hypnotized persons, often unrecognized by those less familiar with hypnosis.

5. *Therapeutic practices within the hypnotic condition.* The experienced hypnotherapist has a number of practices available which can utilize the patient's hypnotic condition in order to achieve therapeutic benefit. In Jennie's case, the therapeutic procedure for restoring her appetite was to incorporate eating fantasies in the midst of hallucinated behavior engendered through her interest in horses. The same fantasies, because they elicited pleasure, assisted in counteracting her depression. As noted previously, we have found imaginative behavior an important resource not only for inducing hypnosis but for utilizing the hypnotic condition for therapeutic purposes. The use of other resources in hypnotherapy is illustrated in other cases in this and later chapters. Most of them depend either upon internally generated fantasies or upon suggestions, whether direct or indirect, for symptom relief.

6. *Termination.* In preparation for ending a hypnotic session, the therapist repeats posthypnotic suggestions for the patient's well-being and relief of symptoms. Termination usually begins with a statement that the hypnotic session will soon be over, that the therapist will count backward from 10 to 1, and that at the count of 1, the patient will be fully alert. The counting process is usually slow so that reorientation to the real world can take place gradually. Repeated suggestions for alertness accompany the counting. If a child still looks or feels groggy, the procedure can be repeated. Occasionally some further impediment to termination may arise. While the situation is rare among children, the possibility increases by late adolescence. This is one of the reasons why hypnosis cannot be left in the hands of those who are inadequately trained. Professional competence on the part of hypnotherapists is essential in order to understand and cope successfully with unusual circumstances.

Sometimes people wonder what would happen if the hypnotist had to leave, or suddenly became ill. A study entitled "The Disappearing Hypnotist" reported that highly responsive, hypnotized college students gradually roused themselves from hypnosis after the hypnotist disappeared, and that they were completely awake in half-an-hour—even though they expected the hypnotist to return (Evans and Orne, 1971).

The therapeutic practices, just discussed, have rested on the assumption that the older patient was sufficiently hypnotizable for the hypnotic condition to be relied upon in therapy. Individual differences in hypnotizability need to be recognized and accounted for in the design of treatment so that the full range of patients from highly hypnotizable to barely hypnotizable can profit from treatment by hypnotic procedures. Those at the low end of the scale commonly obtain beneficial results through the relaxation and positive expectations that hypnotic procedures facilitate.

The Hypnotic Treatment of the Less Hypnotizable Older Child or Adolescent. The initial steps the therapist undertakes with any patient are based on the assumption that some hypnotic talent is present. That is, the get-acquainted interview and the induction proceed as usual. When it is evident that hypnosis cannot be established, whether by clinical observations or by tests of hypnotic talent on one of the available scales, therapy is modified accordingly. Despite the probability that a deep involvement in fantasied action will not occur, opportunity for it is given, with the suggestions framed in such a way that the patient will not assume failure if involved fantasies are not produced.

How Eleanor Overcame Tension and Anxiety over Her Illness. Eleanor, diagnosed at age 13 as having acute lymphatic leukemia, was referred for hypnotic treatment during the pilot stage of our study by her doctor who felt that the high blood pressure she had developed since diagnosis was related to emotional tension over her disease. Eleanor confirmed that she was worrying a great deal about the leukemia and about the treatment procedures. On the hypnotizability scale, her score indicated that her talent for hypnosis was well below average. During the attempted induction, she relaxed well, but she was not particularly hypnotizable because she lacked the requisite imagination. She described herself as a person who preferred logical rather than "imagined" solutions to problems. Her treatment was planned to accommodate her temperament.

The therapist suggested that Eleanor lie still, breathe slowly and deeply, relax, and then go over in her mind the things that were bothering her. The suggestions given to her in the clinic and then used at home were worded this way: "Get clearly in your mind what is bothering you. Think it through completely. If you can change it or do something about it, do it. If not, give it only a few minutes' attention, then put it away until something can be done . . . Your problems are *important* but they are not all of your life. Give them five minutes a day or so, then use the rest of the day for *you*—for pleasure and fun and enjoyment."

The therapist also asked Eleanor if she wanted to talk about any problems that bothered her, but she declined. The assigned five minutes of relaxation and clear thinking appealed more to her logical nature. Soon she was again participating in and enjoying her previous activities, such as attending 4-H meetings and watching television programs. Her blood pressure went back to normal.

After the tension was relieved and the blood pressure lowered, the therapist maintained a friendly relationship with her when she returned for medical treatment. One playful (and less than logical) incident will illustrate this. After hearing that Eleanor was scheduled for an unexpected lumbar puncture the next day, the therapist telephoned her and said: "I hear you don't want to go . . . I'll tell you what. You enjoy TV tonight, have a good time with your family, and get a good rest. It's my turn to worry about the lumbar puncture tomorrow—you enjoy yourself."

Eleanor's mother reported the next day that Eleanor had had a carefree night since someone else was doing the worrying. During the procedure, the therapist was holding her hand and Eleanor said, "Are you nervous?" The therapist replied with a twinkle in her eye, "Of course I'm a *little* nervous, this is my lumbar puncture, remember?" After this whimsical interaction, Eleanor left in good spirits.

With Eleanor, the primary emphasis was on learning to relax while recalling pleasant past activities. She was told that she might *briefly* entertain worries, then set them aside. This orientation, suggested by a supportive therapist, enabled her to move toward participation in interesting activities again, with the result that her blood pressure returned to normal. No hypnosis was involved. As we shall see, some problems respond to suggestions for relaxation and do not require hypnosis. It is clear that when a patient has been referred for hypnosis, there is a place for sensitive modification of procedures and expectations according to the responses of the patient.

For more highly hypnotizable children and adolescents, as in the earlier case of Jennie, the specific benefits resulting from greater hypnotic talent are evident. For them, the active imaginative involvement carries with it a reality which, through the dissociation it produces, competes strongly with symptoms such as pain and acute anxiety.

Hypnotherapy with the Younger Child

When the standard procedures for inducing hypnosis in older children were tried with younger ones, differences soon became evident. The problem of eye closure in the young was one of the more conspicuous. Most 6-year-old children preferred to keep their eyes open and remain active when eye closure and relaxation were suggested. Age norms are not applicable to all children, and a few 6-year-olds closed their eyes and relaxed. The proportion closing their eyes increased with age. Most

8-year-olds readily responded to the suggestions to close their eyes and sit quietly (Morgan and J. Hilgard, 1978/79). Rather than adopt rigid age protocols, we simply shifted to the procedures used with younger children anytime a patient showed signs of difficulty in accepting eye closure and relaxation.

Before describing the modified practices used with young children, we present the case of Chris to illustrate concretely the differences in responses to hypnosis.

How Chris Overcame a Needle Phobia.   Four months after he had been diagnosed as having cancer, 7-year-old Chris was referred to the hypnosis program by his doctor because of his violent resistance to the frequent "finger sticks" that were necessary.[1] Chris's mother reported that although he had cried and required restraint from the beginning, recently his objections were so strenuous that it took three staff members to restrain him.

Chris, large and strong for his age, was an intelligent, good-natured boy who expressed his anxiety in hyperactive behavior. Although he had been occasionally observed sitting quietly for a long period, working on an absorbing crafts project, for example, his behavior in the hospital was typically very restless, and his attention span brief. When given a modified version of the children's scale to test for hypnotic responsiveness, Chris paced around the room and participated only while standing; even under these unlikely conditions, he became very involved in the first four items of a 6-point scale before his restlessness made it impossible to complete the measurements. The degree of his involvement in the items that he passed indicated high hypnotic ability.

When asked what bothered him about finger sticks Chris said briefly, "They hurt." He rated their typical level of discomfort at 4 on a scale of 0–10, where 0 represented no pain and 10 represented the most pain. When the therapist told Chris that he could learn some secrets to make these procedures easier, Chris appeared very intrigued and eager to share these "secrets." Here is the therapist's account of how the session proceeded:

> We'll have to do some magic. Somebody who has been as bothered as you have can't be helped by just anything. We'll have to use *strong* magic. First, you have to make your hand and fingers go to sleep for a few minutes, so they're not bothered. I'll show you how to do it. Take some big breaths with me . . . That's good—now some more . . . That's how you and I breathe when we relax at night . . . Just relax and listen to my voice.

The therapist's voice lowered gradually to a whisper. Chris concentrated as he stared down at his hand and his breathing became deep and slow:

> Ready to help your hand go to sleep? Okay, good. I'll just put my hand up on your shoulder like this, to help it become numb. Sleepy and numb, just like the numbing medicine . . . you know what that's like, don't you? While your hand is becoming numb, you rub the fingers and hand . . . Good, that's right . . . soft and sleepy.

Chris soon reported, without any suggestion from the therapist about movement, that he felt unable to move his arm or hand; furthermore, he reported that they felt quite numb. Then, suddenly, he said: "This is pretend—I don't know if it will work for a *real* finger stick." The therapist agreed with him, saying that one was never sure how things would turn out but that not knowing made it more fun. Even though Chris was worried, the therapist continued, he could be pleasantly surprised to notice how much easier finger sticks could become.

Chris was then asked to imagine himself in the lab, preparing for a finger stick. He visualized the setting, which included the nurse who was ready to poke his finger. He stated that each time the nurse rubbed his finger with an alcohol wipe, just prior to the finger stick, he felt very scared. He was then asked to close his eyes and picture a flower. He pictured a large yellow one, which he was asked to smell. "Just keep your nose in the flower, so the alcohol smell turns into perfume." He grinned at this suggestion. After some practice, using real alcohol wipes, he reported that he no longer smelled the alcohol—only the flower.

As he left this session Chris was told by a nurse that, contrary to the routine he had been anticipating that day, he was due for a finger stick. His voice trembling and tears in his eyes, he loudly denied that it was time. When the nurse insisted, he stated that he would not cooperate. Clearly this sudden test of what he was just learning was premature. Fortunately, his doctor agreed to postpone some of the tests for which the finger stick was required until the following Monday.

Given the limited time available, Chris's mother was asked to work with Chris over the weekend. She took home with her the equipment for the finger stick, and was asked to let Chris examine and hold it, then to pretend he was poking her finger. They were instructed to use alcohol wipes, to make the simulation more real. After the weekend, Chris's mother reported that the practice sessions had gone very well, and that Chris had proudly demonstrated to her his newfound ability to "change the alcohol smell to perfume." As if to demonstrate to the therapist that he had now achieved total mastery over the technique, he tore open an alcohol wipe and rubbed it on his nose. His eyes half-closed, he sniffed with the ecstatic look of a gardener smelling a prize-winning rose. It was clear that he no longer required further direction in order to produce this change in perception. The therapist asked Chris to demonstrate to his mother how he put his hand to sleep. With the therapist's hand placed on his shoulder and again with the same suggestions as before, he reinstated the numbness. Chris then pleasantly walked to the lab, where he proudly pointed to his "numb" hand which dangled lifelessly. His mother and the lab nurse reinforced his behavior with appropriate appreciation of his ability. As the nurse prepared to do the finger stick, he suddenly hid his hand behind his back. After a moment he asked for help again to make his hand "go to sleep." This was accomplished in the same manner as before. The finger stick was then done quickly. Chris showed no active resistance, tears, or expressions of discomfort and seemed very pleased by the nurse's invitation to help her gather some drops of blood. In previous instances, he had been too distraught to take part in this. He rated this finger stick at 1, saying that he felt a poke, but that it had not hurt.

When the therapist arrived at the hospital a few days later, prior to the next scheduled finger stick, Chris was excited and in good spirits. Chris announced that he was going to surprise the other lab nurse who did not know that he had learned how to make his hand go to sleep. He requested that he and the therapist go to the project office immediately to prepare his hand so that he could surprise her. Once in the office, he directed the therapist to touch his left shoulder while he rubbed the fingers of his left hand to make them numb. It was clear that he was in control of the sensations in his hand and used the therapist only as one might use a consultant. He now described his hand as "numb," "tingly," and "sleepy." Meanwhile the two conspirators conjectured together how surprised the nurse would be, since she was accustomed to Chris's putting up a big fight. After a few moments, Chris ran out into the clinic where he encountered several nurses and doctors. He proudly called their attention to the hand that had "fallen asleep." He appeared even more pleased when the director of the clinic replied in a serious tone of voice: "That's good, but don't talk too loud, you might wake it up!"

During the next two or three minutes Chris pursued the lab nurse around the clinic until she finally agreed to do his finger stick next. He waited impatiently for her to be ready with the needle and then told her to proceed. He grinned and laughed as she dramatically displayed an appropriate degree of amazement and appreciation for his behavior. Again, he rated this finger stick at 1.

Follow-up indicated that Chris continued to receive finger sticks with no difficulty. His mother, in answer to a questionnaire several months later, rated the hypnosis treatment program as having been very helpful. "Chris feels less anxiety when making trips to the hospital," she wrote. "He no longer worries in advance about finger sticks . . . he just makes his fingers numb." Furthermore, she felt that Chris's hypnosis program had been of benefit to her as well: "With less anxiety over finger sticks I am more at ease with my role in Chris's treatment. No mother likes to see her child go through so much anxiety, and now that Chris responds better I feel better."

Steps in the Hypnotic Treatment of the Younger Child. Just as Jennie was a representative of high hypnotizability in her group, so Chris was a representative of high hypnotizability in his age group. We will therefore follow the same steps used in hypnotic practices with older children in order to indicate how they are modified in hypnotherapy with hypnotizable younger children.

1. The preliminary interview. A get-acquainted interview precedes hypnosis with the younger child, as with the older one. The hypnotherapist made friends with Chris to help him overcome any uneasiness about the presence of another stranger in the treatment room. Emphasis was placed on eliciting from Chris the kinds of activities he most liked. He proved to be a cheerful child—as long as no needle appeared.

2. Measurement of hypnotic potential. Typically, measurement provided an opportunity both for the young child's initial experience of hypnosis and for appraising the level of hypnotizability. Differences associated with age were often revealed, as in Chris's degree of activity during the test. Even so, in his case there was ample evidence of his hypnotizability.

3. Induction. With Chris, the induction relied upon fantasy from the beginning. After the hypnotherapist suggested that he and Chris play a game of magic, the therapist then heightened the drama of the game by lowering his voice to a whisper. Chris must now listen intently to the whispered words so that he does not miss any of the directions for producing magic. The whispers suggest continued concentration on the hand, general relaxation, and *thoughts* of how the hand is becoming numb. (At no time did Chris close his eyes, nor did he significantly relax, although he markedly restrained his usual hyperactive behavior.)

With most of the very young children we used the fantasy induction. Ordinarily the fantasies were built around the interests and activities discovered in the initial interview. In Chris's case, "magic" substituted for his special interests. Many children of this age are intrigued by ideas of magic, as we shall see with other patients.

4. The hypnotic condition. The induction game of whispered magic moved into the phase of hypnosis for Chris when he perceived his hand as numb. The onset of numbness marked a transition to a limited dissociation—limited because it relates only to a part of the body. A second dissociation appeared when Chris placed his nose in hallucinated flowers so that the smell of a real alcohol wipe turned into the perfume of flowers. The profound degree of dissociation was reflected by his smiling report that an actual alcohol-saturated wipe had a delightful aroma. Chris achieved more than visual and olfactory imagery—the key ingredient in his success was that a part of him—a dissociated part—participated in the fantasy. These dissociations involved no altered state of consciousness. It is clear that both dissociations (the hand analgesia and the olfactory hallucination) were confined to discrete parts of the body consciousness. At all times Chris demonstrated an alert awareness of his accomplishment in producing the dissociations.

5. *Therapeutic practices within the hypnotic condition.* In Chris's case, the hypnotic condition permitted his hand to be made numb by the therapist's suggestions and Chris's own rubbing. This procedure enabled Chris to produce the numbness by himself. The second use of the hypnotic condition neutralized anxiety over the alcohol wash by changing the odor of alcohol to that of flowers. His self-control became a source of pride, supported by the comments of nurse and physician which included playful humor. These effects were produced by partial dissociations without any pervasive change in his consciousness.

The hypnotherapist used ingenuity in sustaining Chris's attentive involvement by such devices as the use of whispering. The effective use of therapy is far from routine and has what may be described as an artistic component that supplements scientific understanding. With patients who have other symptoms, the use of their internal resources as made available by the hypnotic condition, may call for different tactics. Instead of attempting to list these, some of the variations appear in the treatment of subsequent patients.

6. *Termination.* The hypnotic condition is reversed by the same methods that were used in producing it. If fantasies or "magical" practices were employed, they are cancelled. Chris, for example, was told that his hand felt normal again, and that alcohol would smell like alcohol. This reversal takes but little time with younger children because they move back and forth so easily between fantasy and reality.

Characteristics of a Hypnotherapist

A distinction can be made between a capable hypnotist and a capable hypnotherapist. A hypnotist is skilled in adapting induction procedures to achieve as extensive a hypnotic involvement as a subject is capable of. Once the hypnotic condition is established, the hypnotist may use direct or indirect suggestions to produce the varied phenomena of hypnosis, such as age regression or posthypnotic amnesia. These are skills that the hypnotherapist shares with the skilled hypnotist. In addition, however, the therapeutic skills of the hypnotherapist go beyond the practices of hypnosis. Merely becoming hypnotized does not suffice to meet a patient's problems. The hypnotic condition makes the resources of the patient available for therapeutic use.

A skilled hypnotist with little understanding of psychotherapy may conduct very successful experiments relevant to clinical work, such as the reduction of experimentally produced pains in nonpatient subjects. While any qualified hypnotist who works in a nonclinical laboratory setting is sensitive to the interpersonal relationship between hypnotist and subject, there is little need for the hypnotist to have experience in psychological therapy.

A distinction between the qualifications required of a hypnotist and those required of a hypnotherapist recognizes that the hypnotherapist possesses particular skills in the utilization of hypnosis for therapy. In addition, he or she needs broader training and experience in nonhypnotic therapy. In some instances, the therapeutic practices belong to a specialty within the healing arts—as in dentistry—so that hypnotherapy is related to, and restricted to, that specialty. If a patient's symptoms represent behavioral and emotional disorders, the basic requisite skills are those of a psychotherapist. A more complete statement relevant to these broad issues can be found in Appendix A.

Our young patients saw the hypnotherapist as a trusted person helping them gain skill toward all-important goals in their lives. For the hypnotherapist to be perceived in this way, certain characteristics are required: genuine friendliness, an ability to inspire confidence, and the flexibility to respond appropriately to the many unusual circumstances that are confronted in clinical practice.

Assertion of the importance of friendliness and sensitivity to the patient's problems raises a subtle question regarding the relationship between sensitivity, objectivity, and therapeutic effectiveness. Some inexperienced therapists go to the extreme of identifying so closely with the patient's feelings that they are unable to maintain objectivity. They therefore fail to help the patient gain relief through utilization of pertinent coping methods. For example, when Chris complained that the smell of alcohol upset him because of its association with finger sticks, instead of feeling sorry for him, the hypnotherapist cheerfully offered Chris a new coping method. The therapist remained both sensitive and objective. At the other extreme is the beginning therapist who has heard that hypnosis depends upon carefully worded suggestions and therefore uses a routine that is stilted, mechanical, or ill-adapted to the abilities and preferences of the patient. Because these matters are too subtle to categorize adequately at this point, we shall rely on the individual case reports that accompany the quantitative findings of the research.

Notes

1. A "finger stick" describes the needle prick in a finger in order to draw blood for microscopic study. Some children find the repeated pricks very disagreeable.

3   The Stanford Study: Relief of Pain and Anxiety during Bone Marrow Aspirations

In a preliminary phase during the first year of our research grant, 34 young patients ranging in age from 4 to 19 years were referred for hypnotherapy.[1] Of these, 16 were referred for control of pain and anxiety in bone aspirations and lumbar punctures. Another 5 patients were referred for the reduction of pain and anxiety in short procedures such as intravenous injections and the changing of bandages. There were 2 patients with continuous pain from ulcerations and one from the pressure of a tumor. An additional 10 patients asked for help in relieving ancillary symptoms such as diffuse anxiety reactions, depression, insomnia, nausea, and high blood pressure. The results were encouraging, but the referral method, which led to a heterogeneous population of patients, severely limited possible generalizations with respect to the effectiveness of hypnotherapy (J. Hilgard and Morgan, 1978). This exploratory phase resulted in formulating a specific design for the research, more precise instruments of evaluation, and a basic strategy for relieving pain according to a designated treatment procedure.

From observations in the preliminary study, we found that most patients dreaded the invasiveness of the bone marrow procedure. A few, traumatized by prior aspirations, were already screaming as they entered the treatment room and were forced to lie down on the table where the procedure took place. Zeltzer and colleagues (1980) found that most adolescents with cancer spoke of their treatments, including bone marrow aspirations, as worse than the disease itself. We decided that a systematic study should concentrate on children whose distress occurred during bone marrow aspirations and with the source of pain held constant, full attention could be directed toward understanding individual differences between patients. In this way we hoped to account for the greater degree of success with hypnotherapy that some children achieved.

The residue of fear from earlier bone marrow aspirations arises because the procedure is repeated at intervals over an extended period, sometimes several years. The "typical" protocol requires a bone marrow aspiration every six weeks during the active phase of chemotherapy, which lasts approximately two years or longer. During the next phase, that of remission, when the cancerous cells are absent from the blood, bone marrow, and spinal fluid, the procedure is usually repeated every three to six months in order to detect any recurrence. During a recurrence or "relapse," a schedule of chemotherapy and more frequent bone marrow aspirations is reactivated and a new intensive chemotherapy regimen begins.

In the first chapter we described how, in a bone marrow aspiration, a large needle penetrates the iliac crest of the hipbone where there are three areas sensitive to pain: the skin, the periosteum or covering of the bone, and the interior of the bone when the marrow from its central area is sucked into the needle. In addition, heavy pressure is exerted on the bone in order to penetrate the periosteum and bone to reach the marrow. A local anesthetic, 2 percent Xylocaine, was available either through a pressure spray (referred to by many nurses and patients as the "mizzy jet") or through a needle to anesthetize the skin and possibly infiltrate tissues at the periosteal level. Although a local anesthetic could alter the degree of pain felt when the large bone marrow needle penetrated sensitive outer tissues, no local anesthetic could affect the sharp pain that occurred as the aspirate was withdrawn through the needle.

The Systematic Investigation

After our experience in the preliminary phase, we were better able to take into account the restraints upon systematic research in arriving at an appropriate design. We wished to proceed in a manner that would produce conclusive results on the effectiveness of hypnotherapy with patients whose responses to the pain of the bone marrow procedure had been evaluated before any hypnotic intervention.

Four procedural steps were involved in conducting our research: (1) assessment of the degree of pain and anxiety during bone marrow aspirations at baseline, prior to any mention of hypnosis; (2) hypnotic preparation with rehearsal of a simulated bone marrow procedure; (3) assessment of the degree of pain and anxiety during the first and second bone marrow treatments in which hypnotherapy was used; and (4) measurement of hypnotizability. These are discussed in turn.

Assessment of Pain and Anxiety During Bone Marrow Aspirations at Baseline. In order to have a baseline which indicated the degree of pain and anxiety felt by the patient during routine bone marrow aspirations, the first step took place before there had been any mention of hypnosis or prior participation in the study. The study called for observing a consecutive series of patients in the selected age range who were scheduled for bone marrow procedures. We obtained permission from patients and parents for an observer to remain in the treatment room while the patient was undergoing the bone marrow aspiration. At the end of this session, each patient was given the opportunity to enlist in the hypnosis program; that is, the treatment group became a subsample of the baseline group.

A total of 63 patients between the ages of 6 to 19 constituted the baseline sample of children and adolescents. Because we observed them prior to an invitation to participate in the hypnosis program, these patients represented a sample of successive bone marrow aspirations uninfluenced by our planned intervention.

During the baseline procedures, the observer kept a detailed record of the patient's behavior at each stage, from the time of entry to the treatment room through the period after completion. Note was made of behavioral signs of *anxiety* during three periods when no needles were used: (1) entrance to the room and lying down on the treatment table; (2) the sterile wash prior to the procedure; and (3) recovery. Note was made of behavioral signs of *pain and accompanying anxiety* during two periods: (1) administration of local anesthetic, and (2) use of the bone marrow needle (insertion, aspiration of marrow, and withdrawal.) On a scale of 0 to 10, two independent judges subsequently rated the degree of pain and anxiety described in these detailed behavioral reports.

The narrative accounts recorded by the hypnotherapist at the time were sufficiently detailed to produce a basis for later ratings by two experienced judges whose ratings were in substantial agreement. The alternative method of a rating scale by an independent observer present at the time of the procedure was used in research by Katz, Kellerman, and Siegel (1980). In a study subsequent to ours, Zeltzer and LeBaron (1982) supplemented patient self-reports with an observer-recorded checklist similar to the Katz, Kellerman, and Siegel rating scale. Their results, comparable to our judged narrative ratings, are reported later in this chapter.

After the entire procedure was over and the patients had recovered, they were asked to describe what it had been like, how they had felt, and if there were things that helped and things that did not help. We asked for a *self-rating of pain* on a scale of 0, indicating no pain, to 10, indicating the most severe pain they could think of. For the younger children who were unable to report their experience in numerical terms, pictures of facial expressions were used to help in the search for the appropriate degree of felt pain. Self-reports for pain were obtained but not for anxiety. We had found in pretesting that some of the youngest patients seemed confused by the request to distinguish between anxiety and pain (being "scared" and "feeling the hurt").[2] By the time patients had recovered from the procedure and could be questioned, the most recent event, that of the bone marrow needle itself seemed to dominate everything. Therefore, for the estimate of anxiety, we relied on ratings by two judges of the behavior that had been recorded by the observer.

Observation of bone marrow aspirations during the baseline period (before hypnotic intervention) proved to be informative. The percentage of patients accepting the invitation to the hypnosis program showed a direct relationship to the amount of pain they reported. Of the 18 patients with self-ratings of pain between 0 and 2, none volunteered. At successively higher levels of self-reported pain, a larger proportion sought hypnosis as a source of relief. Of the 12 patients in the highest pain group at levels 9 and 10, 9—or 75 percent—of the group volunteered for hypnotherapy. The total group of 24 patients who volunteered had an average self-reported pain of 7.1 on the scale of 0–10. They constituted the treatment group to be studied quantitatively.

Those who did not request treatment were primarily those who experienced less pain, although some patients reported substantial pain. The average level of pain for the 39 patients not accepting hypnosis was 3.7—well below that of those electing hypnotic treatment. Almost all of the 18 with the lowest levels of pain had developed coping methods of their own; their personal coping strategies are discussed in Chapter 6.

We learned during the baseline observations that the routine connected with the local anesthetic varied from patient to patient. Fortunately, from the point of view of the research, once a patient started on a routine with respect to the local anesthetic, the physician tended to follow this routine; in addition, patients expected and insisted upon the routine to which they were accustomed.

At baseline in the hypnotic treatment sample of 24 patients, we noted the following: no anesthetic, 3 patients; pressure spray only, 3 patients; needle only, 13 patients; pressure spray and needle, 5 patients. It was possible to determine if one or another of the several painful episodes (pressure spray, anesthetic needle, bone marrow needle) might have been perceived as most painful by the patient. Analysis of the reports showed that a majority of patients perceived events concerned with the bone marrow needle insertion and aspiration as the most painful. In two patients there was supplementation of the local anesthetic—one with chloral hydrate, and the other with the tranquilizer Valium (diazepam).

An analysis of the baseline measures for anxiety produced findings in the same direction as the baseline measures for pain, but not discriminating as well. Of those patients who did not volunteer for hypnosis, 29 of 39 (74 percent) were rated as expressing a low degree of anxiety (rating 0–2), whereas of those patients who volunteered, 14 of 24 (58 percent) expressed a moderate to high degree of anxiety. Overall, those with a low degree of anxiety were the ones who felt less need for hypnosis.

Always important in studies of change, baseline data are particularly important in pain studies because of initial differences in the expression of pain and anxiety prior to hypnotherapy. If all patients had been treated without baseline measures, the effectiveness of hypnotic intervention would have appeared exaggerated, for many would have shown little pain and anxiety after treatment, yet in many instances hypnosis would not have been responsible. On the other hand, if the untreated group of patients already largely free of pain and anxiety were used as a control, hypnotic intervention might have appeared unsuccessful because the final pain levels of treated and untreated might not have been significantly different. Such a conclusion would have ignored the fact that the initial mean pain at baseline in the treated group was twice the initial mean pain at the baseline in the untreated group.

Hypnotic Treatment and Rehearsal Through Simulation. In our questions to the patient at the end of the baseline observation, one of the goals was to establish a comfortable relationship with patient and parent. When patients who had volunteered for hypnotic treatment returned for their next bone marrow aspiration—usually six weeks later—we reestablished contact through a "get-acquainted" discussion before proceeding with specific therapy. We inquired into the patient's interests and activities, answered questions about hypnosis, and in general clarified how treatment would proceed.

The hypnotherapist then introduced the patient to the experience of hypnosis. With the child seated in a comfortable chair in the project office, hypnosis was induced either by the eye closure or by the fantasy method. Following several minutes of hypnotic involvement, the patient was requested to move to a recumbent position on a nearby treatment table similar to the one used in the bone marrow procedure. The therapist then led the patient step-by-step through a simulation of the aspiration, regardless of the degree of hypnotic involvement. Such a simulation has been termed the rehearsal method.[3] With the skin area of the hip exposed, a cold object held against the skin simulated the sterile wash, a pinch simulated the local anesthetic needle or spray, then the pressure of a finger and a more intense pinch simulated the bone marrow needle insertion and subsequent withdrawal of the marrow. In this way the patient was experiencing the familiar bone marrow procedure at the same time as the resources of hypnosis substituted pleasant fantasies for stresses in the actual bone marrow. Imaginative activity was suggested at critical steps in the simulated aspiration process. The rehearsal ended with a posthypnotic suggestion that the hypnotic experience would be repeated in the actual treatment room and would provide comfort during the bone marrow procedure. The rehearsal, performed at a distance from the treatment room, was conducted without arousing anxiety.

The actual bone marrow aspiration was scheduled to follow on the same day as the hypnotic preparation and simulation, usually immediately afterwards. At the scheduled time, the patient was accompanied to the treatment room by the hypnotherapist. Next, the patient moved to the treatment table and was prepared for the procedure by a sterile wash of the hip area. During this preparation, the child was encouraged to experience pleasant events from the past (age regression) or fantasied events of another type such as flying with the clouds. During the procedure, the hypnotherapist reinforced the hypnotic involvement as needed. For example, at the crucial point of needle insertion, the child might be asked to blow out the birthday candles on a fantasied cake. If candles that relight automatically were used, the intense involvement with blowing could be prolonged.

Because most of the younger patients had been accustomed to holding a parent's hand during the bone marrow aspiration, this was built into the hypnotic preparation. That is, after hypnosis had been induced, it was suggested that the child could squeeze the parent's or the therapist's hand whenever needed and put all bodily feelings into that squeeze—keeping attention on the hand and squeezing it.

Assessment of Pain and Anxiety during Bone Marrow Aspirations with Hypnotherapy. For purposes of assessing the changes taking place from baseline as a consequence of the hypnotic intervention, it was essential to repeat all of the same types of observations and self-reports of pain and anxiety as were obtained in the baseline observation. Within the treatment room where the baseline observations had taken place, the same steps in the bone marrow procedure were observed and recorded. The differences between baseline ratings and treatment ratings served as a basis for determining successes and failures in treatment.

Measurement of Hypnotic Ability. One of the central objectives in our investigation was to determine the relationship between *hypnotic responsiveness and success in using hypnotic treatment to reduce pain.* To accomplish this goal, we measured the hypnotic responsiveness of each patient. (The terms *hypnotizability, hypnotic susceptibility, hypnotic ability or talent,* and *hypnotic responsiveness* are used interchangeably in the field of hypnotic research.) It has long been known that people differ from one another in their capacity to experience hypnosis, even under the most favorable conditions. In our description of the research procedures, we did not specify the time when hypnotic testing should take place because finding a uniform time for this procedure proved to be a problem. For example, when children arrived at the clinic with just enough time for hypnotic rehearsal before the next scheduled bone marrow aspiration, testing had to be delayed until after the procedure. As a consequence, about a quarter of the patients were tested before hypnotic preparation had begun, and the others were tested at some available time in the course of therapy.

The SHCS:Child, a scale for measuring hypnotic responsiveness in children, had been developed and standardized before this investigation was undertaken. To use this scale, the therapist induces hypnosis in the usual ways, and then offers the patient or subject the opportunity to respond to a number of varied suggestions. The greater the number of the person's responses which meet the criteria for passing, the higher the person scores in hypnotic responsiveness.

The SHCS:Child was developed and published in two forms—one for patients ages 6 to 16, and a modified, shortened scale for younger patients ages 4 to 8 (Morgan and Hilgard, 1978/79). To clarify the nature of the suggestions and the criteria for passing, the seven items of the scale for those 6 to 16 years are explained in an abbreviated form in Table 3–1.

The experienced clinician soon learns to detect the signs of hypnotic response which serve as criteria for passing the items. Each item that is passed has a weight of 1, so that the total possible score is 7. The scale was designed to include enough easy items so that almost all children could experience some success. When standardized on a population of 80 well children, the average score for those in the age range of our hypnotherapy sample was 5.1 on the 7-point scale. The hypnotherapy sample of 24 patients scored essentially the same at a mean of 5.4.

The modified form of the SHCS:Child, appropriate for children ages 4 to 8 years, uses a fantasy induction because many prefer to keep their eyes open and do not respond well either to suggestions of eye closure or relaxation. The 6-item scale omits the posthypnotic suggestion so that the highest possible score is 6.

In our investigation, a few patients were older than 16; for them the Stanford Hypnotic Clinical Scale for Adults was used (Morgan and J. Hilgard, 1978/79).

The measurement of hypnotizability proved essential for determining with greater precision the role of hypnosis in the control of pain and

Table 3-1 The Stanford Hypnotic Clinical Scale for Children
(SHCS: Child) Ages 6 to 16*

Test Item	Brief Description	Criteria of Passing	Weight In Score
1) Hand Lowering	Arm extended, palm up; lowering of arm suggested	Hand lowers at least 6 inches in 10 seconds	1
2) Arm Rigidity	Other arm and fingers extended; inability to bend suggested	Arm bends less than 2 inches in 10 seconds	1
3) TV Watching	Visualizing program	Details indicate actual viewing	1
4) TV Auditory	Listening to program	Reports of words and sound effects	1
5) Dream	"Let a dream come into your mind"	Images comparable to a night dream	1
6) Age Regression	Relive an event one or more years in the past	Experience of being at the event	1
7) Posthypnotic Response	Suggestion given that after arousal, a handclap will reinstate hypnosis	Closes eyes; gives evidence of relaxation	1
		Total possible score	7

*The full text of the induction and test items can be found in Morgan and J. Hilgard (1978/79).

anxiety in the investigation. When it is possible to do the testing before hypnotherapy is attempted, it has the further advantage of indicating the kinds of suggestions to which the child is likely to respond favorably.

Results of the Systematic Research

In this section we describe the statistical changes in pain and anxiety between baseline and the subsequent two bone marrow aspirations after the patient has had the benefit of hypnotherapy.[4]

Overall Pain Reduction through Hypnotherapy. When the pain in the baseline aspiration was compared to the first aspiration with hypnosis for the 24 patients treated by hypnotherapy, there was a significant mean reduction of both self-rated pain ($p < .01$) and ratings of pain-related behavior ($p < .001$). This difference was found despite the inclusion of the less hypnotizable patients. There was a further mean reduction of pain during an aspiration on a second day, but the change with hypnosis was not statistically significant.

A study subsequent to the Stanford study, to which reference has already been made in Chapter 1 (Zeltzer and LeBaron, 1982), compared hypnotherapy to nonhypnotic supportive therapy in patients ages 6 to 17 undergoing bone marrow aspirations. While both groups experienced reduction of pain, a significantly greater pain reduction in the group treated by hypnotherapy indicated the advantages of hypnosis.

Pain Reduction as Related to Measured Hypnotizability. In order to compare the changes in pain associated with degree of hypnotizability, scores made by young patients on the SHCS:Child were divided at the mean score into two groups: 19 with scores of 5 through 7 were classified as more hypnotizable, and 5 with scores of 4 and below were classified as less hypnotizable. The 24 patients were dichotomized in respect to their self-report of changes in pain between baseline and the first bone marrow after hypnotherapy: 10 more successful in pain reduction reported a pain reduction of 3 or more points on the 10-point scale of pain, and 14 less successful remained the same, increased slightly, or reduced pain by no more than 2 points on the 10-point scale. The data are presented in Table 3-2.

As seen from the table, 10 of 19 of the more hypnotizable were among the more successful pain reducers, while none of the 5 less hypnotizable were among the more successful. The results in a table of this sort can be

Table 3-2 Reduction in Self-Reported Pain as Related to Hypnotizability: The First Bone Marrow Aspiration after Hypnotherapy*

	Less Successful in Pain Reduction	More Successful in Pain Reduction	Total Patients
More Hypnotizable	9	10	19
Less Hypnotizable	5	0	5
Total Patients	14	10	24

$p < .05$ Fisher's Exact Probability Test.

For criteria of the more and less hypnotizable and more or less successful in pain reduction, see text.

*From J. Hilgard and LeBaron (1982).

tested statistically for the probability that this degree of correspondence could occur by chance. Applying Fisher's Exact Probability Test, the likelihood is less than 5 in 100 that such a result would be found if no true relationship existed between measurements of hypnotizability and ratings of pain reduction. The 10 who reduced pain appreciably on the first day moved from a mean baseline pain of 7.5 to 3.0, a reduction of 4.5 scale points or 60 percent of the originally reported pain. The remaining 14 patients had a baseline pain of 7, and after the first hypnotic treatment, it remained at 6.9.

Even though the results statistically favor the more hypnotizable patients, 9 of the 19 more hypnotizable failed to reduce pain substantially following the first hypnotherapeutic session. It turned out, however, that some of these more hypnotizable patients profited by a second hypnotherapy session at the time of the next bone marrow aspiration. In fact, 5 of the 9 who were less successful the first time moved into the ranks of the more successful pain reducers. Nine of the ten successful in the first session returned for a second session.[5] Because those successful in the first session retained their success, the demonstrated success rate in the second session among the more hypnotizable patients was 14/18, or 78 percent. The 5 more hypnotizable patients who reduced their pain on the second hypnotic session reduced their pain from an average baseline of 7.3 to 3.0, a reduction of 4.3 scale points. None of the other patients, whether high or low in hypnotizability, reduced their pain on the second day.

A further report on the investigation by Zeltzer and LeBaron (1982) related pain reduction in bone marrow aspirations to measured hypnotizability (Zeltzer, LeBaron, and Zeltzer, 1982). Tests of hypnotizability were administered to 17 patients who had received hypnotic treatment and to 15 patients who had received nonhypnotic treatment for pain as described in the earlier report. In the group receiving support of a nonhypnotic type, pain reduction was unrelated to measured hypnotizability. Among those who received hypnotic treatment, 10 were highly hypnotizable and 6 of the 10 (60 percent) reduced pain appreciably, while only 2 of 7 patients (29 percent) who tested low in hypnotizability were able to reduce pain to a comparable extent. Because the numbers are so small, the difference between those high and low in hypnotizability is not statistically significant, although it is in the same direction as that reported in Table 3–2.

Anxiety Reduction as Related to Hypnotherapy. With the same dichotomy of hypnotizability scores as for pain, a correspondence with anxiety reduction could also be computed. The only assessment was by the judged ratings of the behavioral descriptions because the younger children did not seem to distinguish well between anxiety and pain. The source of the anxiety lies largely in the experience of pain so that the two measures do not lend themselves to satisfactory separate appraisal, despite the fact that the anxiety rating was taken at the time of the sterile wash when no needles were involved. For the treatment group of 24, the mean anxiety level at baseline was judged to be 3.2 on the 10-point scale and dropped to 1.9 after the first hypnotherapeutic session ($p < .01$). A slight further decline at the time of the second bone marrow procedure with hypnotherapy was not statistically significant.

The results for anxiety are consistent with the results for pain but, as noted, the two measures cannot be considered independent of one another. When patients were dichotomized on measured hypnotizability, it was found for anxiety as it had been for pain, that anxiety reduction was correlated positively with the level of hypnotizability ($p < .01$ Fisher's Exact Probability Test).

In the later investigation conducted by Zeltzer and LeBaron (1982), separate self-ratings of pain and anxiety were obtained, and hypnotic treatment resulted in significant reductions for both.

Felt Pain and Its Overt Expression as a Function of Age and Sex

In reporting pain, we have noted a satisfactory correlation between self-reports of pain and judged estimates of pain. However, in some instances, particularly among older children and adolescents, the discrepancy between a self-report and judged estimates of pain was marked. By becoming aware of this possible discrepancy, the investigator or hypnotherapist is in a better position to evaluate the actual pain. Because the baseline observations of pain were made on a sample much larger (N = 63) than the treatment sample, they permit an analysis of self-reported pain and the judged expression of pain as related to age and sex.

Since the baseline measures of pain were taken after the patient had experienced a number of bone marrow aspirations, prior experience had provided opportunities for patients to become familiar with the procedure, to develop responses to pain, and possibly to control such responses by individual coping methods. Differences were noted between the reactions of younger and older patients with a dividing line at age 10. The younger patients under age 10 (N = 26) demonstrated their responses to pain so clearly in their behavior that the judged rating of pain was quite consistent with the pain reported by the patient. By contrast, the older children and adolescents above age 10 (N = 37) had learned to control the manifestations of pain so that they were apt to report ratings of pain that were above those estimated by the judges.

For the younger group, the mean self-reported pain of 5.8 did not differ significantly from the mean judged rating of pain of 5.5. For the older group, however, the corresponding values of 4.5 for self-rated pain and 3.1 for the judged rating of pain differed significantly by t test ($p < .001$).

Sex differences also were found. Female patients tended to be somewhat higher than male patients in both self-reported pain ($p < .05$) and in judged ratings of pain ($p < .01$). Sex differences, while consistent, were small, particularly among patients in the older age group.

Age and sex differences in the overt expression of pain were investigated in two related studies that employed somewhat different approaches to the assessment of distress.

In the first of these, Katz, Kellerman, and Siegel (1980) made no distinction between expressions of pain and anxiety in the bone marrow procedure, preferring to call all responses distress. They observed and recorded stress reactions on a 13-item Procedure Behavior Rating Scale. The bone marrow aspiration was divided into three time phases—prior to, during, and following the use of needles. We are making the assumption that the first and third periods reflect anxiety, while the middle period when needles were in use predominantly reflects pain. The differences between the younger and older patients in this middle period were entirely consonant with ours in respect to pain. Their 38 patients aged 6 1/2 to 10 years showed significantly more signs of distress, such as screaming, crying, verbal pain behavior (ouch—it hurts!) than the 39 older patients. Sex differences in the overt expression of distress were slight, with females showing a significant increase over males only when observations during all three phases were added together. Because they did not use self-estimates, there was no information on possible discrepancies between self-rated and observer-rated pain. The evidence in respect to overt expression, however, was in agreement with ours.

A later investigation by LeBaron and Zeltzer (in press) used a modified 8-item behavior checklist similar to the behavior rating scale of Katz, Kellerman, and Siegel. In addition, they used self-ratings and observer ratings of both pain and anxiety. The results obtained on the checklist agreed with those of Katz, Kellerman, and Siegel, and with our own. The incidence of crying, screaming, need for restraint, and verbal anxiety was significantly greater in 26 patients aged 6 to 10 years than in 24 patients aged 10 to 18 years. On the self-estimates of pain they found, as we did, that differences in self-reported pain and anxiety remained comparable between the early and the later ages, indicating that overt expression could be a misleading basis for judging felt pain and anxiety. Significant sex differences were not found, although there was a small tendency for girls to cry, scream, express verbal anxiety, and need more restraint than boys.

These studies alert clinicians to the fact that many older children and adolescents feel pain and are still anxious, even though the external signs from childhood have given way to a system more in keeping with that of the adult world. When adolescents describe their problems in the next chapters, it will be apparent that the inhibition of overt responses has activated defenses such as clenching the hands and gripping the sides of the treatment table.

Although the average differences between self-reported and judged pain are small, in specific instances the differences are great and are therefore important in understanding the pain of individual patients. One dramatic example of the discrepancy between judged pain behavior and self-rated pain occurred when some young patients screamed deliberately as an antidote to pain. This will be discussed in greater detail in Chapter 6.

Summary of Findings

1. Because of baseline observations of pain and anxiety made on successive patients who came for bone marrow aspirations (N = 63), it was shown quantitatively that the patients who accepted treatment by hypnosis (N = 24) were those most traumatized by the bone marrow procedure.

2. For the 24 patients treated by hypnotherapy for distress in bone marrow aspirations, statistically significant reductions over baseline occurred both for pain and anxiety in the first hypnotic treatment session.

3. The reductions of pain and anxiety were related significantly to the degree of measured hypnotizability, a finding that was originally hypothesized on the basis of prior laboratory studies of pain reduction through hypnosis.

4. The advantage of another hypnotherapeutic session during a second bone marrow aspiration (usually six weeks later) was demonstrated for the 19 more hypnotizable patients. While 10 of the 19 (53 percent) reduced their self-reported pain by 3 or more points on the 10-point scale in the first hypnotherapeutic session, 5 more patients succeeded in the second session. Because 9 of the 10 who had succeeded in the first session returned for the second aspiration and retained their gains, a total of 14 of the 18 (78 percent) reduced their pain by 3 points or more in the second session.

5. The 5 (of 24) patients who tested in the low hypnotizable category failed to reduce pain in the first hypnotherapeutic session; those who returned for a second session also failed to reduce pain.

6. Mean differences in group comparisons conceal some individual differences important for investigators and clinicians, such as discrepancies between self-rated pain and judged pain in older children and adolescents. At age 10 and over, values for self-rated pain and judged pain differ significantly as older patients tend to inhibit overt expressions of pain.

7. Some small sex differences appeared, with girls yielding higher ratings of pain than boys.

8. These findings, based on grouping patients according to their degrees of hypnotizability, or by age and sex, provide statistical support for the generalizations summarized above. However, clinical observations made during the course of hypnotherapy present a richer and more varied story. They constitute the content of succeeding chapters.

Notes

1. The preliminary phase was conducted between January 1976 and February 1977 on the Children's Oncology Unit at Children's Hospital at Stanford. The systematic study began in March 1977.

2. In a more recent investigation, children as young as 6 years were able to evaluate separately the pain and anxiety components of the bone marrow aspiration if they were given adequate training in self-reporting (LeBaron and Zeltzer, in press)

3. A corresponding rehearsal method has proved satisfactory in hypnotic preparation for surgery with adults (Kroger, 1977).

4. Detailed findings are available in a published report by J. Hilgard and S. LeBaron, 1982.

5. Not all patients can be counted on to be available for three successive bone marrow aspirations, i.e., the baseline and two hypnotherapy sessions. Attrition in the investigation results from patients' moving away from the area, scheduling difficulties in a clinic setting, and death. In addition, an occasional child finds hypnosis inappropriate.

4 Differential Responses to Hypnotherapy for Pain

Some patients are more successful than others in reducing pain through hypnotherapy, and those who are successful respond at varying tempos. These facts became clear in the statistical analysis of data presented in the last chapter. Now illustrations of what happened in the course of individual hypnotic treatment sessions demonstrate the range of responses.

Hypnotizable Patients Who Differed in Their Responsiveness to Hypnotherapy

The statistical findings in Table 3–2 suggested that we should review four subgroups of patients in the treatment sample of 24 patients. The first subgroup consists of the 10 hypnotizable patients who reduced pain promptly, achieving their maximum reduction in the course of the first hypnotherapeutic treatment; the second group includes 5 hypnotizable patients who required a second treatment before achieving significant relief; the third group consists of 4 hypnotizable patients who failed even in a second treatment to reduce pain; finally, the 5 remaining less hypnotizable patients were all unsuccessful in using hypnosis in pain reduction. Representatives of each of these groups are described in order to illustrate the statistical findings.

Patients Who Reduced Pain Promptly. The 10 more hypnotizable patients in this group whose hypnotic scores averaged 6.0 had given self-ratings of pain in their baseline bone marrow aspiration experience of 7.5 on the 10-point rating scale. After a single hypnotic preparation, they had reduced their pain to a tolerable level of 3.0 on the scale. Their pain levels fluctuated slightly at the time of the second treatment, but were not

57

significantly different from those achieved on the first treatment day. The experiences of the following patients represent what happened in this group.

Annette.   Annette showed how a hypnotizable 6-year-old can be aided in the bone marrow procedure by fantasizing play with her favorite doll, blowing out candles on a (hallucinated) birthday cake, and squeezing any feeling she didn't want out of her own hand as she held her mother's hand. While these responses are typical of treatments used with other patients, the suggestions were always adapted to the particular child.

When observed in the playroom prior to the baseline bone marrow aspiration, as part of the get-acquainted period, Annette was playing at the doll house with other children. Her mother described Annette as a happy child with a vivid imagination. She carried on long conversations with her dolls. She also liked to draw. According to her mother, both she and Annette were outdoor persons, loving the beauty, the colors, and the openness of nature.

Annette had been diagnosed as having acute lymphocytic leukemia seven months before we saw her, and she had already had seven bone marrow apirations. During the baseline bone marrow observation, prior to hypnotic intervention, Annette appeared calm on entering the treatment room. She soon became tense, however, and refused to get up on the treatment table when a nurse asked her to do so; she had to be lifted onto the table where she could easily have placed herself. During the sterile preparation she cried softly. Her crying became loud when the local anesthetic was administered, and throughout the bone marrow aspiration she continued to cry loudly. For some time after the procedure was concluded she continued to cry and complain of pain. Her mother reported that the behavior we had witnessed was typical of her previous bone marrow aspirations. Using the series of faces designed as a rating scale for discomfort with young children, Annette rated her pain during the bone marrow at 7 on the 10-point scale. After this baseline aspiration, Annette —with her mother's encouragement—indicated that she would like to try hypnosis.

When the next bone marrow procedure was scheduled, Annette and her mother arrived early for a practice session with hypnosis. With Annette seated in a large, comfortable chair in the office, hypnosis was induced by the eye-closure method, using a "funny face" drawn with a felt-tip pen on her thumbnail as a fixation target.

After hypnosis was established, as indicated by involuntary closure of her eyes, she squeezed her mother's hand, visualized candles on a birthday cake, and blew them out. Throughout hypnotherapy, Annette not only was willing to close her eyes, but she kept them closed, steps that were unusual in a child of her age. She appeared to become very involved as she imagined the various suggestions.

While hypnotized, but with a suggestion to open her eyes for a few minutes, Annette was asked to move to a treatment table in the office for a rehearsal of the procedure. The therapist's cool hand was used to simulate the sterile wash. While she again practiced blowing out candles on the hallucinated birthday cake, the therapist pinched the skin on her hip to simulate the insertion of a needle. At the same time, she squeezed her mother's hand and was reminded to put all the feelings she wanted to get rid of into that squeeze.

She was calm and cooperative throughout the hypnotic rehearsal, and when she went in a little later for the bone marrow procedures, everything proceeded smoothly. She was relaxed and smiling as she entered the treatment room with her mother and the therapist. Without hesitation, she climbed up on the table. She remained calm, and quietly listened to the suggestions of the therapist during the procedure, with only brief moments of tensing as she squeezed her mother's hand. During aspiration of the marrow, she blew hard on the therapist's fingers, which had become "birthday candles." Toward the end of the procedure she also squeezed the therapist's hand and smiled. She was clearly pleased with herself, and immediately wanted to go downstairs to play. Before she did so, using the rating scale of faces, she rated her pain at the 2 level where she had previously rated it at 7. The pain behaviors observed and recorded by the therapist during this procedure were later rated at 1 by the independent judges. Annette's anxiety level was also rated by the judges at 1.

The SHCS:Child was administered after the first hypnotherapy session. She scored 6 of 7 items.

The hypnotic intervention soon became familiar to Annette and was shortened in subsequent sessions. The parents commented spontaneously on the improvement in her behavior. Her father said, "She used to scream all the time." Her mother said, "The help from you guys made a real difference."

Mary. Although Mary proved to be a highly hypnotizable 9-year-old and hypnotherapy was successful, prospects did not at first appear promising. She is included, however, because she had been so traumatized by prior bone marrow aspirations (36 of them) that her physician had ordered chloral hydrate for sedation prior to several of the most recent procedures. The hypnotherapist deviated from the formal protocol of our investigation while at the same time conforming to its general outline. Hypnotherapy continued beyond the standard sequence of two sessions after baseline, and provided information in addition to that which entered the standard data analysis. Mary had four hypnotic treatments, each six weeks apart.

Mary was sedated as usual by 1.5 grams of chloral hydrate forty-five minutes prior to the baseline observation. Even with that much sedation, she began to cry and struggle as soon as she was on the treatment table. She had to be restrained physically by her mother and a nurse in order for the bone marrow needle to be inserted, the aspirate obtained, and the needle withdrawn. When it was over she continued to cry and complain.

Before the first bone marrow aspiration with hypnotic treatment, the dosage of chloral hydrate was reduced from 1.5 to 1.0 grams by mutual agreement of therapist and physician. Because of the extreme anxiety that Mary had consistently shown, we decided to delay the usual rehearsal under hypnosis in favor of a rehearsal procedure that had some of the characteristics of desensitization and could be accomplished with her remaining awake.

She was taught breathing exercises for relaxation and then shown how to visualize the steps in a bone marrow aspiration. If she became worried at any point, she was told to squeeze the therapist's hand. When she did so, the therapist told her to stop visualizing and reminded her again how to feel pleasantly relaxed. The procedure added about 20–25 minutes to the hypnotic rehearsal, which ordinarily lasted about the same length of time. When it was clear that some of Mary's general anxiety had been controlled, she was hypnotized by the eye-closure-relaxation method and guided through the usual simulation of the bone marrow procedure. The therapist repeatedly suggested that she could be aware of feelings of "pressing" during the bone marrow and that "pressing" did not have to hurt. Finally, she was asked what she would most like to do during the bone marrow procedure. She decided on a visit with *Bambi*—Walt Disney's famous deer.

The therapist took Mary, still hypnotized, from the office where the simulation took place to the treatment room, and once there, suggested relaxing and imagining herself with *Bambi*. As the sterile preparation began, Mary said that she was searching for *Bambi*. Suddenly she complained that the smell of alcohol was making her feel scared and sick. The therapist asked her if she could see the flowers along the path where she was walking. She described beautiful roses. Asked to smell them, she smiled with enjoyment because they smelled so good. She continued the search for *Bambi*, with no further interruptions. Just as the bone marrow needle was inserted, she cried out, "Oh no, I can't!" Once the aspiration was completed, however, she became calm and returned to her imaginative involvement with *Bambi*. She had not required restraint at any time.

Afterward Mary said, "That really helped a lot. I like it that you're here. It really didn't hurt me." Asked to rate the bone marrow procedure, she rated it at 1 on the 10-point scale.

(How did the needles feel?) "They didn't hurt." (What made you cry?) "The poke with the needle." (What was it like?) "It was a big poke, but it didn't hurt me."

When tested on the Stanford scale just before the next treatment session, Mary passed 7 out of 7 items, hence achieving the maximum score for hypnotizability. Because the anxiety-reducing prelude prior to the first hypnotic treatment had taken so much time, testing had been postponed, though it was evident that she was responding well to hypnosis.

The presedation medication was reduced to 0.5 gram before the second aspiration with hypnosis and eliminated after that since it was evident that Mary could manage with hypnosis alone. During the later treatments, the suggested fantasies were varied to sustain her interest. They included trips to a "Magic Candy Store" and a "Bubble Gum House."

A summary of the course of improvement over the four treatment sessions follows. As indicated, the chloral hydrate was reduced progressively over the first two treatment sessions and none was administered at the third and fourth. Self-reported pain dropped from a baseline of 9 to a self-reported 1 at the first treatment session, and at no subsequent session was above 2. The judged rating of expressed pain dropped from 9 to 3.5 at the first session and thereafter fluctuated between 2 and 2.5. The judged rating of anxiety at the time of the sterile wash fell from a baseline of 3.5 to 0.5 on the first day of treatment and then varied between 0 and 1.5.

On a parents' evaluation form, Mary's mother rated the hypnosis program as having been very helpful. She wrote that before Mary's hypnosis, she had been quite upset by Mary's extreme behavior and had felt helpless in dealing with it. Now that Mary was so much calmer, she was better able to help her.

Two years later in a follow-up interview, Mary said to the hypnotherapist, "Bone marrows don't bother me anymore. . . . I just lie down on the table and close my eyes and think of all the things we used to talk about, or I think about other nice things." The nurse reported that Mary sometimes became discouraged and depressed that procedures were still necessary. Considering that the illness, with multiple relapses and remissions, had lasted for years, Mary was showing outstanding courage.

Barbara. The hypnotic treatment of this patient demonstrates how unforeseen changes in clinic routine, such as delays in completing the bone marrow aspiration, require a flexible and spontaneous response from the therapist.

At the time of our baseline observation, Barbara, 13 years old, had experienced ten bone marrow aspirations, the diagnosis of non-Hodgkin's lymphoma having been made a year before. During the aspiration procedure that constituted our baseline observation, Barbara was cooperative, but tense and nervous. Her mother volunteered the information that Barbara had become increasingly anxious prior to and during the past several bone marrows. Barbara watched the doctor's preparations in silence, and cried during the sterile preparation. She squeezed the nurse's hands tightly and began shaking and trembling visibly. As the local anesthetic was injected, she cried out loudly, "No! No!" Then, continuing to cry, asked "Are you done? What's he doing? I'm scared!" Even after the injection, she continued to sob and repeat, "I'm scared! I'm scared!"

While waiting for the bone marrow aspiration to begin, the nurse attempted to distract Barbara by joking with her. Barbara responded briefly with a nervous laugh, and quickly turned her attention back to the procedure: "What's he doing? I'm scared!" She began crying again, and screamed loudly as the doctor picked up the bone marrow needle. "Don't tell me what he's doing!" she cried out, and turned her head away. Again there was loud crying and screaming and a repetition of "I'm scared!" throughout the procedure, with sobs continuing for a few minutes afterward, despite attempts by her mother and the nurse to comfort her. Barbara later rated the discomfort of this bone marrow aspiration at 6.

Several weeks after the initial observation, Barbara had an unscheduled bone marrow aspiration. Because of the very short notice, we had not been notified. Barbara said later that this bone marrow aspiration had been much worse than that of the initial observation, and she would rate it as "worse than 10."

Barbara's interests included watching TV (especially soap operas) with girlfriends, cooking, reading novels, and riding her horse. A very enjoyable recent activity had been driving lessons her father had given her in his truck along some rural roads.

On the SHCS:Child, Barbara passed 5 out of the 7 items. She appeared moderately involved, responding to most of the items with some detail and spontaneity.

When she returned for the next bone marrow aspiration, she told the therapist that she was glad there was help this time, because she had felt very frightened thinking about the bone marrow procedure during the past several days. This was our first opportunity to test the effectiveness of hypnosis with Barbara.

Undertaking the rehearsal in the office as usual, the therapist reassured Barbara that she could prepare herself for a pleasant surprise. "I'm sure that after being so scared for the past week, you are really ready to feel relieved; it's good to be pleasantly surprised when you've been so scared. Let's remember together what the bone marrows were like for you *in the past,* so that we can get ready for having a more relaxed bone marrow." As Barbara described how she remembered previous bone marrows, the therapist agreed with her descriptions of them as frightening and painful in the past, but emphasized that she was describing *what used to be.* She was now going to learn a new way of responding. She could focus her attention on the therapist's voice and visualize, with eyes closed, everything that was described. "My voice is a signal to pay very close attention, not only to my voice, but also to the pleasant surprises, the good, comfortable, calm feelings which you might not have noticed *unless you really paid attention to them.* As you listen to my voice, you can continue to enjoy the comfortable, deep breathing and soft relaxation, as you're now doing . . . That's right . . . and you can notice the sensation of the doctor cleaning your skin . . . that's your signal to look forward, to pay attention to my voice, and carefully watch for any pleasant surprises, as you continue to enjoy relaxing . . ." In this manner, a simulated bone marrow procedure was rehearsed once, and then again a second time with the addition of a fantasy chosen by Barbara. She said that the most fun she had had lately was driving her father's truck on the road beside the river. With the help of further questions, she visualized and described this scene in great detail. As she described the curves in the road, the speed indicated on the speedometer, her careful control of the truck, and her father's approval, the therapist simulated the bone marrow procedure. Afterward, she opened her eyes and said with a smile, "Hey, that was neat! I really was surprised!"

During the actual aspiration, Barbara remained quite calm and relaxed throughout most of the procedure. After a brief induction of hypnosis, she relaxed on the treatment table and began to visualize herself at the wheel of the truck with her father beside her. She described the road, the river, the pleasant aroma of the green fields, and the sound of birds singing. During the local anesthetic, there was a slight, momentary tensing in her face, and a brief flinching. She continued to breathe deeply, however, and to focus on the imagery.

The laboratory nurse had not yet arrived and it was clear that the procedure would be delayed until she came and that Barbara would have to wait on the treatment table. It was important that Barbara not become bored with the driving fantasy, so the therapist quickly shifted the plan: "Stop the truck, get out your TV, and see if any of your favorite soap operas are on." Barbara smiled and, as she described the plot of a soap opera for several minutes, became obviously involved in the story. When it was clear that the bone marrow aspiration was to proceed, the therapist told Barbara, "Now you can get back in the truck and start it up. Keep an eye on the speedometer so that you don't go around this curve too fast." As she continued to describe the fantasy, Barbara flinched a little, then tensed slightly as the bone marrow was completed. For the most part, however, she remained relaxed and calm. She opened her eyes after the aspiration was over, and, with hypnosis terminated, a big smile appeared on her face—"I'm surprised!" she said, laughing. "That was so easy!"

The doctor, the nurse, and Barbara's mother immediately said they had never seen her so calm during a bone marrow procedure. Barbara rated the pain experience at 1, and said that her feelings of fear had been almost completely nonexistent. She also said that approximately 40 percent of her mind had focused on thoughts of the bone marrow aspiration during rehearsal, but only about 15 percent during the actual procedure. As she talked, Barbara's eyes filled with tears, and a tear slid down her cheek. When asked about the tears, she said they were tears of relief, because the procedure had been so much easier for her than ever before. During the time of the hypnosis project, Barbara required no more bone marrow aspirations. According to reports from the nurse, Barbara continued to do well with later bone marrow aspirations without professional assistance.

Harry. This 10-year-old boy showed dramatically during baseline observation why we could rely more on estimates of self-reported pain than on observed responses to pain, especially in the older child.

Harry had been diagnosed as having acute lymphocytic leukemia four years before and, prior to our baseline observation, had experienced 35 bone marrow aspirations.

For the past three years, he had preferred no anesthetic: "It's all shorter without an anesthetic." During the baseline observation, Harry's attitude was cheerful, relaxed, and easy. He participated in casual conversation as he lay on the table. He and an older friend of the family talked of a trip they had enjoyed in Yosemite. He smiled and laughed during the sterile wash. As the physician picked up the bone marrow needle, however, he became quiet, tense, and held the friend's hand. When the needle was inserted, he said "Ouch" softly, and when the aspirate was withdrawn, he again said "Ouch," with no sign of tenseness. Immediately afterward he was laughing at the balloon the physician made out of his rubber gloves. Based on the description of his response to the bone marrow needle, the judges later rated his expressed pain at 1. Harry, however, rated the "hurt" he had felt as 8 on the 10-point scale. He was pleased by the possibility of relieving the pain through hypnotic treatment.

On the SHCS:Child, Harry passed all seven of the tests. His eyes closed quickly and easily. On the hallucinated TV program he saw the "Six Million Dollar Man" throwing a rock a great distance, and he heard the music routinely played on this program. During the age regression test, he found himself in the forest with bluebirds, squirrels, and friends who had been with him on a field trip the year before.

In his first hypnotic session, Harry was introduced to two hypnotic methods he could use together during the bone marrow aspirations. One was the "switch box" technique for turning off the feeling to the bone marrow area, and the other was to return to a pleasant past experience. The "switches" technique is widely used by some hypnotherapists. Harry's switch box was equipped with on-and-off switches located in his brain, and had yellow and blue wires attached to it. The yellow wires went into the switch box and carried his ideas to it—the idea of closing the switch to the bone marrow area, for example. The blue wires that emerged from the box and contacted the bone marrow area were now blocked, causing the area to become numb and go to sleep. The cold feeling of the sterile wash was Harry's signal to turn off the switch to the bone marrow area. The therapist suggested that after he had turned the switch off, he might like to go back in his mind and relive some pleasant experiences. Harry successfully turned off the switches and thoroughly enjoyed a pleasant trip. He later reported that he had been going down hill in a big disc at Yosemite while the bone marrow needle was inserted. He had used both methods to achieve success. He rated the pain of the bone marrow procedure at 3. This indicated an improvement of 5 scale points from the baseline of 8, while the judges detected no change in the overt expression of pain.

In the second hypnotic treatment session, Harry became very involved in watching a rerun of the "Six Million Dollar Man." He was looking at a fight between the Six Million Dollar Man and Big Foot: "He throws Big Foot . . . Big Foot lands on his back but he gets up and starts running toward the Six Million Dollar Man, who hits him in the stomach and knocks him down!"

We had the opportunity to conduct five treatment sessions with Harry. In every hypnotic treatment session the self-reported pain was reduced between 3 and 5 points from the baseline of 8. Because of his control over the physical expression of pain, the pain judged by the observer was always very low; similarly from the beginning, Harry had shown no visible signs of anxiety.

After he learned the hypnotic technique, Harry no longer said "ouch" but at times when the aspirate was being withdrawn, his face would look troubled or a grimace would appear for a few seconds. Since he continued to rate the "hurt" at 3, he was asked specifically about the pain that persisted. He said, "It's a lot better now than it used to be before we started working together. The hurt used to be 8 or 9." To the further question as to what had helped the most, he answered, "Using imagination and pretending." Harry stopped using the switches technique because he found reliving the past experiences much more to his liking.

Hypnotic help continued for a number of sessions in hope of reducing his pain below the 3 level, seemingly quite attainable in this boy who valued and enjoyed his hypnotic experiences. Following the fifth session, we reviewed the technique he now knew well so that he could use it himself in the future: how the cold of the alcohol reminded him to relax, how he could put the feelings he didn't want to have into his fingers as he pressed his friend's hand, how he had learned to concentrate on exciting experiences, how he would feel only a "tingle" when the bone marrow was withdrawn, and, finally, how he would always know when the procedure was over.

For Harry, the plateau level of residual pain had been achieved in the first session and fluctuated around this level thereafter.

These four patients (Annette, Mary, Barbara, and Harry) each illustrated variations in procedure and response generally found among the 19 highly hypnotizable patients who achieved significant pain reduction after the first hypnotic intervention.

Patients Who Needed a Second Hypnotic Session to Reduce Pain. Of the 9 more hypnotizable patients who did not reduce pain at the time of the first hypnotic treatment in a bone marrow aspiration, 5 were successful at the time of a second bone marrow aspiration. To represent this group of 5 patients, we have selected one younger and one older girl.

Carol. Although we have classified the hypnotizable patients as those who made their gains during the first or second hypnotic treatment day, Carol, age 6, who made her initial gain on the second day, continued to reduce pain further on subsequent treatment days. She contrasts with Harry who made his progress on the first day and did not improve thereafter.

Carol was observed in a baseline bone marrow aspiration after she had experienced 25 prior procedures. A diagnosis of acute lymphocytic leukemia had been made when she was 3 years old. During the baseline observation, she showed little anticipatory anxiety about the bone marrow aspiration, but it was evident that she found the bone marrow needle itself painful. She cried continuously and complained; twice she yelled in pain. Both Carol and the judges rated her pain at 5 on the 10-point scale. She accepted the invitation to try hypnosis, and when tested for hypnotic talent, scored at the top of the 7-point scale.

Although she was a friendly child, Carol did not find it easy at first to talk with the hypnotherapist, a stranger to her. At the completion of the baseline observation, her mother told us about Carol's interests—drawing, singing, sewing, playing with her pet cats, and going on picnics to the beach. Her mother volunteered that Carol was creative and enjoyed making things from scraps of leftover materials. As her mother talked, Carol nodded, and added a little confirmatory information.

During seven successive bone marrow aspirations over a period of fifteen months, we continued hypnotherapy and obtained ratings of pain and anxiety. There was no improvement in the first treatment session, but in the second session, pain was reduced 3 scale points to the 2 level. Although the third hypnotic treatment session did not show additional improvement, she progressed further in the fourth hypnotic session when she reported a pain of 1. The level of pain remained between 1 and 2 in the three final sessions. Judged evidence of pain corresponded closely to Carol's self-ratings.

The suggestions that proved effective in hypnotic pain reduction included the familiar blowing out of hallucinated candles on a birthday cake and recurrences of events from her own life. In the fifth hypnotic session, for example, Carol recalled the time when her kitten "Teddy" fell into a shallow creek, and she came to the rescue. She was encouraged to recall in detail everything that happened as if she were there again. She heard Teddy's meows, felt herself wading into the water, and described these events as though they were happening in the present. At the end of this session, when she was asked, "How did it go today," she looked quite vague. A hypnotized person is sometimes momentarily confused before regaining a fully awake orientation. When Carol did not respond, the therapist suggested various adjectives—good, bad, better, worse. Finally Carol volunteered, "Great!" In addition to the relief obtained in the treatment room, Carol's morale improved generally. As her mother said: "Hypnosis relieved her anxiety . . . Carol lets us help more and she is more relaxed at home."

Joan. At age 16, Joan was in the older age range and showed that she could conceal her felt pain and anxiety from an observer. Irregularities in her treatment arose out of scheduling problems, not infrequent in clinical research.

The observation of a baseline bone marrow aspiration took place 1 1/2 years after Joan had been diagnosed as having non-Hodgkin's lymphoma. Twelve bone marrow aspirations had preceded the baseline observation and two hypnotic treatment sessions followed it.

Joan was a bright, attractive girl who enjoyed outdoor activities such as hiking with groups of friends. She liked dating and dancing. She became involved in reading, particularly when it was connected with history and archeology, fields she considered entering one day in the future. Joan was an independent and responsible person. Although her father drove her to the hospital, it was she who made the arrangements and handled the details for her diagnostic and treatment appointments.

During the baseline observation of the bone marrow aspiration, Joan appeared relaxed as she waited on the table for the treatment to begin. Her calm persisted throughout the sterile preparation, but she showed discomfort at the time of local anesthetic. Once the anesthetic was administered, Joan remained calm until the bone marrow needle was inserted; then she winced, jerked her body and bit her lip. The procedure turned out to be a long one, and the needle was inserted twice with considerable gouging and twisting. With each twist, Joan tensed her body and grunted with pain or said "Ow!" Finally she suggested that another doctor should try to obtain the marrow, so a more senior physician was called. She greeted this physician with a smile, tensed her body as he pressed down on the needle, then cried out with a loud "Ouch!" as the aspirate was obtained. Afterward she appeared relieved and calm. She rated this bone marrow procedure at 6.

Joan lived a long distance from the hospital and arrived too late for the hypnotic rehearsal prior to the next bone marrow procedure. Even a short practice session was impossible because of the demands of the clinic. Therefore, the therapist stood beside her as she lay on the treatment table, and induced hypnosis by relaxation and deep breathing, accompanied by suggestions of other pleasant images and thoughts. Throughout the procedure, suggestions that she notice how calm and relaxed she felt were continued. Joan concentrated intensely and remained calm and relaxed during the sterile preparation and the local anesthetic. A few minutes after the physician began pressing the bone marrow needle into her hip, however, he encountered difficulty and again began twisting and gouging as he pushed down. Suddenly Joan jumped and loudly cried out, "Ow!" However, she continued squeezing the therapist's hand tightly and quickly reestablished her calm, relaxed deep breathing. Afterwards, she trembled briefly as she lay quietly taking slow, deep breaths. She said that she would rate the bone marrow procedure at 6. Her self-rating had not changed between baseline and the first hypnotic treatment day, but her more quiescent behavior led the judges to believe the pain had been reduced slightly.

Before it was time for another bone marrow aspiration, Joan called the hypnotherapist for hypnotic help with a lumbar puncture, a procedure that is usually rated less painful than the bone marrow aspiration. Because of Joan's irregular pattern of visits to the clinic, it was evident that there might be difficulties in scheduling the requisite rehearsal time needed to teach hypnosis before the next bone marrow aspiration. Therefore hypnotic practice at the time of the lumbar puncture was substituted for the usual rehearsal. This was fortunate because Joan's next bone marrow was unscheduled.

Joan refused to have the unscheduled bone marrow aspiration until the hypnotherapist had been contacted and had arrived. Upon arrival, she was already on the treatment table, anxious and tense, her eyes full of tears. The busy physician wished to go ahead with his other business without further delay. In spite of the fact that Joan was in tears and asked for preparation time, with strong support for a short delay from the hypnotherapist, the physician replied that he had another immediate obligation.

As the doctor prepared to begin, Joan responded to suggestions for closing her eyes, relaxing her body, breathing deeply and focusing her mind on what she would most like to think of. She concentrated on her plan to attend the junior prom with her boyfriend. She visualized how her boyfriend would look dressed in a tuxedo, how she would appear in her new dress, how wonderful the dinner would be, and finally, how they would enjoy the prom itself.

Throughout the entire procedure, Joan remained entirely relaxed, calm, and involved in her visualization—in spite of the fact that the doctor, a rather large and strong man, pressed down hard and made several twists and gouges with the needle. Joan later described the bone marrow procedure as "real good—the best I've had." She rated it at 1.

In the midst of this irregular schedule, the formal testing of hypnosis occurred between sessions. On the SHCS, Joan passed all seven tests with evidence of deep involvement. She said she very much enjoyed the experience.

A final interview was arranged to inquire about her reactions to the hypnosis program. She stated that it had been immensely helpful to her. Prior to contact with hypnosis, she had always experienced anticipatory anxiety symptoms, including nausea and headaches, during the week preceding a bone marrow or a lumbar puncture. The procedures themselves had been consistently very painful for her, although she tried to control her feelings as much as possible. Despite her exceedingly competent exterior in handling all details connected with her treatment and remaining pleasant in the treatment room, Joan had actually been in a prolonged state of anxiety and tension prior to hypnosis.

By contrast, Joan said that "with hypnosis, I felt like I was floating on a cloud . . . Part of my mind was aware of the bone marrow or lumbar puncture, but there wasn't any pain with it; most of my mind wasn't even aware I was in the room . . . It's really helped me a lot." She described her experience in terms that we have come to recognize as typically adult responses to hypnosis.

Joan's progress was probably impeded in the first session by lack of a rehearsal in which hypnosis could be practiced in a nonthreatening setting.

Hypnotizable Patients Who Failed to Reduce Pain. Though hypnotic ability can often be used to relieve pain, there is no magic that makes it successful in all cases. What can be learned from instances when it is not successful?

In the group of 19 highly hypnotizable patients, four were unable to use hypnosis to relieve the pain they experienced. On the average, their baseline pain level measured 7.3 and remained unchanged during the two subsequent treatment sessions. The average hypnotic score of these four was 6.3. Two boys and one girl were 10 or older and one girl was 7. We have chosen to use one older boy and the younger girl as illustrating the reactions of this group.

Don. The problems of 14-year-old Don were much more extensive than problems of pain. His anger at his condition, shown by a general lack of cooperation during medical procedures, carried over into the hypnotic situation in a lack of motivation to use his hypnotic talent. He was upset about the "bad luck" that had produced a diagnosis of cancer two months before. During the baseline observation of a bone marrow aspiration, he rated his pain at 9 of a possible 10. Unlike most boys of his age, he did not attempt to conceal the suppression of pain, and the judges evaluated the behavioral signs of pain at about the same level as he did. At the urging of his mother, he reluctantly accepted the invitation to participate in the hypnosis program. He passed six of the seven tests of the SHCS and apparently enjoyed this experience because it was carried out independently of any potentially painful procedure. His participation in hypnotic preparation for a bone marrow aspiration, however, was always halfhearted. After two bone marrow aspirations, with attempted hypnotic preparation during which his attitude and his reported pain remained essentially the same, he said he did not wish to continue. Because we recognized the extent of his general problems, we did not persist in attempts to change Don's attitude. To do this meant embarking on psychotherapy with pain control as a subsidiary issue in the midst of pervasive attitudes of anger and fear. Don was referred for psychological help on a broader basis.

Interestingly, several months after termination of the attempted hypnotherapy, Don's mother indicated on the parent's evaluation form that the program had exerted some positive influence on herself and her son. During subsequent procedures, Don tried to recall how he had learned to relax in hypnosis, and she had learned ways of offering more effective support from watching the hypnotherapist. Thus, although Don continued to experience anxiety and pain during bone marrow aspirations, his mother felt that he was better able to cope with the situation.

Marcia. Marcia, a 7-year-old child with acute lymphocytic leukemia, proved to be a fascinating combination of high hypnotizability and a tendency to emphasize concrete facts over imagination. During a first treatment session, the factual Marcia triumphed. During the second, which was proceeding in an encouraging way with its emphasis on imagination, the physician responsible for the bone marrow procedure effectively blocked Marcia's further participation. Most of the physicians who worked with the young patients were sensitive to their needs, but a few could not seem to grasp the fact that protection of the child's psychological well-being in the midst of frightening and painful procedures was essential, and that necessary procedures could go forward without sacrificing those needs.

Marcia had experienced nine prior bone marrow aspirations. During the baseline observation she showed evidence of extreme anxiety as she entered the room. She cried continuously until the end of the procedure, with frequent loud yelling. When it was over, she rated the pain at 10—the top of the scale.

The first practice session prior to the next bone marrow aspiration began with an inquiry regarding her interests. Although she enjoyed playing with dolls, she said that her favorite activities were: (1) having a birthday party, and (2) watching Christmas tree lights. The fact that her birthday was on December 24 suggested a natural relationship between these two.

During the hypnosis practice session prior to the next bone marrow procedure, she tended to respond more practically than imaginatively to suggestions. For example, when told about squeezing any feelings she didn't like into the therapist's hand, she replied, "I already tried squeezing my Mom's hand and that didn't help." In order to induce more relaxation, she was asked if she would like to imagine floating on a cloud. "I never did it," she replied, "so how can I imagine it?" Because of Marcia's tendency to think through problems and produce an intellectual answer for each contingency, this practice session turned out to be chiefly a review of a bone marrow procedure. During the actual procedure, she behaved as she had at the baseline of the observation: she again showed signs of extreme anxiety and discomfort, and again rated the ordeal at 10 despite attempts to focus her attention on a birthday party which she had spoken of enjoying.

Before the next bone marrow aspiration, Marcia was introduced to the SHCS: Child. She not only passed 6 out of 7 tests, but she enjoyed the items and became very involved. Her participation represented the imaginative play so often seen in children of this age. She seldom closed her eyes and responded to the tests as "pretend games."

By the second bone marrow practice session, Marcia's attitude had changed. She no longer offered intellectual objections to suggestions, and she was clearly interested in imaginative games. The practice session, held in the treatment room, was progressing well when suddenly Marcia's doctor strode into the room and announced in a loud voice, "Okay, no more make-believe now. It's time to do the bone marrow." Marcia appeared startled and began to cry. The doctor dominated the communication with Marcia and from that point on, effectively prevented any further hypnotic treatment from taking place. During this procedure, Marcia's behavior was essentially unchanged from the two previous sessions. It had been our last opportunity to offer help to her because our program was closing. What was developing into a promising hypnotic situation could not be reestablished, and hypnotic treatment in Marcia's case had to be considered a failure.

Both of these patients show how much information is lacking when they are merely classified and counted. In neither case was there any doubt about hypnotic potential. In Don's case, it appeared later that if his other personal problems about the illness had been dealt with, he might then have been ready for the hypnotic treatment. In Marcia's case, she was making progress with hypnosis until the physician used his authority to deprecate fantasy involvement. For the most part, we received full cooperation from the physicians—this was the only incident of this kind.

Lack of Success in Pain Reduction by Patients Low in Hypnotizability

Of the 24 young patients in the treatment sample, five scored 2, 3, 3, 3, and 4 on the Hypnotizability Scale of 7 points. Hypnotic treatment did not succeed in reducing pain below baseline levels. Treatment of the less hypnotizable patient challenges the skill of the therapist, and we have chosen to describe all of those in this group.

Joel. When we saw 8-year-old Joel, he had recently been diagnosed as having acute myelogenous leukemia. He had experienced only two bone marrow aspirations before our baseline observation session, during which he appeared to be terrified by the whole experience. He had to be carried out to the treatment room, crying and screaming, arms and legs flailing about. Three adults were required to restrain him on the treatment table where he continued to struggle throughout the procedure. He later rated his pain and anxiety at 10—the top of the scale—and remarked that bone marrows were the worst things that had ever happened to him. The judged rating of Joel's pain was 8.5, as was the judged rating of his expressed anxiety. Joel readily accepted the invitation to try hypnosis.

We took the opportunity to treat Joel hypnotically for four bone marrow aspirations over a period of five months.

Hypnotic testing on the SHCS occurred between the third and fourth hypnotic treatment sessions. He passed only the two motor items—hand lowering and arm rigidity—with a score of 2 out of a possible 7, although he was cooperative throughout.

Joel enjoyed a variety of interests that included swimming, playing games with his friends (especially "cowboys"), and watching cartoons on TV. He hoped someday to have a horse of his own. Although he was quite shy, the initial interactions were facilitated by Joel's mother who was very enthusiastic about the prospect of help for her son.

Prior to each of the four bone marrow aspirations in which hypnosis was involved, there was a practice session. Deviating slightly from the usual hypnotic procedure, we gave Joel an opportunity to describe aspects of the bone marrow procedure that particularly bothered him, the ones that he would like not to think of anymore—that he *need not* think of anymore, we told him, because he would be busy with more interesting thoughts. It was clear that Joel was considerably reassured.

He was shown how to relax by breathing deeply and how to help his body become limp and soft. Drawing on the interests he had mentioned, we encouraged him to imagine himself participating in them. For example, he was encouraged to think of riding a horse and if he liked, to feel himself riding. Although he was fully cooperative, his attention span was so brief that he did not really become involved in the imaginative activities suggested.

In the successive hypnotic treatments, Joel became much more relaxed than previously, no longer resisted entering the treatment room, and even joked with the nurses. He could remain completely calm until the insertion of the bone marrow needle. During the bone marrow manipulation itself, he screamed piercingly until the needle was completely withdrawn. Joel said the procedure had gone "a little better" because he wasn't as scared as before. Joel's mother, and the nurses who knew him well, agreed that his anxiety had been reduced considerably. During the four hypnotic treatments, Joel reported his pain as 10, 10, 10, and 9, while the observable signs of pain were judged to be 8.5, 6.5, 7.0, and 6.0. Judged anxiety gradually declined from 8.5 to 0.

Cases such as this one have led us to adopt a two-component interpretation of the success in treatment, one having to do with relaxation and anxiety-reduction, for which hypnotic talent is helpful but not necessary, and the other the reduction of sensory pain, with which there is a correlation with the person's hypnotizability.

Bob. Almost three years earlier, Bob, 15 years old at the time of our study, had been diagnosed as having acute lymphocytic leukemia. He had experienced nineteen bone marrow aspirations prior to the one we observed. During the initial baseline observation, Bob, a pleasant, quiet, rather shy person, demonstrated considerable ability to control his behavior. He remained calm and quiet through the sterile wash and until the injection of the local analgesia, at which time he tensed his body and groaned softly. This behavior continued during the insertion of the bone marrow needle and the withdrawal of the marrow. Immediately afterward he appeared calm and relaxed. He rated his degree of discomfort with the bone marrow needle at 5, and said he would like to try hypnosis.

Bob's score of 4 on the hypnotizability scale was only a point below the average, though even in the tests he passed, he did not appear to be deeply involved. His interests included, among others, constructing truck models, and he particularly enjoyed camping and baseball. Favorite television programs included "Star Trek," "Godzilla," and other science fiction movies.

In the rehearsal preceding the first treatment session, with Bob sitting in a chair, the therapist attempted hypnosis through relaxation and finally suggested eye closure. Although Bob closed his eyes, he opened them again almost immediately. The usual suggestions for relaxing, setting aside worries and cares, and concentrating on the therapist's voice appeared to produce a light hypnosis. After Bob moved to the treatment table in the actual procedure, he appeared to relax still more; finally his eyes closed and remained closed until the end of the procedure. He seemed to become deeply involved in details of the hiking scenes and action. He hiked up a mountain and reached the summit at the moment the insertion of the bone marrow needle began. The therapist suggested that he take deep breaths and feel *very* comfortable. The therapist reported that Bob continued his involvement in fantasy, continued to breathe deeply, and appeared very relaxed. As the aspiration occurred, his attention was directed also to the view of the valley which he described. There were no behavioral signs of anxiety or discomfort, as he appeared to be completely relaxed and comfortable. Suggestions were given that in the future the procedures would become even easier and he could return to this pleasant place again. When he was aroused from hypnosis, Bob blinked a few times, then looked around with a huge grin on his face. He was asked what it had been like. "Really relaxing," he replied. He reported that the procedure went much better than previously, and that what helped the most was concentration on the hiking trip and deep breathing, because those thoughts kept him from thinking about the needle. Nevertheless he rated the degree of discomfort he had felt at 5, the same as during the baseline observation. During three subsequent bone marrow aspirations, he again had appeared to become very involved in his fantasy, but gave reports of 7, 6, and 5.

An unusual feature in this 15-year-old patient's hypnosis was his reluctance to close his eyes and to keep them closed. It may be that he retained more vigilance than was apparent. While the situation is perplexing, it is possible that future studies of young patients with these marginal scores will assist in understanding the greater ability of highly hypnotizable subjects and patients to relieve marked degrees of pain. It is worth noting again that the *relaxation* component in Bob's description of hypnosis was outstanding. The main effect of hypnosis by Bob's own report was that it capitalized on his ability to relax. This ability showed in the absence of overt signs of anxiety, even at baseline. Thus the effects which might be attributed to hypnosis were related to relaxation without bearing on pain. He was also able to reduce the outward signs of pain which at baseline were judged to be 2.5. and which declined to evaluations of 1 and 0.

Ken. Our reference to 17-year-old Ken, who stayed for only one hypnotic treatment session, will be brief. Ken's comment was that others needed hypnosis more than he.

Ken had undergone seven bone marrow aspirations prior to the baseline one. When he was observed at baseline, he tensed his body, occasionally grimaced, and silently formed the word "ow" with his mouth. Afterward, he rated his pain at the level of 5. The judged expression of anxiety was 0.

Ken described himself as sociable, easygoing, and not easily upset. He scored 3 (of 7) on the hypnotic responsiveness scale. Asked what activity he would enjoy participating in during the bone marrow aspiration, he replied "flying a plane." He cooperated during the rehearsal. At the time of the actual procedure, he was guided in relaxing and focusing on a fantasy of flying while feeling the sensations of flying and seeing details of the sky around him and the earth below. He remained calm, and the only evidence of discomfort was a prolonged tensing of his body. There was no grimacing or quiet "ow." He reported that he felt better and more relaxed than in the previous bone marrow aspirations. He rated pain at 4, only 1 point below baseline.

Hypnosis appeared to be relatively successful in making him more comfortable, but subjective pain was not appreciably reduced.

Bill. At the time of the baseline observation, 15-year-old Bill, with acute lymphocytic leukemia, reported pain at the relatively tolerable level of 3. Observed pain was judged at 3.5 and anticipatory anxiety at 0. Signs of discomfort included occasional tensing, wincing, perspiration, and several "ows." He talked with the nurse throughout.

Bill was pleasant and cooperative. He said he enjoyed physical activity such as basketball, football, or riding his motorcycle. In the area of fantasy, he liked fast action-oriented films like those of James Bond. He passed 3 of 7 items on the hypnotic responsiveness scale.

The usual induction and simulated procedure were followed immediately by the actual bone marrow aspiration. Bill had decided to view a James Bond movie during the aspiration. He was relaxed except for occasional grunting, brief tensing, or momentary strain in his voice as he talked of what was going on in the movie. He rated the discomfort at 2, where baseline had been at the level of 3. Afterward he said that thinking about an activity was all right, but conversation was much better. From his description of his experience, it was clear that there had been very little hypnotic involvement. He elected not to have more hypnosis. Bill may be among those patients we have observed who already had acceptable ways of reducing pain to a manageable level—in his case through conversation.

In the next chapter, we will describe other patients who successfully coped with pain without hypnosis.

Jeff. When Jeff, the fifth member of this group, was not able to gain relief through hypnosis, the hypnotherapist shifted to a nonhypnotic type of therapy, which eventually enabled him to experience a reduction in pain.

When Jeff was observed during a baseline bone marrow aspiration, he had already undergone 27 prior aspirations in the course of treatment for acute lymphocytic leukemia. He was 6 years old.

During the baseline, Jeff resisted vigorously as he was lifted onto the treatment table where three people restrained him throughout the procedure. His crying, which began as soon as he could no longer resist, persisted to the end. Because the needle had to be twisted and turned in order to obtain the aspirate, the session was a long one. Repeatedly, when gasping for breath, Jeff screamed, "Help me, Mommie." Using the picture scale, he rated his "hurt" at the top.

In the clinic playroom, safely separated from the bone marrow threat, Jeff was a pleasant, extremely active boy with a preference for roughhousing or energetically manipulating his fleet of toy cars. We never saw him sit quietly in a game with other children or with his mother. He indicated no imaginative interests. Occasionally, and only for brief periods, he would watch "Sesame Street" on TV.

During the first hypnotic rehearsal of a bone marrow aspiration in the office, Jeff's attention span was very short and his interactions with the therapist quite brief. During the actual bone marrow procedure when hypnosis was attempted, neither his behavior nor his self-report differed from the evaluation made at the baseline observation.

At the time of the second bone marrow aspiration, the hypnotic rehearsal session was described in the therapist's words: "Jeff was friendly and playful, though he seemed so full of energy that it was very difficult to practice with him. He was reluctant to relax on the table, preferring to giggle and avoid the practice." Finally he became involved in a game such as blowing out candles on a birthday cake, after first protesting that this could not be done because there were no real candles there. He was finally persuaded to pet his (imaginary) kitty. After this active rehearsal, Jeff went cheerfully to the treatment room, offered no resistance to getting on the treatment table, needed no restraint to keep him there, and remained calm until the sterile wash started the bone marrow procedure. Thereafter he ignored suggestions related to candles and kittens. He cried and screamed almost constantly. Between sobs he asked how soon it would all be over. After completion, he immediately became calm.

At this time, Jeff was tested on the modified 6 point SHCS designed for use with active 6-year-olds. He was cooperative, but frequently broke the continuity of testing in order to pick up a toy or look at a picture. He passed the two motor items, and finally he was given credit for watching "Sesame Street" on a hallucinated TV screen. His score was 3 of a possible 6.

Having had the baseline observation and two attempted hypnotic treatment sessions, the protocol for the formal data gathering was completed, and on this basis he was assigned to the group of low hypnotizables who failed to reduce pain. Therapy continued with him, however, and an opportunity was taken to try an alternative approach.

At the time of the third bone marrow aspiration six weeks later, Jeff again was a bundle of energetic activity. According to the therapist, "During rehearsal it was difficult to focus his attention on anything for more than a moment. He was interested only in rough physical play." For this reason an alternative strategy of therapy was introduced. The decision was made to keep Jeff energetically occupied with one task after another. During the procedure, he followed signals for accelerated action, such as squeezing the therapist's hand, blowing big breaths, moving his head, and so forth, crying almost constantly as he continued to watch what was going on and listen carefully to instructions. This nonhypnotic strategy proved successful. Jeff rated the "hurt" at 1, saying that he hadn't really felt anything. The disease process accelerated, so this was the last bone marrow aspiration before his death.

The success of a nonhypnotic method indicates that hypnotic involvement is only one of the psychological methods for controlling pain. Although such techniques may be used by a hypnotherapist, their success is not attributable to hypnosis. Some of the patients who did not volunteer for hypnotic treatment had discovered some of these alternative methods for pain reduction that will be discussed later.

Interpretation of Treatment

By presenting information about individual patients in some detail, we hope to call attention to the manner in which the hypnotic procedures retained a basic structure and yet were modified to fit each person's characteristics and needs. An essential common thread in all therapeutic interventions included in this research sample is the rehearsal under hypnosis. As pointed out earlier, our sample was composed predominantly of those who were having the most distressing experiences in bone marrow aspirations. The hypnotic rehearsal method served to reduce initial anxiety, which was based on prior bone marrow procedures, by reviewing the sequence of events in a nonthreatening context. It also acquainted the patient with usable hypnotic skills, such as involvement in pleasant, imagined activities. Within this fixed framework, the therapist was flexible in tailoring the suggestions to the patient's own interests, rather than adhering to a fixed scenario.

With Mary, a deviation in the protocol was a brief desensitization session in advance of the hypnotic rehearsal so that she would be less anxious and therefore be able to pay close attention to the hypnotist's suggestions. The primary advantage of the hypnotic rehearsal method is that it permits patients to learn how to become involved (and to witness that they can) in whatever pleasant experience is chosen as the focus of their hypnotic consciousness, and to do so at a time when there is no strong competing demand for attention. In the actual bone marrow procedure, the hypnotic consciousness must compete with the awareness of pain that normally compels full attention. As stated earlier, the dissociations characteristic of hypnosis permit a division of consciousness between these two claims for attention. When hypnosis is successful, attention is primarily on the planned content of the hypnotic involvement with only marginal awareness of the reality of the setting. For example, Barbara estimated that, under hypnosis, about 15 percent of her attention was on the bone marrow procedure.

While we have stressed the rehearsal method, the highly hypnotizable patient can reduce pain through imaginative involvements within hypnosis in a variety of ways. The following case, which lies outside our sample, illustrates an alternative method.

Mario, a 13-year-old patient with acute lymphocytic leukemia, had made a prior, but reportedly unsuccessful, attempt to use hypnosis during a bone marrow procedure. Because the design of our investigation required a baseline measurement be taken before hypnotic treatment, he did not fit into the study. When he asked for assistance, however, we agreed to help him.

At this point in his illness, he was weak and frightened of the suffering he always experienced during a bone marrow aspiration. He was accustomed to counting out loud during the aspirations and wished to continue with this distraction method because it had helped a little.

Mario was highly hypnotizable, passing 7 of 7 items on the SHCS. At the beginning of the first session, he said he felt "shaky—scared all over—especially in my stomach and legs." Instructions for deep breathing with the therapist's "comfortable, calm hand" resting on Mario's stomach were followed by suggestions of tingling in the toes and all the way up to the face. Emphasis on relaxation, deep breathing and "drifting" served as an introduction to hypnosis. Mario gradually became very relaxed and attentive to the therapist. Building on his interest in the counting technique he had already used, Mario was asked to practice visualizing numbers in various combinations of size, color, and movement:

. . . I want you to imagine that inside your head you can see the number 1. I wonder what size it might be? It could be tiny, medium-sized, or gigantic—as big as a skyscraper. As soon as you can see it, tell me how big it is—a couple of inches or a couple of feet high?

"About 2 inches."

Good. You're doing well. Next you'll see the number 2 in your head. I wonder how big it will be? I don't think it will be the same size as number 1—it will be either larger or smaller.

"It's smaller. It's really tiny."

Good. You're doing well seeing these numbers. Now I want you to visualize number 3; but you'll notice something interesting about this number: It's *huge!* It's the biggest number 3 you've ever seen. You're starting to visualize it right now. There's a surprise too. As this *huge* number 3 is coming into your mind, you notice that it has some kind of color. What color will it be? As soon as you see how big the number 3 is, and what color it is, let me know.

"It's so tall I can't see the top of it. It's colored black."

Good. Next you'll see the number 4. Again, it will be very large, and it will have two colors on it, or perhaps some shiny spots, or different spots or patterns of color. I wonder what you'll see.

"I see a big 4, about as big as a house, and it's green with purple stripes on part of it, and orange stripes on another part."

What a beautiful number! I've never seen such a number before! I wonder what the next one will look like. As the number 5 comes into your mind, you'll notice how it wiggles a little, then starts to shake and turn. By the time you see its size and color clearly, that number 5 will be dancing around and around.

"Yeah, I see it. It's colored bright red and gold, and it's dancing around."

Mario and the therapist continued in this manner up to number 10, by which time Mario was not only seeing the numbers in a variety of sizes and colors, but was also becoming involved in the scenes he visualized. As he saw the number 10, for example, he began feeling the number to see if it was soft or hard, light or heavy. As the visualization developed from 1 to 10, Mario was smiling and occasionally laughing over the unusual shapes and color combinations. He was told that during the bone marrow procedure, he would be able to combine the visualization of numbers with deep breathing and relaxation, and that the use of all of them together would make the procedure go much better and easier for him.

At the beginning of the actual bone marrow procedure, the progressive relaxation techniques practiced earlier proved to be effective in keeping Mario calm. Just as the physician began the actual procedure, Mario was told he could start visualizing and describing the numbers. He visualized numbers in different shapes, sizes, textures, movements, and beautiful colors. As the bone marrow needle was inserted, and again at the time of the aspiration, the therapist told Mario that there would suddenly appear in his mind a very large number, and that he was to take a deep breath or two, which would make the colors of the number much brighter and more intense. With the anesthetic needle, Mario winced briefly, and at the time the bone marrow needle was inserted, he groaned briefly and began to speak more rapidly.

After the bone marrow procedure was over, Mario looked surprised, commenting, "This is the best bone marrow I've ever had! I just didn't feel anything." When questioned about each phase of the procedure in detail, Mario rated the anesthetic needle, insertion of bone marrow needle, and the withdrawal of the bone marrow all at zero. Why had he groaned? He had expected pain, but it hadn't happened.

Mario said that he thought the hypnotic treatment had been effective in reducing pain because it made him keep his mind on the therapist's voice and on the interesting numbers more than on the pain. He added that there seemed to be a small part of his mind on the medical procedure, too.

As in the preceding case of Barbara, we have in these final comments a statement about reliance on partial dissociations.

Why a Response to Treatment among Hypnotizable Patients Was Prompt, Delayed, or Did Not Occur. We have given illustrations of three groups of highly hypnotizable patients, two that were successful in reducing self-reported pain, though at varying rates, and a third that was unsuccessful. Discussion of each of these three groups helps to explain the responses. We turn first to those who were successful.

Prompt and delayed pain reduction. At their first hypnotic intervention, many of the highly hypnotizable patients were able to reduce their pain substantially to a level that was as low as any they were able to attain. Others, unsuccessful in reducing felt pain at the time of the first treatment, by a second or later treatment were as successful as those who had succeeded immediately.

In the delayed respondents, however, control of the *symptoms* of pain was achieved to some extent at the first hypnotic intervention as indicated by the judged ratings of expressed pain. What this means is that the lack of success on the first day was based on their self-ratings of felt pain while at the same time they were becoming more relaxed. By the time of the second hypnotic treatment day, they were able to take advantage of their hypnotic abilities to reduce the felt pain.

Something similar to individual differences in rate of learning was demonstrated by what happened in the sessions beyond the two that entered into the quantitative data. Some patients quickly reached plateau level in the control of pain while others, such as Carol, did not reach a low plateau level until several additional hypnotic treatment sessions were completed.

Parental reaction to the possibility of help was sometimes a factor in promptness. One mother of a prompt responder said that she and her young daughter had both been feeling much better since the end of the previous bone marrow aspiration (baseline) when they had discussed the possibility of receiving help through hypnosis. During this discussion, the 6-year-old patient had described her reactions to the bone marrow procedure—what she didn't like, and what helped her. Hypnosis had been explained to the parent and child, and the opportunity to use it for the potential relief of pain had been accepted by both. In this case, we had an unbeatable combination of excellent motivation, a high degree of hypnotic talent, and favorable circumstances at the clinic.

Certainly the presence of delayed responses highlights the need for those doing clinical research to continue after an initial seemingly unsuccessful session.

Unsuccessful pain reduction. Those highly hypnotizable patients who were unsuccessful in reducing felt pain showed no consistent pattern. It will be recalled that, in one case, a strong counter-suggestion against hypnosis came from the physician, and, in another, the patient was negative about all treatment. Although not part of this sample but of the pilot study, Otis, a young patient who enjoyed hypnosis and was successful at it as long as it was a form of play, objected quite openly to the effort involved in using it in the bone marrow context (i.e., concentrating) and said he refused to work that hard. He returned to the previous high decibel level of screaming.

If we look at reports of observers instead of patients' self-reports, we find indications of some success among patients classified as unsuccessful. For example, in the four highly hypnotizable patients whose self-reported pain remained undiminished throughout our study, judged pain, based on overt facial and other expressions, fell from an average baseline of 7 to a level of 4 by the end of treatment. Because our criterion for success was the reduction of felt pain, these cases were regarded as unsuccessful. On the other hand, it is apparent that members of this group were becoming less agitated and learning to control their overt expressions of pain with repeated hypnotic experience.

While the less hypnotizable patients in this study were not able to reduce felt pain through hypnosis, other advantages associated with the hypnotic procedures helped them achieve marked relaxation and lessen anxiety. Joel and Bob, for example, showed satisfaction with the hypnotic program and felt that treatment had been helpful. Bill, who already had discovered that the distraction of talking made pain more tolerable, preferred to return to this earlier method.

The Effect of Hypnotic Testing upon Hypnotherapy. The concern is sometimes expressed that hypnotic responsiveness should not be measured because failure to perform according to expectations on the test items will discourage the patient and undermine the confidence of the hypnotherapist. We have presented two cases that bear on this problem—8-year-old Joel, who was tested at the time of the last or fourth intervention and 15-year-old Bob, who was tested just before the third intervention out of a total of four. In these two instances, the information on hypnotic responsiveness available to both patient and therapist during the early sessions was only that which any observing hypnotherapist would have. Since there was no self-reported pain reduction in either case prior to the testing, the testing could not have been responsible for either the patient's motivation or the therapist's expectations.

Bob's score of 4 out of a possible 7 on the hypnotic scale (below the average of 5.1 when the scale was standardized on well children) meant that only a moderate degree of imagination was available for use in hypnosis. He and we did our best, but his reported pain never changed. Where hypnotic responsiveness has been measured in the laboratory or in the clinic, only the highly hypnotizable have been able to reduce severe self-reported pain through hypnotic suggestions.

The relationship between hypnosis and pain reduction is sufficiently strong that testing is of service in understanding the course of therapy. Because it does not have the disadvantages that some practitioners fear, it can be recommended for wider use in the clinical setting, particularly in clinical research.

Lack of Talent for Hypnosis or Resistance to Hypnosis? Some clinical practitioners of hypnotherapy for pain relief, in their belief that everyone is sufficiently hypnotizable to share in the benefits of hypnosis, interpret all failures as resistance. Thus the essential problem for them is to overcome resistance when it is encountered. For 150 years, however, it has been known that people who are willing and eager to gain from hypnosis may, nevertheless, differ in their degree of hypnotizability. When confronted with an occasion to use hypnosis, there may be those people who lack sufficient talent or there may be those who resist using the talent they possess.

When we compare the highly hypnotizable patients who were unsuccessful in reducing pain, with the less hypnotizable patients who were also unsuccessful, signs of noncooperation that could be interpreted as open resistance were limited to the highly hypnotizable, such as Don, whose negativism extended to hypnosis, and Otis, who refused to make the effort to use hypnosis in therapy.

The failures to reduce pain by the less hypnotizable could not be assigned to resistance. The one patient, Jeff, who was minimally hypnotizable, reduced pain in a later session by another method. His success was not attributed to overcoming resistance, but instead to the abandonment of hypnotic therapy and substitution of a method appropriate to his hyperactivity. Hyperactivity has been found by others to inhibit the development of fantasy, so essential to hypnotic involvement (see Chapter 9).

Special Problems Connected with the Assessment and Treatment of Anxiety

In our treatment of children suffering from cancer and receiving repeated bone marrow aspirations, there were two chief sources of anxiety. The first of these was the general anxiety associated with a disease which is highly disruptive of normal living and potentially fatal. This anxiety is shared by the child, the family, and their friends. The second source of anxiety—the one with which we dealt directly—was that associated with the threat of induced pain associated with the bone marrow procedures. In the discussion that follows, it is this second source of anxiety which will be the primary focus, although it must not be forgotten that the more pervasive anxiety is part of the background.

Our measurements of anxiety were confined to observations made in the treatment room where no needles were being used. However, a patient's anxiety frequently covers a much longer time span, and there is information about this that comes from other sources. For example, some patients who demonstrated little anxiety in the treatment room had been sleepless during the night preceding the bone marrow aspiration and others had suffered with nausea for days prior to the procedure.

Patients in older childhood or adolescence, such as 16-year-old Joan, have shown the difference between overtly expressed anxiety and underlying anxiety. In talking with Joan after the baseline bone marrow observation, she explained how she tried to talk and laugh a lot in an effort to keep from thinking about how bad the procedure was. Her anxiety at baseline had been judged at 0. How readily the anxiety could be reinstated was indicated by her remark that when a decision to do a bone marrow was announced suddenly, without allowing her time to "prepare," she reacted with nausea and vomiting. Joan also reported the presence of frequent nausea and headaches during the week preceding a bone marrow aspiration. Such knowledge alerted us to the long duration of anticipatory anxiety and its occasional conversion into symptom formation. In Joan's case, we believe that her nausea indicated active rejection of the painful procedure in which she was trapped, and the headache indicated conflict over recognition of the need to face the procedure on the one hand and her intense desire to avoid it on the other. After hypnotherapy was successful in relieving her pain in the bone marrow, these symptoms disappeared. Sleeplessness the night before the procedure is another anxiety symptom not present in the treatment room. It may be recalled how 15-year-old Eleanor was completely relieved of her usual worry over the next day's events by the hypnotherapist's playful remark that she could have a carefree night because the hypnotherapist would do the worrying.

Lisa, a 9-year-old with acute lymphocytic leukemia, whom we have not mentioned before, was a relaxed, outgoing, and friendly child. At the time of the incident to be reported, she had successfully learned to use her hypnotic skills to handle bone marrow aspirations, and she no longer suffered from anticipatory symptoms of anxiety. However, she had become upset by two events: (1) during the preceding bone marrow aspiration an inexperienced house officer twisted, turned, removed, and then reinserted the bone marrow needle resulting in a high degree of pain, and (2) a relapse necessitated additional medications and trips to the hospital which she feared and resented.

From past experience, we knew that anxieties generated under these circumstances could be destructive and long lasting, so in order to counteract this possibility, we tried to reinstate the favorable setting and mood that had prevailed earlier. Because Lisa's favorite activity was tap dancing, at which she was very proficient, she was encouraged to bring along her tap dancing slippers, costume, and music tape for the next bone marrow procedure. After a hypnotic practice session during which specific suggestions were given to counteract the unfortunate previous experience and to elevate her discouraged mood, Lisa gave a splendid tap dancing performance for the staff, other patients, and their parents. She threw herself into this event with skill, enthusiasm, and vigor. In return she received much applause. The bone marrow aspiration followed immediately, and Lisa hopped up on the table and practically took charge. She participated in conversation and smiled. During the actual bone marrow, she held her father's hand, breathed deeply, and told us afterward that she had watched the Three Stooges. She described her one "ouch," when the aspirate was withdrawn, as a little "pinch," and she rated it at the 2 level—lower than the previous time.

As we have already indicated, the course of anxiety before a scheduled bone marrow procedure can begin a few days before the trip to the clinic and is often evidenced in sleeplessness, nausea, and vomiting. Once in the clinic setting, delays before the procedure starts will tend to enhance this anticipatory anxiety. When we were able to meet the patient upon arrival at the clinic, the hypnotic procedures and the rehearsal practices in the office usually allayed anxiety, so that moving to the treatment room was not as traumatic, whether or not the hypnotic practice would relieve the felt pain. In the initial baseline observation, we did not participate in this preparatory stage, so that many of the children were reluctant to enter the treatment room. Their signs of distress were not in response to needles or other direct sources of pain, but were manifestations of anticipatory anxiety. To call the anxiety anticipatory means simply that all of the children we treated had experienced prior bone marrow aspirations, so that they knew what was coming. Their distress was related to pain which they had felt in prior sessions. This relationship between anxiety (or fear) and subsequent aversive stimulation has been studied in animal experimentation and is well known to psychologists.

What then, is the role of hypnotherapy in reducing pain and anxiety? For the less hypnotizable patient, procedures of attempted hypnosis and rehearsal in the office can produce benefits so that the patient enters the treatment room with less anxiety, due to the relaxation component. Although we see a "more comfortable" and "more manageable" patient, for the less hypnotizable individual there may be only a mild reduction in severe pain.

For the more hypnotizable, the initial effect of the hypnotic procedures and rehearsal in the office is essentially the same as for the low hypnotizable. The patient is "more comfortable" and "more manageable." However, the more hypnotizable enjoy an additonal advantage: because of their hypnotic talent, they can reduce severe felt pain through appropriate hypnotic suggestion. Therefore, there will commonly be a correlation between pain reduction and anxiety reduction in the highly hypnotizable, but this relationship is not necessarily present for the less hypnotizable.

This distinctiveness of the role of hypnosis applies chiefly to severe pain. Mild pain, which may be distressing when it persists, can be controlled by many methods. For the reduction of severe pain, however, comparative studies have shown advantages of hypnosis over other psychological methods, such as behavior therapy and biofeedback.

5   Adapting Hypnosis to Specific Symptoms of Distress Connected with Cancer

Many young patients, aware of the hypnosis program on the oncology units, asked for assistance with problems that lay outside the planned research. The therapy of patients who were trying to cope with other types of pain produced a broader understanding of the spectrum of pain in cancer and of how hypnotherapy could help. In addition, a variety of problems, troublesome to patients, resulted from chemotherapy (nausea, vomiting, loss of hair), from surgery (disfigurement), and from general anxiety including fears of recurrence.

Varied Manifestations of Pain

Some self-referred patients were troubled by chronic pain, some by phantom limb pain, and others by pain connected with lumbar punctures. We will describe our interventions for one patient in each category.

Chronic Pain.   Severe continuing pain is commonly called chronic pain, in contrast to the brief acute pain of bone marrow aspirations. Richard was a patient referred for pain caused by the pressure of an abdominal tumor.

Three years earlier, when he was 17, a diagnosis of leiomyosarcoma had been made. This is a malignant tumor of the smooth muscle of the gastrointestinal tract. A large abdominal tumor combined with ascites (an accumulation of abdominal fluid) was now exerting pressure on sensitive nerve endings, and the cancer was metastatic. The oncologist had asked that we do whatever would be possible to make life more comfortable for Richard in this terminal situation. Richard himself, hoping to obtain relief from chronic pain in his back, abdomen, and hips, as well as relief from occasional nausea, had asked to be referred to the hypnosis program. He was receiving 3 mg. of morphine per hour in addition to "Brompton's mixture"[1] for pain. In spite of this amount of medication, he rated his pain at an average of 6 on a scale of 0 to 10 and said that it was sometimes much stronger, at a rating of 9. Whenever he had tried going home for short periods, he had been unable to stay because of the intense pain and constant need for medication. Richard was eager to learn some way to control the pain so that he could be free to enjoy the out-of-doors which he loved. A very imaginative young man, he had entertained fantasies on his own initiative but had not obtained any pain relief from doing so.

When tested on the Adult Clinical Scale of Hypnotic Responsiveness, Morgan and J. Hilgard (1978/79), he became very absorbed in suggestions involving fantasy, and he proved to be highly hypnotizable. The initial treatment sessions took place with Richard lying in bed in his hospital room. Though weak and thin, he was alert.

Hypnosis was induced by progressive deep relaxation followed by suggestions which related to his own interests that he had previously described: images of freedom of movement and comfort such as birds gliding, truck engines oiled and running smoothly, or the surf rolling onto a beach. Richard described the movement of the water, the colors, the light, and the aromas associated with surfing experiences at the ocean and beach. As the therapist participated in these vivid images that Richard described, he began to add more detail and feeling. He confided that he had always enjoyed such fantasies but that he had never shared them with anyone. When asked what other fantasies he had produced during his hospitalizations, he described in great detail driving an old truck up into the mountains. Richard liked the therapist's suggestion that, just like the birds, he could glide effortlessly among pleasant images of the hills, the ocean, the inside of a car motor, remaining relaxed and ready to notice any pleasant surprises. Like the gliding birds, there was no work or effort needed. Rather, he could simply allow things to happen, while noticing any lessening of the pain.

Two days later, Richard said that continuing with self-induced fantasies had made him feel better. He now rated his average pain at 2. By the following day he reported that morphine had been reduced from 3 mg. to 1 mg. per hour at his request and his pain rating was 3. Feeling better than he had in six months, he planned to go home for a short visit.

In hypnosis, he was shown an alternative means of pain reduction which could help turn off unpleasant sensations when he was home. By visualizing switches turned on and off in various parts of his body, he might well discover one that would be very effective for turning off pain. He discovered this to be a master control switch in his elbow. He likened it to a "dimmer switch in a house where you can gradually make the light dimmer." By the end of the session his pain was "a mild discomfort" and he rated it at 1.

On the following day, Richard practiced the "switches" technique during hypnosis induced by the therapist. In addition, he imagined himself going up into the hills on a motorcycle and stopping to watch the birds as they glided above him. Afterward, he commented on how comfortable he felt, reporting his level of pain between 0 and 1. He repeated, as though still surprised, that the level of pain throughout the day now fluctuated between 2 and 4 where previously it had ranged between 6 and 8. His morphine continued at 1 mg. per hour. About a week later Richard mentioned that he no longer used the "dimmer switch" technique. In spite of its apparent effectiveness, it seemed that imaginative activity having to do with birds and trucks, a natural continuation of interests he had enjoyed for many years, was a more congenial approach for him.

One day Richard requested help with pain control during a paracentesis, a procedure for draining excess fluid from his abdomen. While the physician washed Richard's abdomen to prepare a sterile field for insertion of the needle, the therapist assisted Richard in becoming hypnotically relaxed and imagining birds soaring over the hills. Despite the fact that no local anesthetic had been used, Richard appeared oblivious to any discomfort. When he asked if the tube had been inserted yet, he was surprised to learn that the first half-liter of fluid had already been drained.

During the next few weeks, Richard made several visits to his home, some of them overnight. Although he was not always able to eliminate his pain completely by self-hypnosis, he was successful enough to spend longer periods of time away from the hospital. After several weeks during which his confidence, energy and positive outlook increased, he was discharged from the in-patient ward.

On a visit to the outpatient clinic a few weeks later, he reported that self-hypnosis did not always work, and that he coped with these periods by telling himself that at another time he would be able to reduce the pain. For the most part, he said he found it easy to take care of pains "by just sitting back and closing my eyes and imagining."

Richard also reported that he had engaged in the same fantasies before hypnosis but had experienced no pain relief. When asked what made the difference, Richard was puzzled and thoughtful. He answered that prior to hypnosis, he had just "thought about" them. In hypnosis, his experience was of entering into them—of becoming part of them.

Phantom Limb Pain.   Painful sensations in an arm or leg that has been amputated continue to be a puzzling phenomenon from both a neurological and psychological standpoint. Most of the cases of phantom limb pain following surgical removal of an arm or leg have been reported by adults, for whom hypnosis has often proved successful (e.g., Cedercreutz and Uusitalo, 1967; Siegel, 1979). Ten days before referral, 18-year-old Tom had his right leg amputated at the pelvis because of a diagnosis of osteosarcoma, a malignancy of the bone.

Following referral by his oncologist, Tom was enthusiastic about hypnotic help. In the get-acquainted interview, before planning the hypnotic treatment, he talked freely about what was troubling him and was quite ready to talk about his interests prior to the illness. Tom described a variety of uncomfortable sensations he had experienced in his absent leg and foot since the surgery. They ranged from mild tingling and itching, to moderate jerking and aching, to severe stabbing pains "like a thousand pins" in the sole of the amputated foot. He rated the pain as varying at times between 5 and 9 on a scale of 0–10. He found also that an occasional involuntary jerking of the lower phantom limb was both painful and emotionally distressing. At times the joints in the phantom of a toe cracked very unpleasantly. Periodic sleeplessness added to the discomfort and made him feel constantly tired and irritable.

Despite the symptoms from the phantom limb, Tom was cheerful and optimistic about being able to return to high school within a few weeks. He talked eagerly about his wrestling experiences, and about how much he enjoyed driving his car. As he talked, it was clear that he cherished being in control and liked to tackle difficult problems in a critical, analytic manner. Tom passed all of the items on the SHCS:Adults. The experience of hypnotic testing appeared enjoyable to him, and he seemed intensely involved, so that he was ready to begin hypnotic treatment scheduled for three days after the initial interview.

In planning hypnotic treatment, the therapist wanted to help Tom integrate his strong critical faculties and need for independence with the high hypnotic skills that allowed him to become involved in fantasy. At the first hypnotherapy session, the therapist told Tom he could practice relaxation that later might relieve his discomfort. Tom learned first how to tighten then deeply relax all of the muscle groups in his body, including the muscles of his phantom limb. The goal here was to teach him deep relaxation, of course, but also to give him a greater degree of physical self-control. If Tom could control the sensations of tension and relaxation in the absent limb, it would demonstrate to him that he could modify other sensations as well.

Thus respect was shown from the start for his desire to be independent and control his own experiences. The therapist pointed out that mental alertness and awareness were compatible with relaxation, and he had Tom pay close attention to the sensations in the back of his left hand, such as warmth or coolness, heaviness or lightness, and perhaps some slight twitching or a tingling sensation. In a dramatic whisper the therapist said that in the midst of any tingling feelings or other sensations, if he paid very close attention, he might notice sensations of numbness. The whispering emphasized the importance of the message. Hence, while not usurping Tom's right to retain control, the "message" was a suggestion for numbness in the left hand.

A short "rational" discourse on how often numbness was experienced in everyday life followed:

> For example, while wrestling you might well have suffered a bruise or strain you didn't really notice until the match was over. In order to win the match, you somehow kept the pain out of your mind, so that it was numb. You enjoy adventures and interesting experiences. What an interesting experience it could be to discover how much of that same numbness you can notice right now in the back of your hand. Why don't you test any numbness in your hand by pinching the back of both hands?

Without asking about the results of the test, the therapist assumed that Tom had detected a difference between the two hands. Tom was told that allowing himself to concentrate completely on the numbness and learning how to use it for his own benefit could prove to be an important discovery.

As a means of terminating hypnosis, Tom was invited to become alert to his environment in the same way that he had just been so alert to the experiences inside himself. After termination, he was asked to describe what hypnosis had been like. He then mentioned the extreme relaxation and yet alertness during hypnosis, with close concentration on the therapist's words which became "very real and true" to him. The numbness in the back of his hand had been profound. He then added, with considerable enthusiasm, that a numbness in his phantom limb had occurred without any conscious effort. Apparently this was in response to the indirect suggestions about the benefits of concentrating on suggestions of numbness.

After the next hypnotic session, a tape that replicated the progressive relaxation instructions and the suggestions for numbness was given to Tom to take home. At their next meeting approximately two weeks later, he said that he had experienced great improvement—ranging each day from 50 percent to 100 percent relief—in his symptoms. Usually, it seemed, he experienced a complete remission of pain after listening to the tape recording at home. A few other times the pain had not disappeared but "I have learned to just go with the pain now, and it doesn't bother me as much." An unexpected benefit was that a normal sleep pattern had been re-established.

Several months later Tom rated the overall helpfulness of hypnosis as 8 on a scale of 0–10.

Reaction to Lumbar Puncture. Lumbar punctures are similar to bone marrow aspirations in that they are invasive, recurring sources of brief pain imposed upon the patient. In lumbar punctures, a fine-gauge needle is inserted between two lumbar vertebrae, generally the fourth and fifth, in order to enter the subarachnoid space. Some cerebrospinal fluid is withdrawn for examination (the so-called "spinal-tap") and sometimes drugs are injected into the spinal fluid for therapeutic purposes (i.e. intrathecal medication). Patients must be in a curled-up position with the chin touching the chest, either seated or lying on one side so that the back is exposed. They are not only uncomfortable, but they are unable to watch the procedure. As previously noted, a frequent complaint among young patients is the inability to see what is happening. Some patients react with extreme anxiety merely in response to a light touch of the clinician's fingers on their back. Anxiety often increases as the child feels the clinician's fingers probing for the proper site, the cold cleansing agent, and finally, the stinging sensation as the needle is inserted. Unless mechanical difficulties arise, only mild pressure is felt. If a problem arises, severe pain may be experienced as the needle punctures the periosteum and is pushed against the vertebral bone.

Anxiety is a greater problem than pain during lumbar punctures for many children. In the majority of instances, patients complain of some pain, but in a systematic investigation of lumbar punctures and bone marrow aspirations, patients reported significantly less pain during lumbar punctures than during bone marrow aspirations (Zeltzer and LeBaron, 1982).

Lumbar puncture in an older child. Anna was 12 years old when she asked to try hypnosis in the hope of feeling less pain during lumbar punctures. Three years before, the diagnosis of a malignancy had been made.

Anna said that she trembled and was always very scared. She estimated the level of pain at 5 (0–10). She told of her interests and activities—how she took great delight in activities at the beach and in the woods and thoroughly enjoyed acting in school plays like *The Wizard of Oz.* She gave the impression of being a vibrant and sociable person.

During a hypnotic practice session in the office, Anna curled up on a treatment table in the position used for a lumbar puncture. Listening to suggestions for relaxation and deep regular breathing, she quickly achieved eye closure. Asked to engage in a favorite activity, she described herself as wearing a yellow swimsuit while she surfed at the beach, coming into shore on huge blue and green waves and hearing them crash. At this point the therapist assumed two roles: one, the person who was holding Anna's hand

and helping her to relax, and the second, the physician who was touching her back to find the right place for the needle. She was told that when she felt this touch and gentle pushing on her back, it would be a signal to relax. Twice she went through the cycle of tightening at the touch and then relaxing. Finally, she remained completely relaxed whenever the hypnotherapist's fingers probed spaces between the lumbar vertebrae. Anna then returned to an imaginary scene at the beach, as the therapist gave her suggestions for being able to reinstate what she had just experienced, and thus make the actual lumbar puncture much easier. After she was aroused from hypnosis, she and the therapist went upstairs to the treatment room.

The lumbar puncture proved to be a long one. As sometimes happens, the physician was unable to find the right spot during the first insertion so he was obliged to try a second time. While the therapist held Anna's hand and occasionally made suggestions, Anna remained relaxed. Although the session lasted longer than usual, the physician reported that at no time had there been tightening or flinching.

In the discussion that followed completion of the procedure, Anna thought she might have been aware of the first needle but she was completely surprised to hear that there had been a second. All she had *felt* during the entire process was a little pushing and all that she had *noticed* was a "little poking." Pain was rated at 0; pressure at 1.

During this long lumbar puncture, the therapist, aware from experience that patients sometimes tire of a single activity during a long procedure, had suggested a change—acting in a scene from *The Wizard of Oz* with her friends, for example. She had followed this suggestion, enjoyed it, and then returned to surfing. After she had surfed again for a considerable period of time, the therapist suggested that she watch the clouds, even get up on one to view the coast. This, too, she enjoyed for a while, before returning to more surfing adventures. According to Anna's report, surfing had helped the most. She added an interesting insight, "When you're surfing, you have to think of a *fun problem* like getting back to where the waves are." She described how she had substituted this problem for the worry she had always felt during the lumbar puncture. She was asked if she could say how much of her attention had been directed toward the "poking" and how much toward the surfing. She was thoughtful before responding, "Maybe 15 percent noticed the poking. The rest was at the beach."

An interesting aspect of Anna's experience was her previous (ineffectual) search for methods to use during procedures. She had tried "chattering" to the nurse but found she continued to be nervous and tense. She had also tried imagination. The imaginative play she had chosen, however, turned out to be the story of her life in which she was playing the lead, and this hadn't been right at all. It is clear that guidance in hypnosis not only served to focus her imaginative talents on happy experiences that were particularly well adapted to the situation she had to face, but also enabled her to become *involved* in those happy times.

Anna shows again that a highly hypnotizable person often does not learn how to use a natural ability until helped by someone else to discover the available talent. Because of the last-minute referral, her ability had not been precisely assessed at the time of the lumbar puncture. On a later testing with the SHCS, she passed six of the seven items.

Lumbar puncture in a younger child. One of us happened to meet a mother and child outside the treatment room following a lumbar puncture. Jerry, a 5-year-old boy, was complaining loudly of the pain in his leg. Finally, refusing to move, he insisted that he be carried to the car. His mother indicated to the therapist in an exasperated way that this behavior occurred frequently after a lumbar puncture. The therapist took advantage of this opportunity to assist informally in alleviating the pain in Jerry's leg. He turned with a smile toward Jerry and said that he had some "magic medicine" that could really help and would Jerry like to try it? Jerry was immediately intrigued.

The therapist cupped his hands, bent down close to Jerry and whispered, "The magic medicine is in this hand. I'm going to rub a little bit of it on your shoulder. You'll feel it soon . . . Can you feel it now?" As he rubbed Jerry's shoulder, he suggested that Jerry would feel tingling there. After a few moments, Jerry agreed that he felt the tingling. Next the therapist announced that Jerry would soon notice that the feeling of tingling was moving downward—as the magic medicine was rubbed down the side of the body to the hip, down the leg to the knee, and finally to the foot. Throughout this period there had been suggestions that only *pleasant tingling* would be felt and that the leg could soon *feel so very good.* As Jerry followed each step of the explanation and the maneuver intently and soberly, he kept agreeing that all of this was indeed happening to him. The tingling did feel wonderful.

The therapist ended with a gift—"Now I'm going to give you enough to last all day. Hold out your hand." As Jerry cupped his hand just the way the therapist's hand was cupped, the latter said, "Now you have enough to last all day. Anytime you need more, just rub it on wherever you need it." Almost in tears with pleasure, Jerry said "thank you" and went skipping to the car.

The story speaks for itself. While externally it might appear to be a game, for the child involved in make-believe play, it was a serious project, solemnly participated in. The therapist, too, communicated a sense of gravity as well as a conviction that the outcome would be successful.

Reaction to Medication: Nausea and Vomiting

Intensive chemotherapy is widely used in the treatment of many types of cancer. During the period of time that patients receive this drug treatment, they commonly experience the disagreeable side effects of nausea, vomiting, and loss of appetite. A number of patients asked for help with this problem.

Scott.   Scott was 16 years old. Two months after a diagnosis of non-Hodgkin's lymphoma, he came for hypnotic treatment because of severe nausea, vomiting, and burning in his stomach of several weeks' duration. The symptoms coincided with chemotherapy and cranial irradiation.

Scott enjoyed adventure, both physical and mental. As a member of the school track team, he used to spend hours at a time running and concentrating on sensations of rhythm in his body as he ran. He also enjoyed fantasy, especially tales of the supernatural and the occult. On the SHCS: Child, he passed all seven items and gave evidence of becoming intensely involved in each of the items. Afterwards, he said of hypnosis:

> It seemed like daydreaming . . . like when I was a kid . . . at first I didn't think it was going to work. Then I noticed I was becoming really relaxed. Later when you were going to count backwards and you told me I would come out of it, or wake up, I didn't think I was in anything to wake up from. But when I opened my eyes, I realized things really had been different.

How had things been different?

> I felt like I was out of my body. It was like being outside and watching myself.

Techniques of self-hypnosis that Scott could use at home to overcome symptoms of nausea and burning in his stomach were geared to the interests he had expressed. First, he was asked to recall how, during the testing, he had re-entered hypnosis at the clap of a hand and then he was asked to reinstate the same experience now. He liked this idea. Almost immediately he reported that he felt as hypnotized as he had before. After a reminder of how much he had enjoyed adventures of the mind in the past, it was suggested that hypnosis would provide new adventures in the present. If he searched long enough, just like a long-distance runner, he could notice many good feelings that he had not noticed when he had concentrated only on his discomfort. Instead, he could be aware of sensations of floating, tingling, or perhaps peaceful and happy feelings. He would be able to pay close attention to any pleasant surprises that might occur. After he had focused his mind only on pleasant thoughts and sensations, he could expect some desirable and perhaps unexpected changes to occur in his experience. Whatever happened, he was to report it at the next session. He took home a short tape of relaxation induction in case he needed it.

Five days later at the clinic Scott reported that when he had experienced nausea and burning in his stomach, he had recalled the instructions, closed his eyes until he reexperienced the feeling of being hypnotized, and concentrated on thoughts about his girlfriend. He felt how enjoyable it was to be with her. Afterward he was aware that the unpleasant symptoms had disappeared completely. The tape recording had been unnecessary. In the following weeks, Scott reported that the frequent use of these techniques resulted either in a reduction or in a complete elimination of symptoms. Because he was able to control the side effects so well, he felt much less anxiety about his treatment in general.

The potential of hypnosis for treating symptoms of nausea and vomiting associated with chemotherapy has been confirmed by individual case studies and by a few reports based on groups of patients. A successful method of control reported by Gardner (1976) was employed with 12-year-old David, who learned to reduce his nausea and vomiting in one therapy session. In hypnosis the therapist asked David to recall special foods that he enjoyed, to visualize them vividly, and to recall sensations of mild hunger and anticipatory pleasure. She told him that gradually these good feelings would fill his entire body and mind more and more until there was no longer any room for the unpleasant ones. After David had immersed himself in the good feelings and the bad ones had disappeared, he was given posthypnotic suggestions for maintaining the good feelings, enjoying food, and taking medications without difficulty. Immediately after arousal from hypnosis, he was pleasantly surprised to find he could eat a small meal with ease. Subsequently, no more problems with appetite or eating arose.

In a study by Gardner and Olness (1981), a hypnotherapy session provided in advance of the next course of chemotherapy prevented nausea and vomiting in a young patient who had vomited during previous courses of chemotherapy. Similar success in another adolescent was described by Zeltzer (1980).

Hypnotic interventions were also successful in reducing nausea and vomiting in two separate groups of adolescents (Zeltzer, Kellerman, Ellenberg, and Dash, 1983; LeBaron and Zeltzer, in press). Neither of these pilot investigations compared the effectiveness of hypnosis to any other type of therapy, nor were there sufficient data regarding hypnotic susceptibility, so it was difficult to determine whether the improvements were due to hypnosis *per se* or other factors in the therapeutic situation.

In another pilot study, hypnosis and nonhypnotic supportive counseling were compared for nineteen pediatric patients receiving chemotherapy

(Zeltzer, LeBaron, and Zeltzer, in press). Both hypnosis and supportive counseling were found to be effective in reducing these symptoms. When the severity and duration of nausea were recorded separately, it was found that hypnosis and supportive treatment were equally effective in reducing severity of symptoms, though hypnosis was more effective in reducing their duration.

Some of the methodological problems in assessing nausea and vomiting in children have been described by Zeltzer, LeBaron, and Zeltzer (1984) and Zeltzer and LeBaron (1984).

Acute Anxiety Related to Other Procedures

We observed acute anxiety crises resulting from anticipation of other painful medical procedures which, like the bone marrow aspirations, recur repeatedly. Signs of the disturbance appear in advance of the procedure, during it, and sometimes after it. As illustrative of acute anxiety, we present patients in which anxiety reactions were engendered by relatively minor procedures such as finger sticks and intravenous injections.

The Anxiety over Finger Sticks. The needle used to prick the finger to draw blood—"finger sticks" in pediatric parlance—are sources of fear and anxiety for some children. In our initial discussion of hypnosis with the younger child, we discussed 7-year-old Chris, who reacted with violent resistance to frequent finger sticks (Chapter 2). Another young patient illustrates the control he achieved over his reaction to finger sticks and at the same time shows the modifications of hypnotherapy which, as with Jerry, draw upon the child's acceptance of magic.

Fred was a 6-year-old boy with acute lymphocytic leukemia which had been diagnosed at the age of 4 years. During a recent relapse and hospitalization, he had endured many finger sticks. Screaming throughout the procedure, he resisted to such an extent that two people were required to restrain him. Often, at home, he cried about the soreness and tenderness of his fingers. Fred's mother hoped that hypnosis could help him.

The therapist, who had stopped numerous times for friendly chats with Fred as he passed his bed during the recent hospitalization, realized that because Fred and his mother had been constant companions in all of the recent upsets over needles, they had shared a great deal of trouble. Possibly if she could be involved in a treatment project that was interesting, pleasurable, and apt to be successful, they could both be helped. Asked whether she had a lotion of her own that had never been used on Fred's skin, she indicated that she did. She was instructed to tell her son that the lotion was a very special one, that it had magical properties, and that they were using it under the therapist's direction. He had prescribed the lotion in order to make the fingers feel better and a little tougher each day. She was to spend five minutes a day rubbing it on Fred's finger tips.

A week later, Fred's mother reported that they had faithfully followed the instructions. Fred had been fascinated by the improvement he was feeling. That day at the clinic he received a "finger stick" for which he was completely calm and cooperative. Approximately three weeks later when he was observed again, he voiced no complaints and continued to cooperate fully.

On the evaluation form parents complete at the end of the project, Fred's mother wrote, "Just Fred's knowledge that you had prescribed a special lotion for his fingers seemed to work. The key was your authority, and he knew it would work."

In its everyday form, "magic" is invoked in a powerful way when parents kiss a child's hurt finger. The idea of magic from a powerful outside source carried this project to a happy concluson. A further discussion of magic appears in Chapter 9.

Anxiety over an Intravenous Injection (IV) in a Younger Child. Emphasis on the dramatic power of magic helped 7-year-old Sally achieve acceptance of medication by way of intravenous injections for osteosarcoma, which had been diagnosed one month earlier. Whenever Sally heard that an IV was imminent, she started to cry. By the time the nurse began wiping her arm with alcohol, she was screaming and struggling to escape, becoming so combative that three people were needed to restrain her.

A few minutes prior to one of Sally's IVs, the parents intercepted the therapist and asked for help, saying they had heard about his successful work with another patient, and told him how much the needles bothered her. He decided to convey to Sally the idea that something special, dramatic, and magical could happen, if she allowed it. Sally, an alert and somewhat shy child, smiled briefly and then stared at the floor. He crouched down beside her in the corridor and asked what bothered her. She told him she hated the needles, whereupon he whispered dramatically in her ear, "Do you want to see some magic?" Smiling, Sally nodded. The therapist continued:

> I'll show you some here in my hand. Do you see how my hand is tight? I'm making a fist. Now you use one of your fingers to make a needle. Poke it in my hand, between the fingers. Pretend it's a needle, and try to do an IV in my tight fist. You see how hard it is? Now let's take a deep breath together . . . that's it . . . and see how easy . . . how soft my hand becomes. I want you, when you're having your next IV, to take some deep breaths and let your hand become very soft, just like my hand is now. Now poke my hand again. Do you see how it is now to go into my hand? Let's do it

again, but this time *my* finger will be the needle. Remember how to take the big breath and make your hand soft? Here, take some magic from my hand. I'll rub it into your hand, and when it soaks in, you can feel all soft and relaxed and good, just like my hand. That's good.

Pausing at this point, the therapist's tone of voice conveyed great seriousness and excitement, "You have some magic inside you now." He stood up, and in a more usual tone of voice, continued, "How old are you? You're almost 8? That's good, you're a big girl now. Being a big girl and having that magic inside you means that you can remember to take deep breaths and to let your hand go soft whenever you need to. That means that you can enjoy some happy surprises with IVs."

Sally readily went into the treatment room with her two favorite nurses. After several minutes of silence in the room, all three emerged smiling. The IV had been started easily, and Sally reported that it had been better than ever before because she remembered everything she had just learned. Follow-up accounts over the next several months indicated that, even though she usually cried and flinched a little, she needed no restraint and never resumed her combative, highly anxious behavior; furthermore, she was able to recover rapidly after each IV experience. On the evaluation form, her parents thought that Sally's increased tolerance had been a real step forward.

With 6-year-old Fred and 7-year-old Sally, we were dealing essentially with the relief of anxiety. Blood obtained through pricking the tip of a finger or from inserting a needle into a vein rarely involves much pain. We regret that in view of the brevity and informality of these contacts, the children were not tested for hypnotizability.

Anxiety over an Intravenous Injection (IV) in an Older Child. Conventional hypnosis was used with 10-year-old Virginia when she showed anxiety over needles. She was part of our pilot study. Virginia produced a series of symptoms which disappeared with hypnotic treatment, as we shall describe. She was referred because of her extreme fear of needles. In the treatment of Ewing's sarcoma (a malignancy of the bone), she needed repeated doses of intravenous chemotherapy to which she always reacted with intense anxiety and crying.

Highly hypnotizable, she relaxed immediately during an induction which stressed relaxation, then thoroughly enjoyed the suggested experience of floating on a cloud during the injection. The therapist had continued, "Stay as far up in the quiet, peaceful sky as you can . . . Just keep looking, see as much as you can and then you can talk about it later." Virginia complied but began to complain that the medicine felt *cold* as it went in the hand. The therapist suggested that she think of a warm kitten in that hand.

When roused from hypnosis, she still complained that her hand felt cold. Except for this symptom, everybody, including Virginia, was surprised at how easily the procedure had been accomplished. She had eight IV's with the hypnotherapist always present at her insistence.

A curious series of symptoms had begun with the complaint of coldness. The drug that was being injected into Virginia's vein was known to have two side effects: it produced a feeling of coldness at the point where it entered the bloodstream, as well as a "bad taste" in the mouth. Thus after all overt signs of the intense anxiety had disappeared and Virginia was so calm that she said afterwards she didn't know when the needle had gone in, she began to experience the coldness that had not bothered her earlier. The coldness persisted for three sessions until she found an acceptable method for substituting warmth. Again, however, when the feeling of coldness disappeared, she mentioned the "bad taste" in her mouth. While totally relaxed in the fourth session, she gagged and threw up. Interestingly, she said she was not bothered by this development, which continued in a minor way for two more times before it, too, was treated with hypnotic suggestions. Finally, all symptoms disappeared as hypnotic involvement in fantasies was deepened still further.

The appearance and disappearance of one symptom after another might have led to the interpretation that they were all conversion symptoms, had we not been aware of the side effects attributable to the medication. The progression of symptoms is not difficult to interpret. As long as Virginia's anxiety was expressed in hysterical crying, she paid no attention to the cold or to the bad taste in her mouth. Later we shall meet patients who insisted that when they screamed loudly enough, they avoided recognition of pain. As soon as crying no longer protected her, she first attended to the cold at the injection site, and subsequently when the cold was under control she became aware of the bad taste to which she reacted with gagging and vomiting.

Multiple Symptoms of the Cancer Patient

At any particular time, the cancer patient may present a number of symptoms, one of which can be dominant at a single hypnotherapy session, but that does not mean that other symptoms need be ignored. For example, in the midst of a variety of troubles, sleep difficulties are common. The relief of insomnia was frequently an incidental benefit that occurred automatically in the successful hypnotherapy of pain and anxiety in the bone marrow procedures. That is, when hypnotherapy was successful in reducing pain and anxiety, the anticipatory anxiety during the night or nights prior to this procedure declined and so did the inability to sleep. In some instances, insomnia was made the focus of specific suggestions. Fourteen-year-old

Roger, to be described more fully, was told specifically that when he was ready to fall asleep at night, he could recall the same feelings of relaxation that he had experienced during the hypnotic sessions. This simple direction was all he needed.

We found that older children and adolescents sometimes preferred tapes. Relaxation tapes, which we tailored to individual needs, were useful whether the patient was hypnotizable or not. In general, when a young patient needs to be taught a special method for inducing sleep, the most restful scenes and quiet experiences of relaxed pleasure from the past are helpful. A relaxed pet may be fantasized as going to sleep in the child's arms. For someone who likes to camp, the soft sounds of the forest or the monotonous crashing of the waves can be present for a while and then recede in consciousness as sleep sets in. Muscles might be very tired after imagining a long, enjoyable hike or bicycle ride. In the midst of these scenes, a review or reliving of a "success experience" can restore a sense of confidence because "feeling good" about oneself is also essential. If a child is used to having a parent near at bedtime, gentle stroking of the forehead, in addition to the above, is soothing and maintains the patient's feeling of pleasant security.

In the midst of chemotherapy, many children were troubled by the loss of their hair. Hair loss could be corrected by wearing a wig, but the wigs caused problems. Appearance changed radically as hair disappeared and grew again, and active children had trouble keeping the wigs in place.

The next two cases deal with patients with multiple symptoms that needed to be understood and dealt with. A third case represents an unusual problem in which a resistance to medication by mouth had some of the features of the earlier cases in which IV medication was resisted.

Generalized Anxiety over Recurrence of Cancer. Sixteen-year-old Paul asked for hypnosis because of his fear that cancer would recur. After a diagnosis of Ewing's sarcoma in his leg, he had been treated by surgery, radiation, and chemotherapy. The surgery had resulted in a large scar. For the past five months he had returned to the clinic for periodic routine checkups.

During an initial interview, Paul said that during the first few months, he had not worried, but then he started to wonder about metastases. Upon further inquiry, it appeared that what he described as "nagging anxiety" dated from the death of a friend with whom he had formed a close friendship while both were hospitalized.

Paul looked healthy, was friendly, and spoke of being quite religious. He enjoyed many interests, especially those connected with water: swimming, surfing, sailing, and admiring creatures in the tide pools. He loved to hike in the forest where the colors were beautiful, small animals roamed, and after the rain, everything smelled so good. He also enjoyed reading and watching TV. He had not participated as much with friends since his illness because he felt different from them.

Following this preliminary discussion, Paul was introduced to hypnosis when he took the SHCS:Child. He passed 6 of the 7 items, missing only the item that tests the ability to follow a posthypnotic suggestion. He observed that hypnosis was relaxing, and that it was not at all as though someone else was taking over his mind. He felt that his body had become very responsive to his own mind.

In the first of three therapy sessions to follow, the discussion began by talking about how hard it was to have a friend die. Paul expressed feelings of loss, then he and the therapist together reviewed how vulnerable he felt because he and his friend suffered from a similar illness. Paul was helped to recognize that the course of his recovery was different from that of his friend. After he had become more comfortable, he was hypnotized by the method with which he had become familiar through testing. Once hypnotized, the therapist directed his fantasies to positive thoughts. Paul imagined sailing the Pacific with friends, the boat carried along by the wind, and he guiding it skillfully and confidently. He was told to take deep breaths of fresh air and to sense his mind and body as free and full of energy. In the midst of these invigorating experiences, three ideas were suggested to him. The first was the idea that the drugs had gone to all the places in his body where they were needed. He could feel again how powerful they were and how well he had responded. The second stressed how briefly any anxious thoughts would be entertained from now on. Could he picture them floating into his mind and then floating right out? The third thought was that each person needed to get the most out of each moment, out of each day, making all of them rich and full; for his part, he could be fully involved in interesting activities, sometimes with friends, sometimes alone. When Paul came out of hypnosis, he was thoughtful: "The treatment really was powerful. I felt the power of the drugs as they flowed through my body. I got a chill. Then I just felt good."

The next week he said he had felt "a heck of a lot better—I just feel better about myself, more confident about myself, about my ability to handle the leg and other things. My life is beginning to piece together . . . and I don't get nervous around other people. I'm more open again—hypnosis was neat."

During this second meeting, when Paul was encouraged to talk about his thoughts in regard to the recurrence of cancer, it was clear from his response that anxiety about this subject was already receding. He was embarking on familiar activities, such as swimming and visits to watch the tide pools at the beach. Each of the hypnotic treatment sessions followed the general format of the first treatment, though details varied. Sometimes Paul enjoyed the tide pools where he relaxed and felt refreshed. It was at the beach as he watched the movement of the great waves, that he gathered more strength and confidence to face whatever might happen. Another time he went to a favorite fast food restaurant where he felt completely carefree with a group of friends. Suggestions that stressed the three motifs of the first session continued throughout the subsequent ones. Naturally the details varied so as not to become boring.

What did hypnotherapy do for Paul? The initial psychotherapy was nonhypnotic. It began with feelings that he was prepared to express openly: how profoundly shaken he was by his friend's death, and his anxiety about his own life. The ventilation of his sadness and fear in the presence of a supporting adult reduced his anxiety, at the same time as it acknowledged his vulnerability. Instead of dwelling further on his feelings, the therapist pointed out that the course of his illness and that of his friend had followed divergent paths. Now Paul, no longer as preoccupied with worry and doubts, was ready to turn to hypnosis. The changes which occurred with hypnosis could have been brought about gradually by nonhypnotic therapy, but were accelerated by hypnosis. He immediately began reexperiencing in fantasy the old pleasures, made plans, and these plans resulted in real life activity.

Problems following Surgical Excision of a Malignancy. In the treatment of cancer, surgical intervention can range from minor to major, and from a small excision to amputation or even total removal of an organ. The results may be invisible to the eye of others or strikingly apparent. Whether visible or not, the patient may be quite aware of the body changes. We have already met Tom who developed phantom limb pain after amputation of a leg, and Paul who had a large visible scar on his leg after excision of a tumor. Now we shall consider 14-year-old Roger, who developed multiple problems following excision of a malignancy on his leg. In all of these patients, there is a change in body image, but the situation is much more complicated than that. Usually in the background are concerns about the seriousness of cancer. Each patient needs to make psychological as well as physical adjustments on many fronts. Psychological defenses for coping with anxiety and an ability to take positive steps forward to promote psychological health are both necessary. In this respect, support from family members, peers, and medical staff play an essential role (Zeltzer, Zeltzer, and LeBaron, 1983).

Roger was a tall, good-natured teenager. A radical wide excision of a melanoma from his leg had left a large indentation and scar. Eight months later his physician referred him to the hypnosis program because of his inability to control his weight. In the preliminary interview, Roger said that since the operation he had changed. His weight had increased from a normal of 175 pounds to a high of 205 pounds. At present it was 196 and he had been unable to reduce it further by dieting. His favorite sports had been swimming and football; now he felt so self-conscious about the scar on his leg and his increased weight that he had stopped swimming entirely.

Roger also complained of sleeplessness. He often felt anxious as he lay in bed worrying about grades, about his weight, about not being able to swim, or other problems. The next day he always had difficulty staying awake in school. When he returned home from school, he would feel too tired and tense to exercise. Typically, he snacked and watched TV— successfully perpetuating this negative cycle.

Prior to the beginning of hypnotic therapy, Roger was introduced to hypnosis by administering the Stanford Hypnotic Scale; he passed all 7 of the items. After the test was over, Roger commented that this experience was very similar to experiences he had had by himself, for as long as he could remember. For example, he once wondered what it would be like to be paralyzed, "so I made my arms paralyzed."

There followed nine hypnotherapeutic sessions during a period of four months. Roger made excellent progress in therapy. He and the therapist discovered together how certain cues helped to perpetuate the lack of exercise and compulsive snacking. After he was hypnotized, he was helped to visualize himself going through three or four typical school days, plus a weekend. Some direct suggestions were incorporated into his visualizations. For example, he saw himself returning from school and placing his school books in his own room, rather than in the TV room, where he was most likely to start watching television and feel hungry for snacks. He was encouraged to substitute other sports for swimming, and chose jogging and weightlifting. Together, he and the therapist enthusiastically enjoyed his success all along the way. Over a period of four months of therapy, they shared a pride in the way grades in school improved markedly and weight returned to normal. The insomnia had been brought under control early in treatment by suggestions that when Roger was ready to fall asleep at night, he could recall the same feelings of relaxation that he had experienced during the hypnotic sessions.

On the parent's evaluation form, Roger's mother said that the program had been a "tremendous help . . . The problems you helped Roger with were things I had tried to improve but did not know how to approach."

Dysphagia for Pills. Dysphagia, or difficulty in swallowing pills, is an unusual symptom. Its solution in Michelle's case was guided by the patient's own insights.

Michelle, 14 years old, had always gagged, choked, and been unable to swallow pills. With a diagnosis of metastatic Ewing's sarcoma, she was now on an experimental treatment regimen which required her to take many pills each day. In addition, she was currently taking vitamin and decongestant pills. Her mother would grind and mash these pills, and invent mixtures that Michelle was able to swallow, although with some difficulty. Both Michelle and her mother were hopeful that hypnosis might enable Michelle to take pills more easily.

Michelle proved to be highly hypnotizable, passing 6 of the 7 tests on the SHCS. She showed evidence throughout of a strong ability for imaginative involvement. She enjoyed reading and fantasy. Her mother described her as intense, sometimes emotional, and as having strong friendships, although she occasionally wished to withdraw into her own thoughts.

When asked by the therapist what Michelle felt in her throat when she tried to swallow a pill, she replied that it felt like a "super ball," a very hard lump. To the next question, whether the lump had some kind of feelings, she answered immediately that the lump felt "angry and withdrawn from the whole world." She seemed surprised by this last remark and did not know why she had said it. The therapist acknowledged that the lump seemed to have angry feelings about something and perhaps it would like some help. Michelle was intrigued by the therapist's next statement that, "Maybe the lump can tell us more." The therapist complimented Michelle for her good work so far and suggested that she simply observe herself during the weekend to see whether anything happened. Michelle was puzzled by this instruction, and she asked, "Is there something that is supposed to happen? I don't understand." The therapist responded with reassurance that "Whatever happens is all right. If nothing at all happens, just notice it. That's important."

After the weekend Michelle announced that, in fact, nothing *had* happened. She appeared to be anticipating disappointment in the therapist. She was surprised when the therapist replied, "Good! I'm pleased that you observed everything so carefully!" Michelle revealed that she had spent considerable time thinking about the ideas that she and the therapist had talked about, especially about the tightening of her muscles and the lump. "There's something I realized during the weekend." She said, "If I think I can swallow a pill, then I can. If I think I can't, then I can't. The small slippery ones, I think I can." Such insight about the effect that her thinking could have on her behavior was exciting to both, and Michelle was invited "to discover more about how your thoughts can make it easier for you to do what you want to do." She decided that, with her physician's approval, she would like to try swallowing a Sudafed pill.[2]

After hypnotic induction involving deep relaxation and fantasy, Michelle was told that she could see a picture of a pill in her mouth, "floating in water, like a tiny, tiny grain of sand picked up by the sea . . . you can also observe the feelings in your neck and throat, and how your throat is opening wide . . . whatever happens is O.K.—there's no hurry." There was a pause. Michelle placed the pill in her mouth along with a sip of water. As she sat with eyes closed, she was reminded to breathe deeply so that her throat would open wide; she soon swallowed the pill. In describing the process later, she said, "The pill became like a grain of sand, or smaller. Mostly I thought of my mouth getting wide, like a tunnel. Both helped." Very pleased with her accomplishment, Michelle received compliments from her mother, the nurses, and the physicians, as well as from the therapist.

Two days later when Michelle arrived for a hypnotic session, she reported happily that she had been successful in swallowing a Codeine and two vitamin capsules at home. She had simply closed her eyes and remembered all she had learned. That day, in addition to the decongestant and the vitamin capsules, Michelle had to take a Pyridium tablet, which she had found impossible to swallow because of its large size and vile taste. She was additionally worried because her stomach was upset, which she thought would make it more difficult. A reminder that there was no hurry and that whatever happened was okay produced some improvement in stomach symptoms.

After this conversation, she was hypnotized and asked to close her eyes, to notice the progressive relaxation of each muscle group in her body, and to ride down an escalator. It was suggested that Michelle would arrive at a place where a large TV screen was showing pictures of her stomach in the process of relaxing and feeling better and of her throat in the process of opening wide like a tunnel and letting the pills pass down easily. After this picture had been viewed for a sufficient length of time, the therapist suggested that Michelle open her eyes, take a Sudafed first, and then a vitamin capsule. Suggestions for deep breathing, relaxation, and for the pills to become smaller as she held them in her mouth continued.

After Michelle swallowed these pills without incident, she considered the Pyridium. She described it as very big, hard-surfaced, and almost impossible to swallow. She became tense and anxious. The therapist asked Michelle to open her eyes, then drew a picture depicting her throat as a train tunnel with an outline drawing of a train, a watermelon, a grapefruit, an egg, a vitamin capsule, and a Sudafed in declining size in relation to the large tunnel (Figure 5–1). At the same time the therapist said:

> Even though your throat is as big as the train tunnel, the train just *barely* goes through. There's not much room left. Now here's a

Figure 5–1 Sketch of
a train going through a tunnel,
followed by a watermelon,
a grapefruit, an egg,
a vitamin capsule,
a Sudafed pill, and
a Pyridium pill.

watermelon. It's a lot smaller, but you still wouldn't want to swallow it. Look here, I'm drawing the size of a grapefruit. That goes through the tunnel more easily, with a lot of extra room. And now the egg. Look how tiny it is! But a vitamin pill? It's so tiny, I don't know if I can even draw it!

Finally came the Pyridium, which appeared a little larger than the decongestant, but was still much, much smaller than the tunnel.

Michelle giggled at this story and agreed that everything was true, then she popped the Pyridium in her mouth with some water and closed her eyes. Suggestions for deep breathing, relaxation and for the Pyridium becoming softer and smaller, "as tiny as a vitamin pill, which is so easy for you to swallow," followed. "Whatever happens is all right. Whether you actually swallow the pill is not as important as the fact that you are already doing so well, and learning how to relax." A frown appeared on Michelle's face, next she gulped, then she opened her eyes and smiled happily. "I did it!" she cried out. She ran out to tell her mother who gasped, "Unbelievable! That's the first time you've ever done it!"

Follow-up contacts at approximately one, three, and six months revealed that Michelle was now able to swallow, without the slightest difficulty, even the largest capsules. Even awakened in the middle of the night, she could swallow pills as easily as during the day.

On the parent's evaluation form, Michelle's mother rated the hypnosis program as very helpful. "Michelle had been unable to swallow even the smallest pill. She had a terrible fear of gagging, but now she is able to swallow even a large capsule with no problem. I feel I can help Michelle more now with what she has been taught. It seems to be of benefit when she is facing other unpleasant treatments, too. She becomes calmer and more receptive and we feel as if we are working as a team."

Clinical Case Reports and Research

Patients presented in Chapters 4 and 5 illustrate two approaches to the use of clinical material for substantiating the validity of hypnotherapy. Both approaches have a place. In Chapter 4, the selection of patients for purposes of illustration was based on the division of our research sample into groups derived from quantitative findings reported in Chapter 3. They enriched those findings by showing that innovative or improvised techniques could be adapted to the individual's own experiences while under the constraint of a research design.

In this chapter, the patients were not selected in any standard manner because they were self-referred for symptoms that were peripheral to our research. These symptoms were miscellaneous, as such symptoms usually are in clinical practice; that is, not focused on a target area. The approach to an individual patient could be freer, and more improvisation in treatment was possible and desirable. The accessibility of the patient was not limited by the medical schedule of the bone marrow procedure, which separated contacts by approximately six-week intervals. These cases demonstrate possible practices without subjecting them to the comparative analyses which would define the limits of their applicability. Therapy of unselected cases by innovative methods challenges the therapist to obtain results, whether or not the methods are generalizable.

If hypnosis is to achieve scientific status, which has been so long in coming despite the promising therapeutic results with individual patients over the years, it is important to recognize the values inherent in the selection of cases in Chapter 4 as compared with the miscellaneous cases in Chapter 5. The greater freedom illustrated in Chapter 5 is attractive to us as clinicians, but we recognize that it lacks the discipline that is required when research is designed to arrive at verifiable causal explanations and to direct practice on the basis of replicated results.

Notes

1. Brompton's mixture contains morphine, cocaine, and Thorazine.
2. The size of this pill is smaller than a 5 grain (325 mg.) aspirin.

6   Distraction Techniques in the Relief of Pain

The use of distraction techniques in one form or another is a familiar method of coping with pain. Often a tolerable diffuse pain serves as a counterirritant to a focal pain, as in liniments or mustard plasters that distract from the pain they appear to cure. For a time, audioanalgesia (loud music in the ears) was used as a counterirritant for dental pain, until it was found there was the threat of ear damage. A slap elsewhere can prove helpful to distract from the pain of removing adhesive tape from a hairy arm or leg. Sometimes a greater pain will inhibit a lesser one; one adult patient with arthritic pain in the hands, for example, reported that these pains disappeared when a severe lower back pain developed. Such distractions lie outside hypnosis and are available to both the nonhypnotizable and the hypnotizable.

Distraction that compels attention away from pain may be nonhypnotic (characterized by reality orientation), or it may be hypnotic (characterized by an imaginative orientation). The degree of involvement in fantasy will differentiate them. We are interested in the effectiveness of both the hypnotic and the nonhypnotic in reducing pain of varying degrees of intensity and duration.

Distraction Techniques of Patients Not Introduced to Hypnosis

In the course of observing what happened at baseline in the bone marrow aspiration, we found 18 young patients who were bothered very little by the procedure. Their self-reported pain fell between 0 and 2 on the scale of 10. None of them requested hypnosis. In interviews at the time, they reported what they had learned to do that helped them remain comfortable

111

during the procedure. Of the 18 patients, 14 were able to give significant clues as to how they did it, while 4 were unclear.

In this chapter we report patients who are typical of those whose methods were clear. In addition, we describe two other patients who contributed to an understanding of these nonhypnotic coping methods.

Distraction by Self-Produced Pressure.   Clenching a fist, gripping the side of the table, or squeezing the hands of an accompanying adult require effort and attention and may serve to distract from pain.

Jack, age 16: clenches hands together.   In Jack's case, a diagnosis of acute lymphocytic leukemia had been made two years earlier, and there had been 18 bone marrow aspirations prior to our baseline observation. Actually we observed him during two baseline observations, the first of which he rated at 5 and the second at 2. The first was described by Jack and the medical staff as atypical. Both are presented below.

During the first baseline observation, Jack was calm and relaxed while he chatted with the nurse. Still relaxed as the local anesthetic injection began, he suddenly clenched his teeth and gasped. Presumably the anesthetic needle had penetrated the periosteum of the bone with its sensitive nerve fibers. At the time for the insertion of the bone marrow needle, he was tense and braced himself. He clenched his hands tightly together, repeating as the needle penetrated, "Oh, it's hurting . . . oh, Jesus . . ." With the needle out, he commented, "Usually it doesn't hurt that much," and in less than a minute he and his mother were involved in casual conversation about a hiking trip. He said that for some reason the procedure had been much more painful than usual. He rated the pain of the anesthetic needle at 6 and the bone marrow aspiration at 5.

Usually what helped, he told us, was to clench his hands tightly together and keep all of his attention on them. However, he had been completely unprepared for sharp pain at the time of the anesthetic injection, a fact that he thought had thrown him off balance. We learned that when he was first ill, the aspirations had felt very painful; in retrospect, he rated them at 10. Jack refused help from the program, saying he had developed good control on his own through clenching his hands.

One year later, we observed him during a second baseline bone marrow aspiration. Again, during the preparatory phases he chatted with the nurse, calm and relaxed. His mother was not present. The local anesthetic did not appear to result in any distress. As the bone marrow needle probed, he stiffened his body and clenched his hands tightly together. He kept his eyes fixed on the nurse who advised him to take deep breaths, which he did. He winced and grunted as the aspirate was withdrawn. Almost immediately afterward he was smiling, talkative, and relaxed. He rated the bone marrow aspiration at 2. Jack said that what helped him the most was concentrating on his clenched hands. This is coherent with the control of pain through counterirritants which attract attention to the self-produced source of feeling. After Jack left, the nurse commented, "When he was first ill, he often squeezed my hand very hard, but didn't want anyone to know it."

Randy, age 15: grips the table or the nurse's hand. Randy's distinction between suffering and pain was an unusual one for a teenager to make and his general insight into the process was so interesting that a report about him has been included, even though he was not one of the 14 patients. He rated the pain of the bone marrow at 7 but said it did not trouble him at all—that he did not suffer.

A diagnosis of non-Hodgkin's lymphoma had been made two years before, and 12 bone marrow aspirations had taken place before the baseline observation. The bone marrow aspiration proceeded smoothly, with Randy and the physician talking and joking during stages preliminary to the actual insertion of the bone marrow needle. When that time arrived, Randy alternately gripped the edges of the table or the nurse's hand and grimaced briefly. The physician, pushing hard on three attempts and twisting extensively, asked Randy if he was okay. Randy answered "O.K. It's just pressure." However, as the aspirate was withdrawn he said, "Ouch, that hurt," and rated it at 7.

Randy said he did not need help because he no longer suffered from the pain, having developed a couple of methods over the two years of his illness. He was exceptionally thoughtful in the discussion that followed.

It was important to grip something, he said—either the edge of the table or the nurse's hand. He explained the effectiveness of the technique as follows. "When you put pressure on some other part of the body, like when you're gripping something tightly, then your mind goes partly to your hand that's gripping and partly to the bone marrow. That makes the pain less, so you don't really notice it." Because he had gripped the edge of the table *and* a nurse's hand, we posed the question of whether it made a difference which one he did. He replied that it sometimes embarrassed him to hold a nurse's hand—it made him feel younger, like a little child, but a hand felt more like being cared for and was more comforting than the edge of a table. He concluded the discussion by saying, "It's like being on a cliff and you don't want to let go. You want something to hang on to."

Randy said initial relaxation also helped. He demonstrated by shaking his limbs as if to loosen them. Deep breaths helped too, he noted. He was not sure why relaxation and deep breathing were effective in reducing suffering, but he pointed out that when one is more relaxed, one becomes more comfortable. Asked if anything else had helped him, Randy answered that prayer had helped, not only during the procedures but at other times since the onset of his illness. He prays before and during the bone marrow, asking God for strength, "Dear Jesus, please give me the strength to get through this." This provides a sense of security. Prayer has helped in other ways too. "It keeps me from getting depressed so much. It keeps me from getting into sad thoughts, like 'Oh, I wish I was a normal boy, and I could go out and play sports with the others.' But with prayer, I stay more with positive thinking and try to remember that God has a purpose in all this. That has given me a lot of strength over the past two years." With the aid of these two coping methods, Randy admitted to the perception of pain but denied that it troubled him.

Like Jack, Randy talked of how much the emotional support he derived from the nurse meant to him during the bone marrow aspiration. Both patients provide links between a technique common with younger children (squeezing the hand of a parent, nurse, or therapist) and that used extensively by the adolescents (gripping the treatment table or exerting pressure somewhere in the body). Adolescent patients face the problem of needing the same supportive contact during a crisis situation as their younger counterparts, but they find themselves at a developmental stage when they are *not supposed* to need or want comforting.

Screaming. Ordinarily one thinks that screaming is a response to pain. Some of our young patients found instead that if they screamed voluntarily—beginning just in advance of the needle—the effort and the noise of their screaming had the effect of reducing their felt pain. Some practitioners advocate screaming as an expression of feelings of pain, but a few of the young patients in this research group had discovered for themselves that it could minimize discomfort.

Kent, age 8: screams. In Kent's case, a diagnosis of acute lymphocytic leukemia had been made six years earlier. Kent had had 35 bone marrow aspirations between the ages of 2 and 8 years.

He showed no anticipatory anxiety when placed on the treatment table or during the sterile wash. Instead, he engaged in casual conversation with his mother about an amusing incident with a friend. When the anesthetic needle appeared, however, his manner suddenly changed. He produced loud "ouches" before the needle touched his skin. Prior to insertion of the bone marrow needle, his "ouches" became piercing and continuous. Once the needle was withdrawn, Kent immediately resumed talking and laughing again. He rated the pain of the anesthetic needle at 0, the bone marrow needle at 1, and declared that he had felt scared but that nothing really hurt. He compared the bone marrow discomfort to that of a scratch. Queried about his screaming and "ouches," he said that screaming "ouches" made him feel better—in fact, he confided, he was sure that the screaming kept him from hurting.

Another patient used the same method, calmly and deliberately telling the doctor to let him know when the needle was to start so that he could begin to scream. He would not accept a doctor who did not let him scream. A nurse described a third case of a young "screamer": "He'd always be screaming when the needle went in and he'd never know it had gone in. The only way he'd know was when we showed him the needle after it came out. Oh boy, did he open his lungs!"

Martha, age 10: also screams. Martha had been treated for acute lymphocytic leukemia since the age of 5, and had been in remission for two years. Although chemotherapy had been terminated, bone marrow aspirations continued as monitoring procedures at three-month intervals.

At the time we observed her, Martha was calm in the treatment room until the anesthetic needle appeared—then she screamed as if in pain. Screaming resumed at a higher level during the bone marrow needle insertion and aspiration process. In conversation after the procedure, Martha said she needed no additional help. Her mother said, "She's content if she can scream. It's been the same here for five years." Despite being content with screaming, she rated the pain of the bone marrow procedure at 5. Either she had exaggerated her experience of pain, or the benefit from screaming had come through relieving the suffering or anxiety associated with the sensory pain. We have no way of knowing which interpretation is correct. Her mother had observed that Martha would shed tears over minor procedures that could not really be hurting her. Mother added that Martha was the baby at home, tended to be theatrical, loved the dramatic, and played on everybody's feelings.

In the preliminary phase which preceded our main investigation, we did not fully comprehend the potential effectiveness of screaming as a method of coping with pain and, consequently, made efforts to reduce the screaming. The parents and the staff had been upset by the screaming and referred these patients for hypnosis, unaware that a few of these children had hit upon a method of coping that worked for them. It was the young children who taught us that, at least for some of them, the screaming worked better as an antidote for pain than our efforts to substitute hypnosis for the screaming.

Conversation. Patients and those assisting at the bone marrow aspiration readily discovered that if they engaged in lively conversation, such conversation often served as an effective device for coping with pain and anxiety. Conversation often preserves or enhances a pleasant mood, especially if it is accompanied by humor.

Cynthia, age 18: engages in animated and humorous conversation. In remission after chemotherapy treatment for acute lymphocytic leukemia, Cynthia came to the clinic for bone marrow checks every three months. She was a charming, outgoing, and verbal person. When we observed the procedure, she was clasping the nurse's hand firmly, talking, laughing, and joking throughout the prolonged ordeal in which the physician had to twist the needle four times in order to obtain the aspirate. During this time Cynthia and the nurse were deep in the discussion of a movie they had both seen when she suddenly diverted her attention to the physician who was probing with the needle, "Is it in?" When he replied in the negative she laughed, "Go get the chisel—the rubber one," at which point the doctor joked too, and the nurse presented another movie idea. They resumed talking again in the same involved way. As the twisting continued she interrupted this conversation to suggest, "Go get your hammer! Are you in?" After another negative, the nurse asked, "Are you hurting?" "No," she replied. A little later, however, she said, "Ouch, I think it's in," and it was.

As the conversation resumed in an even more spirited way, continuing without pause, it was doubtful whether Cynthia noticed any pain connected with the withdrawal of the aspirate. She estimated that in the beginning bone marrows hurt at least as high as 5 on a 0–10 scale; now, despite the difficult procedure this time and her one "ouch," she rated the pain at 0. It was only after she became well acquainted with the nurse and they had started to talk together that she realized talking was a good way to distract herself. She also realized that the more they could all laugh and joke together, the better things went. When Cynthia was asked what clasping the nurse's hand meant to her, she replied, "It's a comfort to me. Knowing that someone is with me brings comfort." The nurse reported later that Cynthia used to call her "my mommy." Cynthia's mother preferred to stay outside the treatment room.

Herbert, age 15: talks and jokes. Herbert had received chemotherapy for acute lymphocytic leukemia and had checkups at six-week intervals. During the baseline observation of the bone marrow procedure, he had remained calm, relaxed, and pleasant. He paid no attention to the various steps in the procedure, but, instead, centered his interest on a lively conversation with the nurse and physician. Afterward, he rated his discomfort, which he described as "pressure," at 1.

What made the bone marrow aspiration easy for him? He likes to talk: "I need something to distract me. I have to talk about things I *like* . . . What distracts me most are jokes. Even if one's not funny, I'll laugh." He had not watched the procedure, saying later, "What you don't know won't hurt you."

Herbert reported that he liked football, swimming, tennis, water skiing, hunting, suspense movies, cars, drawing and building models, and playing with friends. He also mentioned a deep reliance upon religion which helped him to cope with his illness and the treatment. In a later discussion with the nurse who knew him well, we learned of some severe problems between his parents which he had tried unsuccessfully to negotiate. The troubles between them meant that they had been unable to help him. Lacking direct parental support, it was fortunate that he had the resources of his religion and a supportive staff to which he could turn.

Dan, age 10: converses and reminisces.   Recently diagnosed as having acute lymphocytic leukemia, Dan, a calm, relaxed, and matter-of-fact boy, had experienced three previous bone marrow aspirations. During the preparation periods when signs of anxiety are recorded, he commented briefly, "I don't like this," then started talking and joking with the nurse and physician. In response to the initial pressure of the large needle, he tensed his body slightly, then relaxed, took deep breaths, and held the nurse's hand. As the two of them continued to talk steadily, Dan's attention appeared to be completely absorbed in their lighthearted exchange of ideas. The observer noted, "He was good humored throughout." Dan rated the discomfort of the procedure at 1. Recovery was immediate and when the physician asked, "Was that hard?," Dan shot back with a smile, "I don't know. Was it hard for you?"

Observed on two occasions and interviewed after each, Dan said that conversations as well as deep breathing kept his mind busy. He added that when the nurse and the doctor did not talk, he kept his mind busy by imagining he was back in Idaho, swimming at grandpa's place. In other words, Dan had available two methods for reducing pain: he would direct his attention outward to a cheerful conversation with staff, or inward to a recall of past pleasurable activities. His decision to distract himself by thinking of swimming at his grandfather's had much in common with the involvement in special fantasies we have encouraged in hypnosis.

Mabel, age 7: listens to her mother.   A diagnosis of acute lymphocytic leukemia had been made when Mabel was 2. Now, 34 bone marrow aspirations later, we observed her during a baseline procedure. While the physician prepared her, Mabel, a spontaneous, friendly, and talkative child, took the initiative and asked if she could tell him a joke. She then told a funny one about a rooster. When asked if she were ready for the bone marrow aspiration, she asked pleasantly, "Will you do it real fast?" During the readiness and sterile preparation periods she was anxious but quiet, holding her mother's hand in both of hers while the mother began to talk. When it was time to insert the bone marrow needle, her mother told her to take deep breaths, which Mabel did—very strongly. At the same time, her mother continued to talk of other things that obviously interested Mabel. All that she said was "Oh, mother," as the aspirate was withdrawn. She recovered quickly from this mild indication of disturbance. Judged evidence of pain was rated at 1; Mabel rated the "hurt" at 2.

According to staff reports, Mabel used to scream vigorously. Her mother explained how the change in Mabel's behavior had been accomplished. "It used to be so much worse. Now I get her to look at me and listen to me." At this point, Mabel interrupted to say, "I want to do stuff with her, talk with her so they can get it done quickly and go faster." Her mother continued, "I keep myself talking. She is on the track with me and on the bone marrow track." This figure of speech suggested a dissociation. Mabel agreed with her mother about dividing attention between the two tracks. Her mother added that Mabel wants her to keep talking. After relating details of the bone marrow aspiration that had preceded this one, she said with pride, "Mabel didn't even know it was done." Mabel again agreed, with an air of pride that matched her mother's. The extent of the positive feedback that Mabel received for her accomplishment also deserves attention.

Religion. The comfort of religion—that God will offer comfort and solace to those who are in need—is expressed in different ways by different people. The belief that God cares may provide a constant source of support and hope; for some, a belief in God provides a focal point for prayer and other rituals which sustain the individual in time of crisis. Familiar prayers may absorb the mind and attention.

Martin, age 6: repeats the 23rd Psalm. Ten months prior to our baseline observation, Martin had been diagnosed as having acute lymphocytic leukemia. At the time we met, he had already received eight bone marrow aspirations.

Martin was an outgoing, friendly, and sturdy boy. As he lay on the treatment table during preparations for the baseline aspiration, his mother leaned close to him and rested her hand on his forehead part of the time. During the aspiration, she held his hand. When the needle was twisted, Martin gave a short cry. Afterward she asked, "Did it hurt more than usual?" He replied, "Yes, but it was all right." He rated the discomfort at the 1 level. It seemed to the observer that Martin's estimate of 1 might be low in view of his assertion that the bone marrow had hurt more than usual.

How did Martin describe his method of managing the bone marrow procedure? When he first went to a hospital for the bone marrows, they hurt a lot and he screamed; but then his dad told him that if he relaxed and repeated the 23rd Psalm, they would not hurt. His father was right. As long as he keeps his mind on the 23rd Psalm while he relaxes, they don't hurt. Pressed to describe what happens, he said, "I relax. It's like going to sleep but you don't close your eyes." Martin's family is devoutly religious and it is likely that Martin becomes deeply involved in reciting the Psalm.

Clara, age 16: prays during the bone marrow. This friendly, outgoing girl, who had been ill with acute lymphocytic leukemia for almost three years, was in good spirits during the preparations. At the time the bone marrow needle was used, the only sign of discomfort was tension in her eyes and face. She rated the "pressure" of the bone marrow insertion at 4 and said that was the reason she had tensed. When the bone marrow aspirate was sucked out, however, she estimated the pain at 2. What helped her? "Squeezing the nurse's hand and working with the Lord . . . I pray everytime at least three times, that it won't hurt." She added, "I give thanks for the good and for the bad."

Some dependence on religion and prayer was noted earlier for Randy and for Herbert, both of whom were adolescents. Clara used her own prayers. Martin, much younger, was guided by his father into a ritual repetition of the Lord's Prayer, illustrating an alternative employment of religion as a coping device particularly appropriate to his age.

Self-Induced Involvement in Fantasy. The benefits of hypnosis have been shown through previous studies to be available to those who are capable of setting ordinary reality aside through becoming imaginatively involved. Some of the patients we met, without experience or training in hypnosis, had discovered that they could reduce pain by becoming involved in pleasant fantasized experiences.

Albert, age 7: thinks of a hamburger and a milkshake. After a recent diagnosis of acute lymphocytic leukemia, Albert had experienced only one previous bone marrow aspiration. During the preparatory phases of the observed baseline bone marrow aspiration, Albert was calm and talked with the nurse. In response to the pressure of the large bone marrow needle, he tensed his body moderately but remained quiet and did not appear anxious. Immediately afterward he relaxed. He rated the bone marrow aspiration at the 1 level.

As we talked with him, he said the previous bone marrow aspiration had hurt a lot . . . "I cried—I was so scared and that made it hurt even more." What had happened between the first and second bone marrow aspirations? He said his father had talked to him about how it would not hurt because he could be thinking of something else, of something fun, instead of the bone marrow. Today he had thought of going to his favorite restaurant and having a hamburger and a milkshake. As a consequence of his father's insightful advice, Albert showed no anxiety and reported that he had felt almost no pain.

Edward, age 16: watches a fantasied TV program. Acute lymphocytic leukemia had been diagnosed when Edward was 11 years old. After chemotherapy for three years, he had been in continuous remission and off treatment for two years until a relapse occurred two months before.

During the baseline bone marrow aspiration we observed no visible sign of discomfort at any time. He lay calmly on the treatment table, his feet dangling off one end because he was so large. As the female physician (who was rather small) was about to insert the bone marrow needle, Edward said in a humorous way, "Dig in," and later as she was pushing hard to get through the bone, he continued to tease her: "You're getting some exercise." Afterwards, he reported the bone marrow discomfort at 1, describing it as pressure, not pain.

Edward was shy but friendly. After a little hesitation, he explained that during the bone marrow aspiration he was watching an imaginary TV program. "On 'Emergency' they rescue people, take people to hospitals, and they've got some comedy on there. I think about the comedy of it while I'm on the gurney. I think of what I've seen." An effort was made to understand the type and degree of fantasy involvement Edward felt. "I'm related to the movie. I'm actually a part of it. Today I was thinking about the old man who is always complaining of something. The doctors know it's a fake. First day it's his back, the next day it's his leg. Next day he thinks he's having a heart attack. I seemed to be really there. I was a part of it." Asked if this had always been the case, Edward said, "No." He rated his first and second bone marrow procedures at the 5 level, or like "a bad toothache." Then he hit on the idea of watching the imaginary TV program and, when he did, the pain diminished to practically nothing. He estimated that at least 50 percent and probably more of his attention was on the television program rather than on the bone marrow.

On a later occasion when he returned for another bone marrow aspiration, the observer commented that Edward's reaction was no greater than if he were having a physical examination—this in spite of the fact that two bone marrow needle insertions had been necessary. Again he reported that he had watched an imagined television program.

When he was asked about related experiences, Edward described two situations other than bone marrows when he had dealt with pain. At age 8 he had cut his hand on a plate glass window and required 20 stitches. He played Monopoly with his mother and found that attention to the game took his mind away from the pain, most of the time allowing him to forget about it completely. He reported similar success a few years later when a toenail was removed; he made the pain disappear by concentrating on ice around the toe and thinking that the toe was too cold to feel anything.

It was clear that Edward had been able to successfully divide his conscious awareness under a number of different circumstances and by different approaches. During the bone marrow procedure, by centering attention on imaginary TV programs, he was able to convert the pain to mild pressure, just as we had suggested in a previously cited case where the patient was under hypnosis. During the plate glass window incident and the stitches, he involved himself in playing a game, and during the painful treatment of a damaged toenail, he successfully suggested the sensation of coldness to himself. An induction procedure proved to be unnecessary. What he had already accomplished during all of these experiences was a form of self-hypnosis, producing the achievements of a gifted hypnotic subject trained in pain control.

We have a brief note in regard to the way Edward developed his rich imagination. In our conversations with him, we found out that he was an only child and had spent much time alone. He liked to read, watch TV, and make up stories of his own (the relationship between early childhood experiences and the development of hypnotic talent is discussed in Chapter 9). As we talked with Edward, he was cheerful and optimistic, and stated that he had not been depressed by the relapse. His leukemia did not interfere with his plans for the future. His major project at this time was building a model Boeing 707 for which he had drafted his own plans. When he grew up, he intended to become a commercial airline pilot.

A year after we last saw Edward, a staff member who was close to him said he was doing as well as ever with the bone marrow aspirations and that the disease process again appeared to be in remission.

Distraction as Related to Hypnosis

Distractions of a nonhypnotic type range greatly in the degree to which they command attention.

The type of distraction that our young patients used which bore the least relationship to hypnosis included activities such as gripping the treatment table or a nurse's hand, taking deep breaths, and, in a few cases, screaming. These served as distractors because they directed attention away from the unpleasant stimulus, required considerable effort, and provided sensory stimulation that counteracted the pain to some extent. Intense muscle contraction in gripping the table is not a naturally interesting or absorbing activity and thus is capable of producing only a mild involvement that is apt to be less successful in the relief of acute pain. In addition, it is fatiguing. Screaming, because it includes more widespread muscular activity and produces a greater sensory "bombardment," results in a higher degree of involvement and appears to provide a rather successful distraction for a few children; but again, because of fatigue, is useful only over a limited time period. Some cognitive methods of distraction such as counting or describing objects around the room become boring if carried on for any length of time.

Conversations can be more interesting and involving, if a concerted effort is made by both adult and patient. Success probably depends upon the skill of the adult in capturing the child's interest. Conversation may also elicit fantasy material from memories, current movies or TV programs, and thereby overlap with hypnoticlike experiences. Hence, while nonhypnotic and hypnotic involvements generally can be differentiated, there are areas in which sharp distinctions cannot be made.

As we turn to experiences related to hypnosis, coping methods can be classified from least hypnotic to most hypnotic on the basis of *degree of involvement* in fantasy that is required to make them successful. In Chapter 4 we described young patients like Jeff and Joel who possessed little capacity for fantasy and little aptitude for hypnosis. At the other end of the spectrum is Edward whom we have just described; he involved himself in fantasized television programs to reduce the pain of bone marrow aspirations. On a later occasion, he readily agreed to a test for hypnotic talent and passed all 7 items. In the dream, which he described as very pleasant, he said, "I was flying into the sunset. The sky was purple, and I was flying a purple cub airplane." In the age regression, he vividly described a trip to Disneyland when he was 7 years old: "It felt like I was right there." Before the session ended, it was suggested that after he had awakened from hypnosis, he would immediately re-enter the hypnotic state at the clap of the hypnotist's hands. Subsequently, this hand clap produced a sudden, complete relaxing of all muscles and immediate closure of eyes. Afterward, when asked how he felt, he stated, "I feel dazed." What Edward did, when hypnotized, was so similar to what he had done spontaneously during the bone marrow aspiration that it is possible to interpret the spontaneous experience as self-hypnosis.

It would have been helpful had the circumstances of our investigation permitted more measurement of the hypnotizability of those who were successful in pain reduction without hypnosis. As it happened, we were able to test only one other patient in this group. Herbert, who reduced pain through conversation, passed all tests of hypnotic ability on the Children's Scale with evidence of marked involvement. In his conversation, it is likely that he was using the same resources in pain control that underlie hypnosis, for he said he wanted to talk only about things he really liked. Among the interests to be discussed were sports, movies, and religion.

Religious ceremonies based on faith and ritual among devout believers can approximate hypnotic involvement. We recall 6-year-old Martin's statement after he had repeated the 23rd Psalm during the bone marrow: "I relax. It's like going to sleep, but you don't close your eyes."

A remark of this nature by a young child is often descriptive of the hypnotic experience.

The imaginative involvements commonly take a narrative form, whether reproducing pleasant, recalled experiences, or invented, pleasurable ones of riding on a cloud or exploring magic islands. Because the narrative form takes time to unfold, these hypnoticlike fantasies can cover pains varying in duration from short ones to longer ones. Most of the pains considered in this chapter were of relatively short duration—chiefly those connected with bone marrow aspirations—so that such short fantasies as blowing out the candles on a birthday cake often served adequately. Even then, the ability to fantasize the relighting of the candles produced a narrative element to prolong the experience if difficulty was encountered in inserting the bone marrow needle. Another important feature of the hypnotic fantasy of longer duration is that, once aroused, it can continue with a minimum of effort so that fatigue is rarely a problem.

We have been touching on two important variables in clinical pain, namely its intensity and duration. A "finger stick" usually involves little pain and is extremely brief, a lumbar puncture involves a longer-lasting and more severe pain, and a bone marrow aspiration generally elicits the most pain. Pains associated with solid tumors, as discussed in the previous chapter, were continuing ones and raised the issue of pains of longer duration. Thus the various distraction methods must be prepared to meet challenges posed by pains of varying intensities and durations.

Because our observations of nonhypnotic methods were restricted to bone marrow aspirations, we have reported the experiences of relatively few patients: those who took deep breaths, gripped the table, or screamed to distract themselves. In unusual circumstances, nonhypnotic methods may be successful in counteracting extreme pain from a persisting source. A common story is that of the injured person who is not aware of pain during an athletic event to which he or she is deeply committed until the contest is over. It has been reported that some severely wounded soldiers experienced no pain from serious wounds during a battle although they were still sensitive to painful stimulation at a later time as shown by their wincing at the puncture of a hypodermic needle (Beecher, 1956). Both on the playing field and on the battle field, the participants had been engaged in all-engrossing, reality-oriented distractions of extraordinary importance.

In a comparison of the ability of the nonhypnotic and hypnotic distractions to relieve clinical pain, hypnosis presents some advantages. Its major component, imaginative activity, is inherently interesting to almost all children and to many adults, a characteristic that promotes deep involvement. The experienced hypnotic fantasies can subsequently become so profound and absorbing as to relieve severe pain, including pain of long duration. Further, the hypnotic experience entails little effort and little fatigue. The nonhypnotic distractions, except in unusual circumstances, tend not to be so profound, and, because they are fatiguing, are not as successful in longer lasting types of pain.

7 Parents, Nurses, and Physicians: How They Help Patients Cope

Coping methods that compete successfully with pain, whether they be listening to stories or using hypnosis, operate best in an atmosphere of understanding, confidence, and hope. Practices that contribute to this type of therapeutic atmosphere are apt to increase the patient's comfort and fulfill the wish expressed by many—to live life as fully as possible in the present.

The Therapeutic Atmosphere

The therapeutic atmosphere in the oncology unit depends upon pleasant surroundings, but even more on the personal relationships fostered by the staff members who deal with the patient—the receptionist, laboratory technician, recreational and occupational specialists, social worker, nurse, nursing aide, and physician. Initial impressions are very important to patients, and to their parents who are struggling to cope with the diagnosis of cancer.

Preparing for the Initial Procedures. Ordinarily the patient comes to the oncology center either for early diagnostic tests or to confirm a presumptive diagnosis made elsewhere. Children and parents alike are naturally apprehensive about a nebulous unknown in a strange environment. Increasingly, nurses and physicians advocate education in advance of a new procedure and even in advance of a familiar procedure when carried out in a new setting. How this is done will depend upon the age and developmental level of the child (Eland and Anderson, 1977). A first and essential step is to acquaint the patient with the purpose of the procedure.

125

When no pain is involved—in radiation therapy, for example—the child needs to know this fact and how long the procedure will last. A patient who is to be left alone during any procedure, or a part of it, should be told when someone will return.

Clinical staff members have found that they can be honest in speaking to the patient about possible pain without dwelling on it, for a child's vivid imagination often enhances anticipated events. The message should be clear that other parts don't hurt at all; for instance, when doctors apply alcohol to clean the skin, it will feel cool or cold. Nursing staffs in large oncology centers have prepared specific directions on how to help children of different ages prepare for various diagnostic and treatment measures. Frequently an explanation of the purpose of the prospective procedure and a verbal description are accompanied by educational materials appropriate to the child's age, ability to understand, and personality. These may include a mini-rehearsal either with the patient or a doll as the subject, a prepared movie version, a simplified anatomical drawing, or other aid. Ideally, the particular aid that is used will stimulate questions by both patients and parents, perhaps elicit worries, and clear up misunderstandings. Deeply concerned about their child's welfare, parents need and appreciate explanations as much as the patients. With more knowledge, many parents will be better able to assist a child in the procedure.

Careful preliminary planning is required to determine the best way to introduce the subject of noxious stimulation, usually needles, that result in pain. A pertinent investigation by a team of nurses who dealt with orthopedic cast removal illustrates the importance of appropriate description (Johnson, Kirchhoff, and Endress, 1975). Orthopedic cast removal includes sawing and cutting a heavy cast. Even though this does not involve pain, it is known to be a threatening experience for children. To determine the most useful amount and kind of information to reduce anxiety during the procedure, 84 children aged 6 to 11 years were divided randomly into three groups of approximately equal number. A control group received the procedure without any information about what to expect. A second group listened to a 2 1/2-minute tape recording that described steps in the procedure and how the cast would be sawed off and removed. The third group heard a tape of the same length as that of group two, with added information about the sensory experiences the child could expect. The sound of the saw was audible on the tape, along with statements that the saw would not cut the skin, the skin would look scaly and dirty, there would be chalk dust in the air, and, afterwards, the arm or leg might feel a little stiff and seem light because the cast had been so heavy.

Following the removal of the cast, a novel experience for each child, a distress score was derived from self-reports and observational data. The result was clear-cut: those receiving the sensory information showed the least distress, those receiving the procedural information were next, and those given no information showed the most distress.

In contrast to cast removal, a first-time bone marrow aspiration includes the threat of pain in addition to anxiety. The patient, in advance of the bone marrow, may be informed not only of the procedural steps, but also of the sensory impressions expected at each step. This account should include opportunities for the child to ask about any "hurt" or "pain" to be expected. When a child is not advised beforehand, he/she fears that, once pain starts, its duration may be unlimited. One boy who was not told what a bone marrow aspiration would be like said afterward: "I was afraid it would never end." In a second comment, this boy also described his sense of power-lessness: "I felt I couldn't stop it." Another problem is the fear of pain escalation, for there is no way of knowing how much worse a pain may become. An explanation of a bone marrow aspiration should note the cool feeling of alcohol, the feeling of a short sting when a small needle delivers the numbing medicine, then a wait of a few minutes while this medicine takes effect. After this pause, the physician or nurse will be ready to push the needle into the center of the bone, and this will feel like quite a bit of pressing. When the needle is in the right place, the bone marrow will be withdrawn, and this may hurt for just a few moments. Then it will be all over.

In the actual procedure, whether or not it is the initial one, some patients wish to know what is going on at the time it is happening. For them it is appropriate to announce each step as it occurs. Because anxiety mounts when there are periods of time when nothing seems to happen, methods need to be devised for filling such blank times. The wait for a local anesthetic to take effect is particularly important because in many children anxiety increases rapidly just before insertion of the second needle—the large needle for the actual aspiration. Resources for filling such time with items that interest the child are considered in detail later in this chapter.

Empathy for the Child or Adolescent in Pain. The atmosphere that affects the young patient's outlook is, to a large extent, produced by those who provide care. One aspect of the caring person's relation to the patient is described as empathy. Empathy is an acceptance or understanding that is based on an implicit "I know how you feel." The empathic person does not duplicate the feelings and emotions of the child, but understands them from the child's point of view (Deutsch and Madle, 1975; Barnett, King, Howard, and Dino, 1980).

It is important to distinguish between *empathy* and *sympathy*. Sympathy generally means that what affects the person in trouble similarly affects the helping person. By duplicating the patient's feeling, the helper gets caught up in the same emotional state. Sympathy underlies empathy, but sympathy alone tends to bind the parties together in an emotional predicament. The helper needs some distance in order to be supportive and assist the patient to cope. A sympathetic mother, for example, can become so wrapped up in the emotion of her distressed child that, in effect, she sustains the child's emotional state rather than relieves it. Such an overly sympathetic person is trapped, as is the child, in intense feeling. The *empathic* parent, while sympathetic to the child, may achieve enough distance from immersion in feeling to take steps to ameliorate the child's distress.

Some children are unusually empathic toward their parents. We witnessed an illustration by Richard who was aware of what his impending death meant to his mother. She had lost her husband (his father) several years earlier due to a drowning accident and she had lost her sister from cancer. The staff noticed the mature consideration that this 13-year-old boy evidenced for his mother. Because his veins were so poor, he suffered during intravenous injections, and his mother suffered with him. He noticed this and asked her to leave the treatment room, reassuring her that he would be all right and she should not worry.

Some staff members and research team members are recognized by colleagues as being unusually empathic, while others lack this trait. The question arises whether these differences are so deeply rooted in prior experiences that they may be difficult to change. We are optimistic that people can learn to be empathic, provided they are sufficiently motivated.

Researchers who are more accustomed to laboratory investigation occasionally have to be reminded that the patient comes first and the research design second. An emphasis upon objectivity in clinical research may draw the investigator too far toward the pole of detachment, at the expense of important variations in the behavior, needs, and motivation of individual patients.

Clinical staff members who have to protect themselves from emotional strain in dealing with pain and suffering day after day are confronted with the dilemma of becoming overly sympathetic on the one hand or too distant and unfeeling on the other. Their problem is to achieve the middle ground: an awareness of, and personal attention to, the patient's suffering, but with the major emphasis placed on facilitation of the coping processes.

The Patient's Initiative and Control. There is another facet in the understanding required of adults responsible for the treatment of a young patient. This is the recognition that children do not like to feel helpless in treatment, as though relinquishing all responsibility to others who do things *to* them, even though they are doing things *for* them. Self-respect depends upon some measure of initiative and control over circumstances.

A 10-year-old boy suffered from a daily painful irrigation and debridement procedure on his right elbow necessitated by a bleeding purulent discharge from a laceration (Cowherd, 1977). His experience illustrates the value of including the patient as a member of a treatment team that respects his ideas.

His nurse reported the precipitating event that led to a modification of the relationship between patient and staff. One day the physician was impatient and started removing the bandages before John could get into bed to have this done. The purulent discharge ran down his arm to the floor. From then on John struggled and made obscene remarks. The physician completed the procedure by using physical force. John felt so intimidated that he wished to leave the hospital and in fact packed his bag to do so. The friendly nurse who had been present during the encounter persuaded him to remain. When he talked with a psychiatric nurse specialist afterwards, he spoke of his anxieties and of his frustration over how much was done *to* him. The debridement felt as though the skin were being pulled off and the peroxide burned. When the nurse asked John for suggestions about ways treatment could be made less painful, he suggested that he be responsible for removing the old bandage, the physician proceed more slowly so that the pain would not be so overwhelming, and the peroxide be a different temperature. He also wanted to grip something when the pain became intense so that he wouldn't cry, because he said crying didn't make him feel good afterward. Both John and the nurse transmitted these suggestions to the physician, who agreed to comply with John's ideas. On the following day, all went as planned: the nurse continually supported John's efforts with statements noting how helpful he was and how well he was doing. Although John cried out a few times, he managed to remain steady throughout the procedure.

John had been able to cope with his problem after a therapeutic discussion in which he was allowed to express his anxiety, describe the pain, and finally propose treatment strategies that made sense to him. After developing an acceptable program with the encouragement of the nurse who facilitated his communication with the physician, John resumed partial control by removing the bandages himself. Subsequently, the pace of the procedure represented his and not the physician's. John's wish to grip something, a familiar choice of older patients undergoing bone marrow aspirations, also enabled him to adopt a "grown-up role." In the precipitating episode, John recognized that if he did not fight, he would cry, which would be childish and a threat to his developing maturity. Under these psychological pressures, he had tried to escape.

The willingness of the physician to cooperate by slowing his tempo to meet John's, and the encouragement of the nurse throughout the procedure contributed significantly to John's feeling of accomplishment. There are many demands upon the staff, and to meet the patients' requests is, at times, difficult. On the other hand, the patients' sense of well-being contributes to the success of the therapeutic program. Most physicians and nurses recognize that the inconveniences incurred to meet a patient's requests usually are justified by the gains.

Reuben, a patient who had been in remission for a long time, told how important it had been to him to have control over the time of needle insertion: "I wanted the doctors to check with me to see how *I* wanted things done." He went on to say that he wanted to call "Now" to signal when the needle was to be inserted so he could brace himself. He had been very upset when one doctor hadn't let him do this. At another hospital where he had received his first spinal puncture, he reported that "the doctor made me roll up in a tight ball. He didn't tell me what was happening and that scared me. I like to see what they're doing and I can't see in the back." He added approvingly, "Here, people listened to me; they waited with the needle in the back until I said 'ready.' They didn't surprise me so I didn't jump around. Sometimes when I had a spinal tap they pressed a thumb on me where they were going in, and I could get prepared to say 'ready.'"

Martie, a little older than Reuben, had returned for a periodic recheck. In an interview she emphasized a similar point, volunteering that when she had to drink very disagreeable tasting medicine, it made her feel sick: "They'd let you do it by yourself instead of forcing it on you." Even though she knew she would have to take the medicine in any case, she found this a great help.

Martie understood, as did Reuben, that there were good reasons for the specific medical regimens they were undergoing. She put it simply, "You cannot have a choice in the big medical decisions. You don't know the research." Reuben arrived at the same point somewhat indirectly. He said that he felt better about himself after he and the physician had talked together about his illness and treatment. At first he had been too scared to talk about having cancer because he felt he was no longer like other children. After his talk with the physician, he realized, "I wasn't different. I was still a regular kid. I had a disease that needed attention." He was then ready to accept the medications.

The cooperative relationship among the physician, nurse, and patient respects the differences in their areas of competence. Respect for the child's initiative and desire to retain some measure of control serves to reinforce the authority of those responsible for treatment. By having some measure of control over clinical procedures, children are better able to mobilize their coping abilities and become more cooperative patients.

The Power of Praise: The Warm Glow of Success. Isen (1970) proposed that a difference in feeling between those who experience success and those who experience failure had to do with what she called the "warm glow of success." The experience led to a willingness to be generous and helpful to others. The relevance of Isen's remarks to the treatment situation is evident in that the desirable consequences of success can be achieved only when small gains are recognized and commended. Large gains carry their own sense of success whereas small gains may go unrecognized. One child who had cried and protested throughout a procedure was given recognition for how much calmer she had gradually become during the procedure and how much better she had been able to hold still throughout, even though crying. In the bone marrow situation, two consequences of acknowledging a patient's efforts could include a greater feeling of competence in coping with the disturbing experience, and a willingness to become more helpful to the staff.

In some instances the patient appreciates a reward that is contingent simply upon having endured a difficult procedure such as a bone marrow aspiration or a lumbar puncture. That is, the reward is not contingent upon improved performance. At Children's Hospital at Stanford, for example, at the end of a distressing procedure, the child is invited to go to a locked box, brightly colored in red lacquer, and choose any toy that suits his or her fancy. The contents of the box are changed from time to time, and thus retain the fascination of a secret surprise. Access to the box is never based on "good" or "bad" behavior. The nurse coordinator at Children's Hospital reported that children up to the age of 12 looked forward to it and enjoyed the experience: "They love it!" In the box for the young set, from age 3, are toy cars, toy pinball machines, jacks, stuffed animals; for older girls there are bath beads, Disney caper stickers (girls trade them), earrings; for older boys, a baseball bat, softball, blank cassettes, batteries, flashlights, fabric wallets.

Psychologically this reward system makes sense: it assures that the last part of the experience is a happy one for the child and helps to associate a pleasurable experience with the nurse who was present throughout the less pleasant period. In addition, the anticipation of receiving a surprise helps to ease the child's return visits to the clinic.

If the family plans to treat the child to something special after a procedure, it is wise to put the reward on the same basis as the secret surprise box—contingent upon finishing the procedure and not promised for good behavior. There is nothing positive to be gained from criticizing behavior over which the child has not been able to exert control. If possible, it is best not to lecture, ridicule, or hold up another child as a model. Better that the family can draw a deep breath and celebrate the completion of a difficult procedure.

Those Who Help the Patient to Cope:
The Supporting Team

The supporting team begins with the assumption that both patient and parents are going to do their best to deal with the difficult problems they face. Prior to the diagnosis of cancer, people have developed many internal resources and coping skills, designated as strengths, through life experiences. These strengths will vary greatly from family to family, and individual differences will be apparent to the supporting team. Problems will need to be tolerated while efforts are made to effect gradual changes where these seem feasible. Initial adjustments will be easy for some families and difficult for others. To deal effectively with the patient and parents, members of the team need time to become acquainted with strengths already evident in the way the family has faced other unexpected or frightening situations. Recommendations to the parents for assisting the child to cope can be adjusted as further knowledge about the reactions of all members of the family become clearer.

Parental Coping with a Child's Pain. When a child receives a diagnosis of cancer and enters upon protracted treatment, the parents are placed under unusual strain. Varying greatly in reaction, their resourcefulness takes many different forms. A study by Kupst and others (in press, 1984) followed 60 families from the time leukemia was diagnosed in one of their children through two years of treatment. The investigators were impressed by the families' eventual success in coping. During the first few months, the problems in family adjustment mounted at the same time the child was beginning a series of often painful procedures; it was during this period parents found psychological consultation particularly helpful. Even though the circumstances of stress persisted, families were able to adjust; two years after diagnosis, most of them were coping well, including those who had had to come to grips with the death of a child.

Unless parents are able to adopt a supporting and positive attitude, it is difficult for them to help their children develop coping strategies that will work. In a pain-producing procedure, the parents are caught in a dilemma: they do not wish to see their child suffer, but they can no longer protect the child from pain. The haunting question for many is, "Can I really stand by while my child suffers?" The child benefits most if the parent can express empathy, as previously described, without giving evidence of actual suffering with the child. This attitude, however, is an ideal behavior that many parents are quite unpreparerd to assume because of their own past experiences. For instance, the mother of a 7-year-old boy who was diagnosed as having leukemia had seen how her brother had suffered during a sternal biopsy several years before.[1] She was certain that her son must be suffering each time as intensely as her brother had suffered. Trying to comfort him during a procedure, she held his hand, but when he cried, she fell apart and was unable to give him any reassurance. Through discussion with a staff member, she was helped to understand the distinction between the two experiences and to observe how brief the painful experience was for her son and how rapidly he recovered. Afterwards she was able to be of greater assistance to the boy.

Some parents, again for reasons of their past experiences, find it impossible to remain in a treatment room. One father of a teenage girl suffered from claustrophobia in the small treatment room with its doors closed. He remained in the open waiting room. The nurse substituted for the father as the caring companion; the patient understood her father's predicament and accepted his need to stay outside the room.

In another instance, a mother became so distraught when her young son cried and struggled that she could not remain in the treatment room. Hypnotic treatment was initiated with her son, and although his distress was not completely alleviated, his struggling disappeared and his crying was reduced. At this point she could return and take her place as a supportive mother.

Sometimes a disturbed child has to be restrained so that a needle can be placed accurately in a target area. Occasionally several people are required to keep the child absolutely quiet. Knowing that parents often were expected to help "pin down" the child, a visiting group of psychiatrists raised the question of whether or not physical restraint of a struggling child during a procedure contradicted the supporting and sympathetic parental role. There is no one answer for all children. The child recognizes that some restraint is necessary if he or she is to lie perfectly still and often states a preference as to who should do it. It is reassuring to the child to have the preference respected. Nurses have reported that some children say, "I want my mom to hold me down . . . I want my dad to hold me down . . . I *don't* want the nurse to hold me down." By assigning this role to a trusted parent, the child may feel assured that the constraint comes from a caring person.

When the child is not willing to accept any restraint and a parent imposes it by force, the parent often feels both angry that it is necessary and guilty for doing it. Sometimes a nurse or other staff member will recognize the parent's upset and take charge until the child becomes less negative and more willing to cooperate.

The Central Role of the Physician.   Usually the family physician or pediatrician is the one who first detects the possibility of cancer in a child or adolescent and refers the patient to a pediatric oncologist to confirm the diagnosis and recommend the course of treatment. Medical practice in connection with cancer is highly technological and calls upon a wide range of specialized knowledge. The expertness of the oncologist, therefore, is what first brings patient and parents together for a consultation. Although the physician's expertness is what brings them together, what holds them together is the establishment of a relationship of confidence, trust, and friendliness. During a long and life-threatening illness, the decisions that have to be faced often constitute crises for patient and family. For example, the first of these crises is the confirmation of the diagnosis of cancer, a reality the physician assists the family in facing. Subsequently, from time to time, the patient and parents will wish to discuss the course of the disease with the physician who continues in the role of an understanding advisor.

A decision of vital importance to a patient with pain concerns the use of medication. Studies now indicate that pain can be controlled as effectively at home as in the hospital. Consequently, current programs call for more home care of patients suffering with persistent pain. While the physician makes decisions about medication for pain relief, it is more apt to be the discharge-coordinator nurse who visits the home and instructs patient and parents in its administration. Under appropriate circumstances, even narcotics are now given on a regular basis at home.

From the point of view of the young patients, it is important that they receive attention from the physician as persons in their own right. Like adult patients, they wish to be recognized by name in the corridor, they like the bedside visit in the hospital when the physician asks how their favorite baseball team is doing, and they appreciate a friendly, humorous remark.

A more detailed discussion of the physician's role in supportive care of the young cancer patient may be found in other sources (Zeltzer, Zeltzer, and LeBaron, 1983); Zeltzer and LeBaron (in press).

The Strategic Role of the Nurse.   Thomas (1983) noted that high technology has reduced the amount of personal attention the physician gives to the patient. Among nurses, however, he finds a persistence of the personal care that once was the basis of all medical practice. Although widely experienced as a physician, it was through his personal experience as a patient that he was particularly impressed by the nurses:

> My discovery, as a patient on the medical service and later in surgery, is that the institution is held together, *glued* together, enabled to function as an organism, by the nurses and nobody else (Thomas, 1983, p. 67).

Our observations of nurses on the oncology units support Thomas' high estimate of the nurse's role. Nursing personnel now take a prominent role in investigating the psychological and social aspects of pain in child patients undergoing medical treatments that entail anxiety and pain. Several studies by nurses have already been cited, e.g., Abu-Saad and Holzemer (1981); Cowherd (1977); Eland and Anderson (1977); Johnson et al (1975); Schultz (1971), and additional articles are cited elsewhere in the book.

In the treatment room, the nurse functions as a coordinator of physician, child, parent, and other personnel. While she is sensitively caring for the child's needs, she anticipates that the physician may need her help. When she finds it necessary to leave the child temporarily to assist the physician, she plans for someone else to take over. This is generally the mother, if the patient is a young child. A short absence is not critical for an older child.

Throughout a procedure, the nurse is sensitive to the parent's needs as well as to the child's. During her initial acquaintance with the family, she observes the interactions between parent and child and inquires about prior experiences with treatment. She realizes that it is important to utilize coping abilities that the families bring with them. What has worked before has been pretested. The finale of a treatment procedure requires a skilled hand. The hope is that the patient will leave with a positive outlook that will reduce anxiety about subsequent treatment. The nurse contributes praise at the end and, in the Children's Hospital at Stanford, enhances good feeling by leading the way to the locked red box with its selection of surprises.

The Team. The child and adolescent in a treatment program for cancer cope with problems in a number of settings: hospital clinic and ward, home, and school. In each setting they meet a variety of people, all of whom influence them. Also, in each setting a few persons can be thought of as responsible members of the therapeutic team: the hospital staff, the family, and the teacher.

We have already discussed the roles of parents, physicians, and nurses in the hospital setting. When the patient is resident in the hospital, other significant staff members include social workers, occupational therapists, recreational therapists, religious advisors, and teachers. They contribute to the general well being of the patient and, by providing interesting activities, they often divert attention away from pain, the primary symptom with which we are dealing.

A philosophy that makes sense is that sick children feel much better at home in the midst of family, pets, friends, and home cooking. Now much of the treatment that formerly required a prolonged stay in the hospital can be conducted on an outpatient basis in the home. The shift away from a predominantly hospital-based program has been made possible because certain procedures traditionally associated with hospital practice have been improved to the point where it is feasible to carry them out elsewhere. For example, a catheter inserted in a vein for a period of weeks, known as the Hickman catheter, permits the drawing of blood, and the infusion of chemotherapeutic agents, antibiotics, or narcotics to a patient while at home. For these and other procedures, a discharge-coordinator nurse paves the path for the move from hospital to home. The child's condition dictates what else is needed, whether it is a wheel chair, hospital bed, continuous oxygen, medication for pain control, the planning of a school reentry program, or a community referral for adaptive driving aids. The nurse may need to check every day, twice a week, or less frequently. In some cases the patient will feel well enough that no special attention is needed.

Most children at home, whether in active treatment or remission, face social adjustments at home and school. At home, a sick child necessarily receives more attention, sometimes at the expense of other siblings. The normal balance of relationships is altered and various adjustments then need to be made. In a study of children's reentry into school after an absence due to cancer treatment, fears were common among children of all ages—fear of teasing from peers, fear of embarrassment from changes in appearance, and fear of difficulties in talking about the illness (Henning and Fritz, 1983). Ross and Ross in interviews with school age children with leukemia found that ridicule or teasing by peers greatly troubled a number of them as they returned to school bald or obese due to the side effects of medications; they suggest ways in which patients can be taught to cope with such attitudes and, in the process, restore their self-confidence (in press, 1984). Many children worry about their ability to participate fully. The discharge-coordinator nurse sometimes found it necessary to discuss with the teachers their own fear that a child with a malignancy would require too much classroom time, or that the child's further illness, even death, would disturb the other children. Despite the possible problems, there were teachers who met the problem creatively. One 11-year-old boy treated at Stanford was invited by his teacher to talk to the whole class about his illness, about life at the hospital, and how the doctors and nurses paid attention to what he wanted. After this discussion, which captured the children's attention, his differences from the other children did not lead to teasing, but led to his acceptance by the group. In a similar instance, a girl of 14 spoke glowingly of how her teacher had asked her to speak of her experience. She had given her classmates a vivid account of how she felt she was the possessor of a special experience.

In the varied settings of clinic, inpatient ward, or home, different members of the staff carry primary responsibility. At the same time the cooperative relationships continue through an integrated approach, in which all members of the team—physician, nurse, nurse-coordinator, parents, and teacher—strive to help the patient feel secure. The organized effort provides coherence for the therapeutic program.

The Role of Medication in Pain Relief

It is true that the greatest medical advance in pain relief came by way of chemical agents that produce analgesia. The possibility of reducing pain through analgesics, including narcotics, is so widely recognized that the major issue is simply how often and in what quantities they should be used. Even very young patients know the effectiveness of medication. In one study of over 100 children hospitalized for medical and surgical problems, when they were asked "What makes you feel better when you are in pain?", they answered most frequently, "medicine, shots, and pills" (Tesler, Wegner, Savedra, Gibbons and Ward, 1981).

Because patients welcome the relief medication brings, the issue of frequency of use becomes important. In general the warnings against addiction favor the use of as little medication as possible. It is quite possible, however, that this restriction in use has been carried too far, particularly with children. Eland and Anderson (1977) studied 25 children ages 4 through 7 who were hospitalized for surgery in a large teaching hospital. All had had surgery under general anesthesia. Thirteen of the 25 children were not given any medication for pain relief during their hospitalizations. Although 21 of the children had orders for pain medication to be given at the discretion of the nurses, members of the nursing staff apparently were reluctant to administer the medication. A comparison was made with 18 adults in the same hospital whose diagnoses and surgical conditions were matched with 18 of the 25 children. All had undergone surgery under general anesthesia. These 18 adults had received 671 doses of narcotic and nonnarcotic analgesics. By contrast, all 25 of the children had received only 24 doses. Those who hesitate to give pain medication to children support their actions with various reasons, such as the assertion that children feel less pain, that narcotics might be harmful or addictive to a young child, that children fail to localize the pain, and in any case, recover rapidly. These reasons have little basis in fact. For example, Haslam (1969), in a careful study of pain thresholds in children 5 to 18 years of age, found that the younger the child, the more susceptible he or she was to pain. In a further discussion by a nursing pain consultant and a pediatric staff nurse, it was concluded that children in pain were seriously undermedicated (McGuire and Dizard, 1982).

The use of pain medication is essential for management of chronic pain in children with cancer. If medication is warranted, then it should be of a sufficient dosage and frequency so as to maximize the therapeutic value. If initial dosages achieve only minimal pain reduction, not only are patients deprived of significant relief, but they may lose confidence in the physician's and nurse's ability to help and in the potential efficacy of the medication. It is now generally agreed that adequate doses of medication for pain should be administered on a regular schedule around the clock so that a patient does not have to experience pain in order to request and receive a drug (Twycross, 1983; Zeltzer, Zeltzer, and LeBaron, 1983).

Another point to consider in using medication for chronic pain is that many patients have greater need of it at night when outside stimuli are minimal. During the day, medication doses may be lowered for many patients by providing interesting age-appropriate activities which occupy a child's mind. Often the physician or nurse can discuss these issues with children or adolescents and their families to determine their preferences, then recommend the best combinations of activity and medication for the individual patient (Zeltzer, LeBaron, and Zeltzer, 1984).

Psychological Resources for the Management of Anxiety and Pain

Our major topic has been the hypnotic control of pain, but we have repeatedly recognized other methods that have helped the patient threatened by pain and suffering. The desirable practice is to combine whatever resources may be needed and available for the benefit of the patient.

The Importance of Personal Contact. In his charming book on the nature of medicine and medical practice, *The Youngest Science* (1983), Dr. Lewis Thomas stressed the importance of human contact between physician and patient, particularly the "laying on of hands."

> The doctor's oldest skill in trade was to place his hands on the patient . . . Most of the men who practiced this laying on of hands must have possessed, to begin with, the gift of affection (pp. 56–57).

The importance of personal contact is not limited to physicians. Most patients found contact with a supporting adult helpful. Some parents stroke the child's forehead. Wally, age 8, said, "Holding my mom's hand makes it easier. It makes me feel as though it won't hurt as much." Dale, age 21 years, had started treatment seven years before. Throughout the procedure, his wife was at his side clasping his hand. Asked afterward what had helped, Dale replied that holding his wife's hand was "a comfort, a relief of tension."

When a child complains of pain, it is important to learn what the pain is about. The pain complaint may be loud, though the pain stimulus appears minor, or the reverse may be true. Sometimes, anxiety more than pain is involved. In any case, the complaint needs to be recognized. The severity of the pain may necessitate further exploration of the cause, a sympathetic rub, a warm washcloth to the spot that hurts, or medication. Whether physical relief is obtained, this contact reassures the patient that someone cares and is taking time to help. Sometimes people forget the value of old-fashioned remedies administered with a dose of personal concern. Parents may fear that the more attention they give the child, the more the child will demand. On the contrary, the result is apt to be a feeling of greater security.

Thus far, we have spoken of physical contact through the hands. Eye contact is also an important way of establishing intimacy between two people (Ellsworth and Ross, 1976). In the bone marrow aspiration, children who comply with the nurse's suggestion, "Look at me," experience a greater sense of affiliation with the nurse as well as a distraction from the procedure. Parents have long recognized looking as a form of touching in their advice to children passing a display of delectable cookies or fascinating toys: "Touch only with your eyes." Particularly for an older school child or adolescent, who may feel uneasy about clasping hands during a procedure, keeping in touch with friendly, reassuring eyes can be a primary source of comfort.

Conversation represents another type of contact, this time by way of an encouraging voice. Closeness through conversation is a cognitive equivalent of physical contact through touch. For the young child, the adult may do most of the talking, maintaining interest by telling a story or recounting pleasant experiences from the child's past. Older children and adolescents often participate with animation and sometimes wish to direct such a conversation.

The treatment room can be arranged so as to facilitate these types of contact. For example, some nurses seat parents at the head of the treatment table so that patient and parent can see each other, clasp hands if desired, and communicate in words.

All of these caring approaches contribute to the comfort and well-being of the patient and have as their by-product the relaxation that is so essential for a patient dealing with pain or the prospect of pain.

Activities that Counteract Pain. We turn now to a discussion of stories, games, and other activities that divert the patient's attention from pain, reduce anxiety generally, and fill in waiting periods that invite apprehensions and fears. When it commands attention, pain can feed upon itself and become exaggerated.

Effective pain reduction occurs when the patient's attention is diverted by some other compelling interest. The advantage of hypnosis for this purpose is that it does not require environmental supports. Under hypnosis, whether guided by a hypnotist or accomplished through self-hypnotic techniques, the patient's interest is captured by fantasies produced out of his own experiences. The less hypnotizable may require attention-diversion through realistic distractions rather than through hypnotic fantasy. The relative use of distraction by way of environmental supports such as conversation and action, to distraction by way of hypnotic fantasy, varies from child to child. What is merely a distraction of attention for one child may be the beginning of hypnotic involvement for another. As children grow older, the truly hypnotizable will be capable of reducing pain through the use of fantasy, but the less hypnotizable will require external distraction or other coping strategies.

The activities to be described are applicable to all children regardless of their hypnotizability. Individual differences in interests and preferences will determine how attractive and successful the various activities will be for any one child or adolescent.

Storytelling and Story Reading. Over 60 years ago, Bartlett wrote that storytelling was concerned with the shared enjoyment of make-believe (1920). More recently, Hunter, discussing folk tales, commented how both narrator and listener enjoyed the stories (1981). The narrator frequently uses gestures, mimicry, dramatic devices, and skillful improvisation as well as words to entice the listener into living a story in imagination.

A young boy at the hospital was so frightened of intravenous injections that he shook uncontrollably during their administration. He did not want hypnotic treatment, but the therapist involved him in stories, both the ones that he told and the ones that the therapist told him. According to instructions, at the moment an IV was to be inserted, instead of watching the needle, he was to watch the blood pressure gauge. He did so, and did not shake. Afterward he commented, "It was pretty good." It is not clear from his comment whether the pain had been reduced or, equally important, he had found a way to tolerate the residual pain.

There are many hours to be filled for a child who is ill. Because normal activities are restricted, those responsible for helping the child occupy time need to provide other suitable activities, of which storytelling is one. Some parents are more gifted than others at storytelling, but one source of stories offers advantages to parents who are less accustomed to telling fabricated stories: children love to hear about themselves. Recollections of anecdotes about earlier experiences can be most enjoyable. Each family has its own memory bank of good times. With an emphasis always on the positive, these "stories" can include adventures, perhaps the trip to Disneyland, how funny it was when Aunt Lulu spilled her coffee on Grandpa's white suit, or the great baseball game he (the patient) pitched. Tales from the past cover the fun times, the silly times, and the proud times accompanied by the warm glow of success. Children love to hear these same stories over and over again.

Storytelling has advantages over silent reading because another person is involved to share the interest and excitement. Reading a story to a child provides new material, while at the same time it is a shared experience.

As the child grows older, stories suited to individual reading ability and preference can be enjoyed by the child alone. For suggestions about books that children find challenging and attractive, we found a discussion with the librarian in the children's division of the local library helpful. Books adapted to each age group, some of them the old reliables known to parents and even grandparents, and some quite new, are present in abundance. Many are interesting enough to be read and reread.

One series called "Choose Your Own Adventure" permits readers to make their own decisions in solving mysteries and science fiction plots. For ages 9 and up, stories such as "Who Killed Harlow Thrombey?" (Packard, 1981) or "The Abominable Snowman" (Izzard, 1955) contain options and allow for choices among them, permitting the reader to make decisions all along the way. Depending on how the clues are evaluated, the child is directed to read a section of the book that continues that particular line of thought. Some decisions bring a young detective closer to the answer and some lead away from the main track. Success in solving the mystery depends on the kind of decisions that are made.

A librarian can also direct a reader to authors who show that they really understand teenage concerns. Young Adult fiction is directed toward ages 13 to 15.

Stories Transmitted by Television. If the goal is to fascinate and occupy the time of a sedentary child, as parents know well, there is nothing more successful than television. Studies of children's TV viewing habits show that the average number of hours spent per day viewing television varies from 3 per day for the older preschoolers to 5 or more for elementary school children (Singer, Singer, and Zuckerman, 1981). Any child who is ill at home is likely to be watching television.

When used with discretion, television has a place in pain control. If the objective is to promote a feeling of well-being, it is important that someone observe the reactions of each child to various programs. Some children say they haven't felt good while they watched violence on TV, or that they felt "jumpy" after a fast-paced and noisy program. There are many programs of this type on television today, and for children who are anxious, distressed, or ill, great care must be exercised in the selection of programs. There is direct evidence from a study of first-grade children that those who spent more time watching TV tended to have the more unpleasant fantasies (McIlwraith and Schallow, 1983). This is a clear warning that excessive TV viewing may be counterproductive for an ill child. A sick child who is already anxious needs experiences that will help him or her feel better, calmer, and more cheerful.

If television viewing is compared with reading, differences in the two media are apparent. Watching a story can feel different from reading it because of the impact of TV's fast action and special effects. When a child reads, he controls the pace. When he views TV he is swept along, whether he understands the material or not, and is often confused as a result.

There are TV programs of moderate length designed specifically for children of various ages. Such children's programs are available on Public Television and, to a more limited extent, on commercial stations. Parents who wish help in selecting appropriate programs have found essential information in the guides issued periodically by local broadcasting stations.

Full enjoyment of a program often requires the presence of another person. The advantage is that recall of interesting scenes or events can be discussed afterwards. To be sure, parents and nurses cannot be with a child all the time, and television will sometimes serve as a convenient babysitter.

The Attraction of Games. Attentive concentration on an interesting game can command the attention of patients faced with pain. Ed described how, as an 8-year-old, he had become so involved in a Monopoly game with his mother that most of the time he was unaware that the surgeon was using a great many stitches to repair an extensive laceration (Chapter 6). Ed also indicated that no medication for pain was used.

Games are helpful to the young patient, not only because of their high intrinsic interest, but because many encourage social interactions. Some games provide an immediate reason for enjoying the company of another person, and such sociability is itself an attractive diversion. One child whom we observed in a bone marrow aspiration reported pain between 4 and 5 (scale 0–10), but did not wish help from the hypnosis program because she would miss playing games with her friend Sybil who regularly accompanied her and her mother to the hospital. During the baseline observation period, the two had played a game until the procedure started. During the procedure, they talked about the game, and though the patient showed signs of discomfort as the bone marrow was withdrawn, she happily resumed playing with Sybil at the first possible moment.

Both children and adults enjoy recreational computer games. They can be exciting and fun. Naturally, some games will be better adapted to individual tastes than others. Again, the children's section of the library often has game cassettes available to lend.

When a child's game partner is older or younger, a game that is partially controlled by chance, like shaking dice in board games such as Parchesi, tends to equalize age differences.

Most large oncology centers have a recreational and occupational unit with suggestions about games that are appropriate for children of various ages. The staff at a children's library is likely to be knowledgeable about current games that appeal to children as well as books and manuals that describe them. Games should be chosen to match a patient's interests and levels of ability if they are to "capture" the player's attention.

When a patient has been weakened by illness, games that do not take too long to play are preferable. The child may tire easily, and it is more satisfying to be able to finish each game than to interrupt it and return later.

Filling Unfilled Time. A special need for diversion arises during the anxious waiting periods that occur in the course of treatment procedures. One such period in the bone marrow aspiration procedure is the wait for local anesthesia to take effect before the needle is inserted. Because the anesthetic does not relieve the deep pain experienced when the marrow is withdrawn, anxiety tends to mount during this quiet period. This is an appropriate time to recall a short, interesting, or happy experience. Lively conversation serves the same purpose. In addition, unexpected delays can occur in the midst of a procedure, and plans for filling in these blanks should also be in readiness.

Unfilled time periods are occasioned by the trip to the hospital, the waiting period before a procedure, the vacuum created by isolation in a hospital bed, the temporary departure of family members, or the difficulty in getting to sleep. After observing the impact of these situations upon the patient, suggestions for needed activities may be made.

In the discussion of time frames, we generally have referred to the past. Just as children enjoy the recall of past experiences, however, they enjoy the anticipation of future events. For the child whose illness makes planning for the future uncertain, it is preferable to base the anticipations on events to occur in the near future. Children always enjoy special treats or surprises, as already mentioned in connection with the surprises kept in the little red locked box in Children's Hospital at Stanford. Small extras planned in the morning for later the same day have been shown to improve mood (Isen and Levin, 1972). Their specific form depends on the wishes and physical condition of the child, as well as on the habits and customs of each family. They might include a freshly baked favorite food, a milkshake, or short recreational trips to interesting spots, such as a toy store or the zoo.

Many of the parents and nurses whom we observed showed great ingenuity and imagination in meeting the continuing needs of a child with cancer. In addition, hospital staff members and volunteers took care to equip children's waiting rooms with interesting toys and books. In this chapter, we have described existing practices as suggestions and reminders of the many ways children can be assisted to meet the problems of serious illness.

Notes

1. In a marrow biopsy a large needle is inserted into the marrow space and a core of bone spicules is withdrawn, along with the marrow. In an aspiration a different type of needle is used to withdraw the marrow only. A sternal biopsy indicates that the sternum (breast bone) is the site of the biopsy.

8 Understanding Hypnosis and Hypnotherapy

As we reflected upon our experiences in the Stanford study, certain generalizations about our understanding of hypnosis and hypnotherapy emerged. These include comments on the relationship between patient and therapist, the facets of hypnotic induction, the utilization of imaginative involvements as related to hypnotic talent, and a discussion of dissociation in the perspective of other contemporary theories of hypnosis.

Relationship between Patient and Hypnotherapist

The role of the hypnotherapist is reminiscent of the role of the family physician in the sense that the therapist deals with the patient not only as an "expert" but as a friend and counselor who, as such, develops a relationship of trust and whose expertness depends on psychological as well as on technical skill. In the early stages of the relationship, however, unlike the situation of patient to family doctor, a patient is often confused about how to deal with a hypnotherapist because of the various popular images of hypnosis. A therapist, consequently, attends first to the patient's preconceptions about hypnosis.

The relationship between patient and hypnotherapist becomes a therapeutic alliance as they discuss the patient's current problems, goals that are desired as a result of treatment, and the possibility that hypnosis can be of benefit. With young children, a short discussion usually suffices. Older children and adolescents appreciate the thought that their own contributions will make a difference in the shared effort. In line with this plan, hypnotherapists explore the skills, interests, and enthusiasms of the patient. Talking about a patient's strengths permits communication on the "high ground" of the patient's self-confidence and self-esteem, and thereby serves as an ego-strengthening technique. Subsequently, some of the patient's interests and enthusiasms are used as a foundation for hypnotic therapy. The hypnotherapist—like any other good therapist—must be a good listener and careful observer. Particularly important for the alliance of patient and therapist is the establishment of an atmosphere of collaboration that contradicts the myth of the hypnotist as a powerful manipulator of the mind. Forceful direct suggestions are used with great discretion. The approach of the hypnotherapist is more likely to include statements such as: "I think that by working together, you'll be able to use your own experiences in such a way that they can help you feel much better."

The Dual Role in Self-Hypnosis.   Hypnosis, guided by a hypnotherapist (heterohypnosis), can prepare the patient to serve the dual role of hypnotist and patient in self-hypnosis (autohypnosis). In heterohypnosis, the hypnotist initially takes over (with the patient's assent) some of the executive functions of the patient and through suggestions influences the direction of therapy, whereas in self-hypnosis the patient retrieves the executive function and represents both the hypnotist and the one who is hypnotized. Patients are able to do this because, at the same time as they are participating in a fantasy, a small observing part of the mind has remained separate as a monitor. Because the monitor is a normal aspect of the hypnotic experience, it can expand its observing role to initiate the kind of executive action required in self-hypnosis. By analogy, it is as if an airplane pilot decides to place the controls on automatic pilot. The pilot is still in charge, but the operations are carried out without requiring his additional voluntary action. In an emergency, however, he can again take charge. It is the same with the patient in hypnosis, whether in hetero- or self-hypnosis: when the time comes to terminate hypnosis, the monitoring or observing self is there to do so.

Self-hypnosis is a valuable adjunct to therapy because, with one's self in charge, not only is the control issue resolved, but also a therapeutic intervention can take place, at the will of the patient, at any hour or place. Initially, the degree of success in self-hypnosis corresponds with the degree of success in heterohypnosis. To the extent that the patient has used initiative and imagination in heterohypnosis, he or she transfers these skills to self-hypnosis.

The Components of Hypnotic Induction

As we have already indicated, spending time in a quiet preparatory phase which may or may not include a formal hypnotic induction, serves to direct attention away from the patient's usual activities and concentrate it on the hypnotherapist's suggestions.

Although there are a variety of induction procedures, they all share common components. The three obvious components of the induction process, each of which has its psychological consequences, are the *enactive* component, represented by either eye closure or arm levitation, the *relaxation* component, emphasized most in the eye-closure procedure but also in the arm levitation one, and the *imagination* component, the essential one in the imaginative induction. Each of these will be examined in turn so that note can be made about the extent to which the components are involved in various inductions and what the consequences of the components are.

The Enactive Component in Induction.   By the enactive component, we refer to actual movements made in response to suggestion. For example, if it is suggested that the hands will move together, the suggestion is fulfilled by the enacted movement of the hands. This contrasts with responses to suggestion that do not show in movement, as in hallucinated age regression. The enactive component is represented both in the induction procedures of eye closure and arm levitation. Although we did not use arm levitation in our present investigation, a cogent description of such an induction by a young adult is illustrative.

Helen, age 45, suffered from arthritis. She wondered whether she would be hypnotizable since this was her first experience with hypnosis. In fact, she proved to be highly hypnotizable and reduced her pain completely.

The induction began while Helen sat in a comfortable chair. The hypnotherapist described to her the usual arm-levitation procedure: How she would *find* her right arm, now resting on the arm of the chair, *rising by itself* as she concentrated on its becoming lighter, and how, when her hand touched her face, she would realize that she had arrived at a condition of *markedly* increased relaxation and ease. The therapist explained that it was important to *"let these things happen."*

Helen's arm and hand remained on the arm of the chair for some time before starting to move, then they rose very gradually until the hand touched her face. After hypnosis, Helen described this phase. "It [the impulse to rise] did not come quickly, but very slowly. I felt within me a struggle. *I wanted to make sure I wasn't doing it myself.* From the elbow down it began to feel quite light, it became ever lighter, until the entire arm felt light and it went up." Had she felt that she was *making this happen, or had she let it happen?* the therapist asked. She spoke with conviction of how important it was for her to let the movement happen by itself. She thought that everything might have occurred more slowly for this reason.

Helen's "struggle" represented the two conflicting demands upon her. To comply with one of the hypnotist's suggestions, she had agreed not to raise the hand voluntarily, yet the hypnotist also had suggested that the hand was supposed to rise. This is the familiar double-bind situation described by Haley as part of the eye-closure induction (Haley, 1958). The solution to Helen's conflict consisted in producing a dissociated condition in which the hand seemed to rise by itself. Part of her (a subordinate cognitive structure) was actually raising the arm, but the fact that she was controlling the action now was absent from her awareness. She experienced what it was like to respond with involuntary action as a consequence of suggestion.

On the second day of hypnosis, hand levitation occurred much more quickly. In addition, Helen was shown how to use hand levitation herself to induce hypnosis and how to terminate it. From this point she used self-hypnosis successfully at home. It should be noted that although Helen could now voluntarily decide when to enter a hypnotic state, the involuntary nature of the hand levitation persisted as did the automaticity of thought and action which is characteristic of hypnosis.

Some tests of hypnotic responsiveness incorporate a hand-levitation induction. For example, the Stanford Profile Scale of Hypnotic Susceptibility, Form I, uses a hand levitation induction accompanied by imaginative suggestions for tingling and lightness in the hand "as if it were a feather ready to float up and away" (Weitzenhoffer and Hilgard, 1963). In a recently constructed Creative Imagination Scale (Wilson and Barber, 1978), the talent for hand levitation is the second item that is measured in the scale. In this test the arm is positioned straight out in front and imaginative suggestions are supplied by the therapist for the subject to picture a garden hose with a strong stream of water pushing it up. The scoring of the item does *not* ask for any movement enactment; rather, the patient rates how the imagined experience compares with a real one. Because the hypnotherapist does not suggest that the movement be made, the person who takes this test loses the opportunity to gain an experience of involuntary movement that meant so much to Helen as an indication that she was hypnotized. The nonenactment features of the Creative Imagination Scale are particularly serious when this scale is adapted for use with children (Myers, 1983). The important role of enactment is prominent in the experience of young children (Morgan and J. Hilgard, 1978/1979). At the earliest ages, enactment is preeminent because the child expresses fantasy portrayed in action (Chapter 9).

Enactment serves as a useful way for the subject to grasp and develop dissociative behavior. Observing their own movements helps patients understand the difference between the waking condition and the dissociated behavior of the hypnotic condition. Two important goals are achieved in this phase of enactment: the patient begins to understand what hypnosis is about, and the hypnotherapist is able to evaluate the patient's ability and continued progress. Enactment, in effect, serves as an important nonverbal form of communication between them.

The Relaxation Component in Induction. Relaxation has enjoyed such a long history of successful use in hypnosis that some psychologists regard it as the central core of the hypnotic state (Edmonston, 1981). Edmonston believes that the essence of induction is to produce relaxation and that the "neutral hypnotic state" is defined by the achieved relaxation. Edmonston considers it the *only* fundamental characteristic of hypnosis, relegating all subsequent phenomena generally accepted as belonging within the domain of hypnosis (dreams, regression, amnesia) to a secondary position. He relates this view to an early one espoused by Pavlov, who thought that hypnotic induction replaced the everyday state of wakefulness with a form of partial sleep. The assumption that hypnosis was sleep became untenable when electroencephalographic (EEG) recordings from hypnotized subjects proved not to match those of sleeping subjects.

For more recent support of his theory, Edmonston leans on a concept popularized by Benson and his coworkers (Benson, Berry, and Carol, 1974) called a "unitary relaxation response," which they claim to be present in progressive relaxation, transcendental meditation, autogenic training, Yoga, Zen, and hypnosis. Regardless of one's view about the primacy of relaxation, the quieting effect of a relaxed induction is therapeutic for an anxious child and is a benefit that is available whether one is but little hypnotizable or highly hypnotizable.

Whether or not relaxation suggestions are used in induction, the patient need not achieve muscular relaxation for the hypnotic condition to develop. As shown by Ruch and Morgan (1971), subjects hypnotized while standing upright with postural muscles tense showed no significant differences in their hypnotic experiences from those hypnotized while sitting or lying down. It seems appropriate to call this a type of cognitive relaxation. Another investigation demonstrated that relaxation suggestions are not necessary for a profound hypnotic experience to occur. Banyai and E. Hilgard (1976) demonstrated that when subjects vigorously pedaled a stationary exercise bicycle, and they received a hypnotic induction which concentrated on suggestions for increased wakefulness, freshness, and alertness, they entered into a hypnotic state similar to that induced by the conventional relaxation approach.

These results were produced under laboratory conditions but bear considerable similarity to those achieved by Balinese dancers (Gill and Brenman, 1959) and by long-distance runners (E. Hilgard, 1977a).

Relaxation may or may not be a feature of an imaginative induction. Whether it is will depend upon the type of imaginative sequence that is chosen. With young children, activity rather than relaxation will characterize any imaginative undertaking.

By contrast with enactment procedures, the specific signs of relaxation, including general quiescence, are not indicative of hypnotic dissociation; the same signs are shown by patients with slight hypnotic talent as by those with much talent. In one respect this is an advantage for therapeutic practice because the subjective effects of relaxation are pleasantly felt by all, regardless of success in producing dissociated activity. In fact, the high degree of subjective comfort may lead to the patients' own belief that they have experienced some degree of hypnosis.

The Imagination Component in Induction.   Just as relaxation plays some part in hypnotic induction, so, too, imagination plays a part in inductions which have relaxation and enactive components. Milton Erickson (1952) asserted his belief that imagery as part of trance induction was useful in many situations to facilitate hypnotic behavior. He noted that a subject or patient who, when originally hypnotized experienced difficulty in developing suggested hallucinations, could often profit from the use of imagery when hypnosis was later reinduced. He cited. an experiment in which medical students were divided into two groups—one group asked to stare at a crystal ball and to imagine a scene in it and the other asked to imagine both the crystal ball and the scene. The latter achieved better results.

By its very title, the Creative Imagination Scale suggests an imaginative induction (Wilson and Barber, 1978). One of the claims for the scale, however, is that it measures hypnosis without an induction. The language in which the first item is phrased is such that it could be regarded as a planned imaginative induction:

> Item I. Arm Heaviness: "By letting your thoughts go along with these instructions, you can make your hand and arm feel heavy. Please close your eyes and place your left arm straight out in front of you at shoulder height with the palm facing up."
>
> (Begin timing.) "Now imagine that a very heavy dictionary is being placed on the palm of your left hand. Let yourself feel the heaviness. Your thoughts make it feel as if there is a heavy dictionary on your hand. You create the feeling of heaviness in your hand by thinking of a large heavy dictionary. Now think of a second

large heavy dictionary being placed on top of the first heavy dictionary. Feel how very heavy your arm begins to feel as you push up on the dictionaries. Push up on the heavy dictionaries as you imagine the weight; notice how your arm feels heavier and heavier as you push up on them. Now tell yourself that a third big heavy dictionary is being piled on top of the other two heavy dictionaries in your hand and your arm is very, very heavy. Let yourself feel as if there are three heavy dictionaries in the palm of your hand and your arm is getting heavier and heavier and heavier. Feel your arm getting heavier and heavier and heavier, very, very, very heavy, getting heavier and heavier and heavier . . . very heavy." (Approximately 1'20" since beginning of timing.) "Now relax your hand and arm and tell yourself that your hand and arm feel perfectly normal again." (Wilson and Barber, 1978, p. 244.)

Each of the suggestions used as an item for testing hypnotic responsiveness after an induction carries on the induction process in the sense of maintaining the hypnotic condition. In other words, when a measurement scale is given without a labeled induction, induction procedures are usually inherent in the items that are used.

In testing hypnotic responsiveness on the SHCS:Child, an imagination induction was found more suitable for many children aged 4 to 8 than the traditional eye-closure/relaxation induction (Chapter 2). The imagination induction is presented below, along with Item 1 of the scale, in order to show how the imaginative component of induction is utilized both in producing the hypnotic condition and in testing for the consequence of hypnotic induction.

The hypnotist begins the imagination induction by saying:

"I'd like to talk with you about how a person can use his imagination to do or feel different kinds of things. Do you know what I mean by imagination?" (If necessary, explain.) "Do you know what it's like to pretend things, to 'make believe'? Do you ever pretend things, or make believe that you are someone else? When you can do anything you want to do, what do you do? That is, what are the things you like to do more than anything else in the world?" (Probe for interests, i.e., swimming, hiking, playing on the slide and merry-go-round (playground), having a picnic, etc. Select a favorite activity and engage child in thinking about it. The picnic described here is an illustration.)

"O.K., let's do that right now.[1] Let's imagine (pretend) that we are on a picnic and there's a big picnic basket right in front of us. What does the basket look like to you? How big is it? . . . I'm going to spread this bright yellow tablecloth on the grass here . . . Why don't you take something out of the basket now? Tell me about it . . . That's fine . . . What else is in the basket?" (Continue until a convincing fantasy is developed, or child shows total lack of involvement.)

"You know, you can do lots of interesting things by thinking about it this way. It's like imagining (pretending) something so strongly that it seems almost real. How real did it seem to you? Good. Now let's try imagining some other things, O.K.?" (Morgan and J. Hilgard, 1978/79, p. 164).

This ends the imagination induction and the first test item follows. Note how imagination facilitates the enactment of the suggested hand-lowering.

Item 1. Hand-Lowering: "Please hold your right (left) arm straight out in front of you, with the palm up. (Assist if necessary.) Imagine that you are holding something heavy in your hand, like a heavy rock. Something very heavy. Shape your fingers around the heavy rock in your hand. What does it feel like? . . . That's good . . . Now think about your arm and hand feeling more and more heavy, as if the rock were pushing down . . . more and more down . . . and as it gets heavier and heavier, the hand and arm begin to move down . . . down . . . heavier and heavier . . . moving . . . down, down, down . . . moving . . . moving . . . more and more down . . . heavier and heavier . . . (Wait 10 seconds; note extent of movement) . . . That's fine. Now you can stop imagining there is a rock in your hand and let your hand relax . . . It is not heavy any more . . ." (Score + if hand lowers at least 6 inches at the end of 10 seconds.) (Morgan and J. Hilgard, 1978/79, pp. 164–165).

To be successful, the imaginative components in inductions used with children need to build upon experiences of involvement similar to the type found in their own experiences. The fantasy draws on the child's favorite activities, a procedure that typically elicits enthusiastic cooperation and overlaps with an enactive induction because of its active expression.

For 4- and 5-year-olds, active participation by the therapist was generally necessary, whereas it was only the occasional 6-year-old who needed extended participation by an adult for a fantasy to unfold.

We have identified three major components of induction—enactment, relaxation, and imagination—which may be variously combined to induce hypnosis. Regardless of the emphasis on one or another of these components, the resulting hypnotic condition is similar: the patient or subject is ready for active participation in experiences associated with the hypnotic condition. Subsequently, within hypnosis, these same elements will continue to operate in varying degrees. Tellegen suggests that what defines a response as hypnotic is the subjects' "ability to represent suggested events and states imaginatively and enactively in such a manner that they are experienced as real" (Tellegen, 1978/79, p. 220).

Waking Suggestion and Hypnosis without Formal Induction.   Most of the phenomena of hypnosis can be produced by direct suggestion without using a formal induction procedure; this approach is described as waking suggestion.[2] Because direct suggestion is effective in producing hypnotic experiences, this has led some investigators to deny any importance to the role of induction and others to assert that induction procedures accentuate a person's responses to suggestion. Regardless of these differences in interpreting the role of induction, all agree that individuals are differentially responsive to waking suggestions, and that those who are more hypnotizable respond better than those who are less hypnotizable. Actually, all induction techniques begin with waking suggestions, whether they employ eye closure, arm levitation, or imagination. In other words, the transition to the established hypnotic condition occurs as a result of the initial response to waking suggestions.

The omission of a formal induction procedure by those who downplay its role is not always convincing evidence of its unimportance. For example, Evans and Paul (1970) joined those who minimized the role of induction. In their study, they hypnotized the experimental group by a formal induction procedure. As a "nonhypnotic" comparison group, the subjects spent 25 minutes in self-relaxation to parallel the time spent by the experimental group. Because results were similar for both groups, they concluded that induction was not effective. For a person with hypnotic talent, 25 minutes spent in self-relaxation can permit the same drift into fantasy and dissociation as occurs in hypnosis. For those with low hypnotic ability, no difference would be expected in any case. The lack of a formal induction procedure by another does not necessarily mean that the modifications associated with hypnosis cannot take place. On the other hand, many individuals find that a slow induction process assists greatly in making the transition from a rational, intellectual mind-set to a more fanciful, uncritical mode of perception.

Imaginative Involvement and Hypnotic Talent

Throughout our discussions, we have referred to *imaginative involvement* as a central concept. The concept of imagination is familiar, but the added component of *involvement,* which is prominent in our interpretation of hypnosis, merits further elaboration.

Briefly, imagination makes use of imagery, memory, and novelty. Children's facility for imagery is generally strong. In terms of imaginative power, individual differences exist and are largely determined by the way memories are put together. In our hypnotic work, we used (and often combined) two major areas of memory: 1) regression to earlier experiences, where the emphasis is on *reproductive memory* (patients returning through memory to surfing experiences, for example, or to viewing reruns of movies), and 2) flights of fancy, with an emphasis on *productive memory* (patients looking down on an earth that lay far below them as they floated on high clouds). *Novelty* (or creativity) has added to these episodes, sometimes more and sometimes less, depending on the person. When the imaginative experience becomes involving or absorbing, an *affective* component which makes the experience important, exciting, or satisfying is added. One way of viewing this is to consider that affect enhances and amplifies the experience (e.g., Tomkins, 1979).

A familiar illustration of how sensory information is affectively enhanced can be a sunset. On one level, an ocean sunset can be seen merely as a series of colors near clouds and water, but it becomes an aesthetic experience when the whole vision is transformed and augmented by feelings of pleasure in the beholder. At this point, it becomes memorable, something to be held in the mind, and enjoyed and savored now. It is because of affective enrichment that a child's imaginative involvements in stories like *Bambi,* TV programs like "The Six Million Dollar Man," vacation trips with exciting activities, and blowing out birthday candles on birthday cakes take on such compelling characteristics as they unfold in hypnotic recall. Such affective experiences possess a quality of effortlessness, and in that sense, of involuntariness.

One account of intense imaginative involvement comes from the longtime friend of Pablo Picasso—Françoise Gilot—who was impressed by Picasso's ability, in his 60s, to paint for extended periods without experiencing fatigue:

> He stood before the canvas for three or four hours at a stretch. He made almost no superfluous gestures. I asked him if it didn't tire him to stand so long in one spot. He shook his head.
> "No," he said. "That's why painters live so long. While I work I leave my body outside the door, the way Moslems take off their shoes before entering a mosque." When daylight began to fade from the canvas, he switched on two spotlights and everything but the picture surface fell away into the shadows.

"There must be darkness everywhere except on the canvas, so that the painter becomes hypnotized by his own work and paints almost as though he were in a trance," he said. "He must stay close to his inner world if he wants to transcend the limitations his reason is always trying to impose upon him" (Gilot and Lake, 1964, pp. 116–117).

The nature of an imaginative orientation becomes clearer when contrasted with a problem-solving orientation, which is reality-oriented, active, and purposive. The imaginative or aesthetic orientation permits immersion in the feelings of the moment. Tellegen, discussing the distinction, regards the imaginative set as "experiential," while the realistic, goal-directed behavior is "instrumental" (Tellegen, 1981).

Involvements as Related to Hypnotic Talent. We have used the concept of imaginative involvement to refer to immersion or absorption in an experience which tends to sustain focused attention to the exclusion of competing sources of stimulation. When the plural form "imaginative involvements" is used, we refer to the many paths of specialized interest or activity which lead to involvement. For example, a person with an habitual interest in reading imaginative literature can quickly become absorbed in a new book, and while involved, may fail to respond to a call for dinner. Hence reading becomes, for that person, one of the pathways into imaginative involvement.

In relating such imaginative involvements to hypnosis, we have two criteria in mind: One of these is the relationship between the involvements and measured hypnotizability; the second is the relationship between the involvements and a capacity for pain reduction. They are all positively correlated, with much in common, but at the same time the correlations are not perfect, and a great deal can be learned from studying deviations from the expected correlations.

That imaginative involvements are predictive of measured hypnotizability was shown in the extensive study with college students (J. Hilgard, 1970). Those with involvements rated as deeply absorbing proved to be more hypnotizable than those with less compelling involvements. Interviews with these young adults showed that many of their involvements had a history going back to childhood and were formed in an atmosphere of contagious enthusiasm with parents. In a follow-up study, a group of highly hypnotizable college students was compared with a comparable group of those only slightly responsive to hypnosis (J. Hilgard, 1974). It turned out that the ability to *enjoy and savor sensory experiences* and a strong interest in either *reading, drama, or both,* was almost universal (93 percent) in the highly hypnotizable group. By contrast, the less responsive hypnotic subjects ranked much lower in these capacities, only 20 percent exhibiting these preferences. Other involvements more strongly exhibited in the highly hypnotizable subjects were daydreaming and adventuresome experiences, either actual or fantasied.

Because the study with college students had demonstrated that this capacity for involvement originated in childhood, it was not surprising to find similar involvements present in the young patients comprising the clinical study group. As previously noted, it was during an initial interview that we uncovered the interests and involvements that could be elaborated in hypnotherapy. Invariably, the more hypnotizable patients provided us with vivid and varied recall of past events and, when tested on the hypnotic scale, embellished the test items with specific and richly detailed fantasies. As reported earlier, these patients had no difficulty in extending still further the scope of their fantasy at the suggestion of the hypnotherapist, and, as a result, the hypnotherapeutic treatment ran smoothly.

That the presence of intense involvements is related to the capacity to reduce pain through hypnotherapy is expected from the correlation between the involvements and success in hypnosis. This leaves the question of causal factors unexplained. Either the imaginative involvements or the hypnosis could be primarily responsible for the pain reduction. One hint that the involvements serve a distinctive role is given by the illustrative experiences in Chapter 6 where individual patients discovered that they could reduce pain through involvement in their favorite fantasies, without having had any preceding experience formally defined as "hypnosis." We recall that Edward capitalized on a fantasy to reduce pain in the bone marrow procedure by fastening his attention on the TV program "Emergency!" throughout the bone marrow aspiration. In this instance, his comment, *"I'm actually a part of it . . . I seem to be really there,"* suggested that the depth of imaginative involvement was equivalent to that attained in hypnosis, and could be termed self-hypnosis.

Important as the imaginative involvements are, there are occasional persons who control pain through practiced dissociations that have little relation to imagination or hypnotic talent. In order to keep our discussion in perspective, we report on the experience of a college student who scored 2 on the 12-point Stanford Hypnotic Susceptibility Scale, Form A, (Weitzenhoffer and Hilgard, 1959) and yet was able to reduce felt pain in a laboratory experiment when her hand and forearm were immersed in ice water. It turned out that for years she had practiced shutting out long and tedious religious services by staring at a spot on her dress and making her mind blank. Using the same technique during the time her arm and hand were in the ice water, she proved that she could reduce pain without using fantasy. Her lack of potential for fantasies probably accounted for her low hypnotic score.

We know that a high level of hypnotizability is required if severe pain is to be reduced by hypnotherapy. In a recent review of the clinical literature relating hypnotizability with the relief of various symptoms, hypnosis was described as having unique value in the treatment of pain in clinical settings (Wadden and Anderton, 1982). By contrast, although hypnosis could be effective in treating cigarette addiction, obesity, and alcoholism, it was generally found that therapeutic success with these patients did not correlate with measured hypnotizability, and, consequently, was attributable to nonhypnotic treatment factors.[3]

When we record the number of items passed on the scale of hypnotic susceptibility, we usually find that the degree of involvement is correlated with the number of items passed, although some items are more involving than others. The advantage of a multiple-item scale is that it assesses the varied resources that can be used in hypnosis. The score itself is an estimate of the variety of these resources and measures the *potential* for deep involvement in hypnosis, not necessarily the depth of involvement of which a person may be capable. In the clinical use of hypnosis, the hypnotherapist combines the resources of each individual in ways that will promote the most effective depth needed in treatment. There are differences among those who are highly responsive, and the several facets can often be combined in unique ways.

The Accentuation of Imaginative Experiences in Formal Hypnotherapy. It is important to recognize that the patient's imaginative involvements must be used adroitly by the hypnotherapist if they are to serve effectively in relieving stressful symptoms. There are two essential ways the hypnotherapist accentuates these involvements:

Choosing the right involvement. A patient often brings a variety of involvements to the attention of the therapist. Some are isolated incidents, others are long-enduring or repeated experiences, and still others represent sources of pleasure or experiences of discomfort. The skilled therapist will assist the patient in focusing on those experiences that are rich and satisfying as well as clear in memory and imagery. To illustrate the process of selection, we refer again to Anna, age 12, who had searched by herself, ineffectually, for a way to use her imagination to help her through a lumbar puncture (Chapter 5). When she tried to think of an imaginative play, the one that occurred to her was the story of her life, which somehow was not right. The hypnotherapist recognized that Anna's life story included unhappy elements that worried her, and that her use of a potentially unhappy fantasy could only add to the anxiety already present. Anna is the patient who found that for her, substituting a "fun problem like surfing" exactly met her needs. It was informative to observe that other involvements were acceptable to her (acting in a play or flying on a cloud to watch other clouds and the coast), but only surfing was "just right." Anna was then shown how to *deepen* the surfing experience by attending carefully to various details of sense perceptions.

Thus, the hypnotherapist helped Anna locate the most appropriate imaginative involvement and then assisted her in channeling it in ways that produced the degree of participation necessary for it to compete successfully with pain for the major pathway to conscious awareness (Anna's pain was reduced from a baseline of 5 to 0 after hypnotic treatment).

Deepening the involvement. As we have noted, once the therapist and Anna had selected the appropriate involvement, the therapist guided her to enhance her immersion in the fantasy by elaborating its sensory detail. For another illustration where emphasis on the details of a fantasy prepared the way for deeper involvement, we refer again to Mario, the patient who had self-selected counting as an activity he had already used and one in which he thought he could become more involved (Chapter 4). The way he was using it, the counting technique was not successful in relieving his pain. The therapist strengthened his visualization of the numbers by suggesting that Mario alter their sizes, colors, movements, combinations, and textures. As the numbers became enriched, exciting, and pleasurable, the experience became deeply absorbing and, as Mario reported, he felt no pain.

A major point here is that even a patient who is highly hypnotizable and capable of using imaginative involvement may not be able to make the maximum use of the talent without guidance.

Prevalent Theories of Hypnosis and Hypnotherapy

In a field as puzzling as hypnosis, many ideas have been advanced to explain it. Over the years, several points of view have had vigorous proponents. In psychoanalytic ego theory, hypnosis has been considered as "adaptive regression." In role theory, hypnosis is interpreted as a special type of social role enactment. T. X. Barber and his colleagues explain the relevant phenomena by other psychological principles, making a special "state of hypnosis" unnecessary. Milton Erickson's approach is more a particular style rather than a theory, and is not easily summarized in a few words.

Psychoanalytic ego theory. From their clinical and experimental observations, which began in the late 1930s, Gill and Brenman advanced the theory that hypnosis could be described in psychoanalytic terms as regression in the service of the ego (Gill and Brenman, 1959). This type of regression refers to capitalizing upon more primitive thinking (hence "regression") to solve contemporary problems. It is sometimes described as an adaptive regression. Gruenewald, Fromm, and Oberlander (1979) also used psychoanalytic ego psychology as their starting point in dealing with hypnosis. Based on the findings from their investigation, they concluded that although adaptive regression can take place in hypnosis, the equation of hypnosis with adaptive regression is not an adequate explanation of hypnosis.

Role theory. Role theory was introduced by the sociologist G. H. Mead (1934), but was first espoused as an explanation for hypnosis by Sarbin (1950). He regarded hypnotic subjects as enacting the role expected of a hypnotized person. Sarbin and Allen (1968) extended the language of role theory to account for practically all of human behavior and experience. Roles include any defined social position, such as professor, shortstop, or mother. Sarbin and Coe (1972) interpreted the hypnotic role as a special form of communication indicated by the title of their book, *Hypnosis: A Social Psychological Analysis of Influence Communication.* They describe several dimensions to the concept of role, of which the most important for hypnosis is "organismic involvement." The degrees of organismic involvement vary by level from a base zero, where the role is latent and therefore without involvement, to level seven in which the involvement is so deep that it may lead to voodoo death. The levels that characterize hypnosis fall in the intermediate zone short of level seven. It takes little translation to move from Sarbin's role-theory construct that postulates levels of organismic involvement in roles to our dissociation construct that postulates degrees of imaginative involvement. That is, despite the difference in the conceptual languages we use, there is an overlap between the dissociation interpretation and the role interpretation.

T. X. Barber's alternative to a unique hypnotic state. Barber's writings have been directed primarily against the special state (trance) paradigm of hypnosis (Barber, 1979). One expression his argument takes is to enclose the word "hypnosis" in quotation marks to indicate that there is nothing in the condition to distinguish it from familiar forms of psychological behavior. Although details of his views have changed, his essential position remains unaltered. He now acknowledges a close affiliation with Sarbin's theory by including what he describes as "the member of the audience" analogy; that is, the subject who is responsive to test suggestions resembles a member of a theater audience who experiences the thoughts, feelings, and emotions that the actors are attempting to arouse. The person responsive to hypnotic test suggestions has "positive" attitudes, motivations, and expectations and is willing to think with and imagine whatever thoughts are suggested, whereas the person who is very unresponsive has "negative" attitudes, motivations, and expectancies toward the communications he or she is receiving. Such a subject does not let himself imagine or think with the suggestions. This point of view deemphasizes the stability of differences in hypnotic talent by suggesting that if attitudes, motivations, and expectancies are modified, individual differences in response would disappear. However, Barber's later discovery of the fantasy-prone personality among 27 women rated as excellent hypnotic subjects has modified his interpretation of hypnosis more in the direction of the imaginative involvements (Wilson and Barber, 1983).

Milton Erickson's innovative approaches to hypnotherapy. Early in his career, Erickson undertook some ingenious experimental studies relevant to psychodynamic theories, and in his later theorizing, he continued to make references to the unconscious. His interpretation of the unconscious, however, was never clarified by theoretical analysis, and he was imprecise in statements such as "Talking to the unconscious." His ingenuity lay, rather, in his therapeutic techniques which were characterized by their dramatic quality. The approach to each patient appeared to be *de novo* and could be described as a dramatic production in which Erickson was both the playwright and the stage director (E. Hilgard, in press). Because the cases are treated in such a varied manner, no coherent theory emerges. Part of the difficulty in pinning down Erickson's theory of hypnosis and his theory of hypnotherapy lies in the use of many techniques that have little to do with hypnosis; thus it is hard to distinguish between the hypnotic features and other aspects of his psychotherapy. Erickson's work is available in a number of collections of his papers, of which the major one is the four volume collection edited by Rossi (1980).

Other theories. The foregoing theories represent a selection from among current attempts to explain hypnosis, but the list is incomplete. Earlier we discussed the equation of hypnosis with relaxation by Edmonston and mention was made in passing of Pavlov's interpretation of hypnosis as partial sleep. We wish to turn now to the dissociative explanation which has had a long history.

The Dissociative Interpretation of Hypnosis and Hypnotherapy

Boris Sidis (1902) and Morton Prince (1906) kept Pierre Janet's concept of dissociation alive during the first decades of this century, after which interest died, except for a brief notation by Hull (1933) that further experimentation on dissociation in relation to hypnosis was called for.

In his book on *Hypnotic susceptibility*, E. Hilgard (1965) noted the relevance of a variety of dissociated experiences to hypnotic phenomena, such as age regression and amnesia. His laboratory continued, through experimentation and clinical observation, to provide data bearing on the dissociative interpretation (E. Hilgard, 1973, 1977a, 1977b). The observations on automatic writing and on pain in studies of hypnotic analgesia further supported dissociation.

Hilgard noted that ordinary nonhypnotic human behavior and consciousness are *not* highly integrated, that the facets of personality form a weak Gestalt, and that many conflicting motives pull in different directions. In an ordinary conversation, individuals can indulge in more than one concurrent stream of thought as they listen to what another individual is saying, formulate an answer, and monitor the appropriate interactions with facial expressions as well as words. Each of these reactions (listening, thinking, talking, monitoring) may be considered structures or substructures of consciousness, a number of which are available to us at any one time. The term "structure" is used because it reflects the fact that specific experiences are embedded in a host of associated memories and thoughts with an executive ego that exerts a shifting control. When the conversation is calm, i.e., when little is at stake, each structure has easy access to the pathway for conscious attention. The situation changes drastically, however, when a structure capable of exerting a much stronger influence than the others enters the picture and establishes a clear dominance. A painful experience, for example, preempts other experiences, and immediately demands its position at the top of a hierarchy of substructures that now form. The essence of a successful hypnotic interaction is that the relative position of one substructure over another changes when the two structures compete for attention: the fantasy becomes the ascendant structure and the pain is thereby dissociated from awareness. Studies of selective attention have clearly demonstrated that attending to one thing reduces the attention to something competing with it (Neisser and Becklin, 1975).

We have indicated how the hypnotherapist capitalizes on the patient's imaginative involvement by helping the patient to select the preferred experience and to augment it. In the context of dissociation, deepening the patient's involvement is what permits the fantasy to hold the attention and divert it from the compelling pain. Hence Anna's surfing fantasies and Mario's number fantasies competed successfully with pain and illustrate the operations of dissociative processes.

All dissociations are a matter of degree. Clearly, if we can speak of degrees of dissociation, we can effect massive perceptual alterations as well as restricted ones. For many years, and still today, the hypnotic condition has been described as a "trance" or as a special state of "altered consciousness." Other theorists believe that the trance concept is superfluous. Dissociation can be viewed as mediating between the extremes of trance and nontrance conceptions (E. Hilgard, 1977b). More massive dissociations, those involving obvious personality alterations, can be accepted as altered states of consciousness, justifiably referred to as trance.

The system of ideas that gain ascendancy or become inhibited in hypnosis can involve large or small cognitive structures, each of which has some degree of coherence. This is as true when the smell of alcohol becomes the fragrance of flowers as when a recollection of the truck driving suppresses the perception of pain. An altered state means simply that a larger fraction of systematized ideas has been dissociated.

A Hidden Observer in Hypnotic Analgesia. The possibility that a person made insensitive to pain by hypnotic suggestion might feel pain at a subconscious level was raised by an anecdote from Estabrooks (1957). He reported a hypnotic experiment with a friend who was reading *Oil for the Lamps of China* while his right hand, screened from view by passing it through a cloth curtain, was engaged in automatic writing. Because of hypnotic procedures the friend was unaware of his hand, which had also become insensitive to pain. When Estabrooks pricked the hand with a needle, it wrote profanity "that would have made a top sergeant blush with shame." This went on for five minutes and included an attack on the hypnotist for having pricked him. The subject continued his reading calmly, "without the slightest idea that his good right arm was fighting a private war."

Because of a similar incident that arose unexpectedly in a demonstration of hypnotic deafness, E. Hilgard undertook a systematic investigation of pain which might be felt at some level during hypnotic analgesia while it was not being experienced consciously. He used the expression *hidden observer* to refer to the cognitive system perceiving pain at a concealed level (E. Hilgard, 1977a). Experiments conducted at the Stanford Laboratory proceeded as follows:

Only those students scoring very high (the upper 10 percent) on the Stanford Hypnotic Susceptibility Scale, Form C, were selected as subjects for the experiment (E. Hilgard, Morgan, and Macdonald, 1975). Pain was produced by lowering the hand and arm in circulating ice water for 45 seconds. Under these circumstances, the pain mounts to a severe level but can be tolerated. In preliminary studies, it had been found that verbal reports on a numerical scale (also used in the Stanford Children's study) were more consistent than physiological indicators, such as blood pressure or heart rate. The first step was to study pain sensitivity while not hypnotized. Therefore pain reports on the verbal scale were requested every 5 seconds while the hand was immersed. In the next step, the subject was hypnotized, given suggestions for analgesia, and the hand was again immersed in ice water, with requests for pain reports.

The highly hypnotizable subjects were all able to reduce pain by hypnotic suggestion, although there was some residual pain so that the mean pain reduction was 70 percent from the pain reported in the nonhypnotic condition. By a method described as automatic talking, similar to the automatic writing familiar in hypnosis, reports were obtained from the hidden observer. The subject was rehypnotized and told that some concealed part might have been aware of more than was reported by the hypnotized part. If that were the case, the therapist continued, this part would be able to supplement or amend the report given under the earlier hypnotic analgesia. Although this method might appear to invite compliance, it is significant that of all subjects able to reduce pain by hypnotic suggestion, only 40 percent reported such a hidden observer. Subsequent in-depth interviews substantiated the fact that the verbal reports of felt pain had indeed been accurate; when faced with these written records, the subjects said in essence, "I *felt* nothing. I was surprised to find that a part of me had felt something." Thus the hypnotic analgesia had been effective, the subjects had reported honestly, and it is also true that certain aspects of the pain experience were available and recoverable from a subordinate cognitive structure.

If one assumes, justifiably, that the presence of the hidden observer is a consequence of hypnotic dissociation, then it is important to ask why the hidden observer is absent in so many highly hypnotizable subjects who are able to reduce pain successfully through hypnotic procedures. One possibility in respect to the differences between those with and those without a hidden observer was advanced by the successive studies of Perry and Laurence (1980), Laurence and Perry (1981), and Nogrady, McConkey, Laurence, and Perry (1983). If we combine the results of their 1980 and 1981 studies, 9 of 23 highly hypnotizable subjects reported hidden observers of the pain experienced in hypnosis, essentially the same proportion as was found in the Stanford investigation. The new finding in their investigation was that during regression to the age of 5, all nine subjects who showed hidden observers experienced duality in age regression (adult-self and child-self simultaneously or in alternation), whereas those without a hidden observer denied all awareness of their adult identity while regressed to childhood. This observation is an important first demonstration of a differentiating characteristic of persons with and without hidden observers.

We made no effort in our research to explore the possibility of a hidden observer in the young patients. However, a few subjects who participated in pain experiments in the Stanford laboratory were high school students and therefore within the age range of our clinical group. The possibilities can be illustrated by one young subject who participated in the laboratory studies in which the hidden observer in pain was studied.

Gwen, a 16-year-old senior in high school, had no prior experiences with hypnosis but proved highly hypnotizable on the adult forms of the Stanford Hypnotic Susceptibility Scales. In the pain study, Gwen was able to reduce the pain of circulating ice water from a felt level of 9 on a 10-point scale when not hypnotized to 0—a total absence of pain under hypnotically induced analgesia which she had achieved by hallucinating an absence of the arm. Her account is unusually informative in relation to the hidden observer.

Prior to the method used for uncovering the hidden observer, when the experimenter raised the question as to whether a part of her might have some additional information about what went on during hypnotic analgesia, the idea seemed to her not at all plausible. However, while she was still hypnotized, the hypnotist initiated the procedure for eliciting the hidden observer, and Gwen then reported a concealed pain at a level almost as high as that felt when not hypnotized. (This is the basis on which a hidden observer is said to be present.) The memory of the pain in the past did not reinstate feelings of pain as she talked about it.

In the interview that followed hypnosis, Gwen expressed surprise at discovering a hidden part of herself, and proceeded to describe her experience in dissociative terms; that is, she used the concepts of "me" for the normal waking part, "me-in-hypnosis" or the "other me" for the hypnotized part, and the "hidden part" for the concealed self who reported pain even when the "me-in-hypnosis" was without pain. In her words, "I was surprised. The hidden part wasn't surprised because it was aware of its own existence as well as the existence of the hypnotized part. The hypnotized part was surprised because it's usually in the foreground [during hypnosis] and now was shocked to be pushed into the background. It isn't used to that; it felt kind of betrayed."

The idea of "betrayal" rested upon her assumption of an implicit understanding between the two parts as to their control over conscious experience. "The hidden part is supposed to stay hidden and not infringe on the property of the 'other me,'" she explained. When encouraged to describe this relationship further, she said, "There's an unspoken agreement that the hidden part is supposed to stay hidden and not come out. He's betraying his agreement; he's not abiding by the rules. He's gone back on his word. He's stealing something from the hypnotized part." She explained that she used the masculine pronoun for the hidden observer because she thinks of males as more logical, females as more intuitive.

In a further experiment on hypnotic deafness, she experienced the hidden observer again. Asked to say something more about what the hidden part was like, she responded: "He seems more mature than the rest of me—more logical and amused by the me-in-hypnosis that couldn't hear because of course you *can* hear."

Because Gwen had been given a variety of tests, including the advanced Stanford Profile Scales, she was asked whether anything else came to mind in relation to the hidden observer. She immediately referred to her experience of age regression in hypnosis when she became a 9-year-old child. She said that she was surprised that a different person, the 9-year-old, came into the foreground. At this point she had also felt the shock of betrayal because, as a 16-year-old, she had agreed to be hypnotized, yet the hypnotized 16-year-old realized that she was displaced by her 9-year-old self which had become so strong that, at least briefly, she was a competing personality. As Gwen explained, "The 9-year-old belongs to me, but because of the suggestion that I would be 9 again, the 9-year-old part was pulled out of me. Most of the time this little person is in the background as a memory or recollection and as an influence on recollection, but it is not an active decision-maker because it's so immature. It seemed like a whole different entity. It went back into the slot when he [the hypnotist] ended the suggestion."

What the two experiences—the hidden observer in pain and the 9-year-old in regression—both evoked in her was a sense of betrayal stemming from the sudden alteration of her personality structure as she knew it. In other words, it was a 16-year-old Gwen who had agreed to a "hypnotized 16-year-old me." In her ability to relieve pain and to experience deafness, her hypnotized ego had a sense of accomplishment or mastery over these perceptual processes. When the hidden observer appeared, however, its report denied the success of which the hypnotized part felt proud, in a sense belittling the hypnotic ego for having been deceived in its perception of what was happening. That is why she called it a betrayal.

Similarly, in her age regression, the observing ego of the 16-year-old, comfortable with having a 16-year-old hypnotized part responding to suggestions, becomes alarmed when the 16-year-old hypnotized part is displaced by the emerging 9-year-old and is shocked by its pervasiveness. Gwen's experience of divided consciousness—aware at once of being a 9-year-old in competition with a 16-year-old—reveals important aspects of dissociation.

This case makes abundantly clear the complexity of the research task that lies ahead if we are to achieve a clear understanding of the phenomena, for the "hidden observer" involves not only distortions of perception and memory that can be produced within hypnosis, but also the modifications of executive control that occur when one or another part is dominant. The dissociations that appeared in our case studies of children were limited ones. Gwen's dissociations, however, were sufficiently extensive to show their resemblance to the more profound dissociations found in multiple personalities. The reports of her experiences point to a continuum from the less extensive dissociations present in the usual hypnotic regression to those of multiple personalities (Watkins and Watkins, 1979/80).

Dissociation theory recognizes the complexity of consciousness and the self system; neither the waking consciousness nor the hypnotic consciousness can be considered as clearly delineated states so that an individual can be either in the nonhypnotic state or the hypnotic state, by analogy with being wide awake or deeply asleep. Dissociation accepts that at any one time, there are several substructures—conscious or unconscious—that may become dominant. These go by various names, such as cognitive structures, ego-structures, apparatuses, habit systems, or social roles—the names implying somewhat different interpretations but all recognizing a degree of fractionation that is overlooked by simplifying the interpretation as an alternation between the two states of nontrance and trance.

The dominance-subordination relationship among the various substructures is not fixed, and that is why hypnotic induction can produce the kinds of changes that it does—by exaggerating some available memories or fantasies (as in age regression or hallucination) and suppressing other substructures (as in amnesia or loss of motor control). It is not necessarily a state of consciousness that has been altered, but the dominance-subordination relationships of some of the available substructures.

In line with this analysis, it is clear that dissociations can be partial (involving single or relatively few substructures) or more widespread (involving many substructures). When the dissociations are widespread, the modifications in consciousness and personality become profound, are recognized as such by the hypnotized person, and deserve to be called altered states.

However, this continuum between partial dissociations and the more extreme ones qualifying as altered states does not follow a single dimension of hypnotic depth or involvement because the changes are in the complexity and articulation of smaller units into *patterns* that dominate consciousness at any one time. These relationships cannot be described simply because patterns or organizations of substructures may be operating together, as in the case of Gwen.

Notes

1. It is not necessary for children to close their eyes. If closing appears desirable, give a choice: "Some children find it easier to imagine with their eyes closed. You may close your eyes if you wish to, but keep them open if you'd rather."

2. The word "waking" harks back to the time when hypnosis was thought to be a form of "sleep." It is used today to represent the ordinary nonhypnotic condition without implying that hypnosis is a condition of sleep.

3. A dissenting opinion was that of J. Barber who claimed that 99 of 100 subjects, of unknown susceptibility, successfully completed dental work under hypnosis (J. Barber, 1977).

9 The Growth of Hypnotic Ability: A Developmental Approach

The presence of developmental factors in hypnosis became evident in the course of an interviewing program at the Stanford laboratory in 1960. The first published communication bore the title "Developmental-Interactive Aspects of Hypnosis" (J. Hilgard and E. Hilgard, 1962). These interviews were conducted with college students who were about to experience hypnosis or had just experienced it. Events that had happened in their childhood appeared to be related to their present responses in hypnosis. It was stated:

> Specific experiences of early childhood will have a central role in providing readiness for hypnotic experience, and this readiness will take specialized forms depending upon later childhood as well (p. 149).

The roles of parents emerged in the interviews:

> A fantasy-life that is regulated by responsible adults, so that a distinction is maintained between reality and unreality, appears to favor tolerance for the regressive and unreal experiences associated with hypnotic hallucinations and other cognitive distortions, e.g. amnesia (p. 171).

In pursuing these leads, an investigation into the fantasy life of children while they were still in the process of growing up in the home provided additional information. Both parents and all children over the age of 5 in six families were independently tested for hypnotic responsiveness and interviewed. Children and parents were queried about the children's interests, activities, and personalities. Because of the possible links between generations, parents were asked to report the same type of data about themselves (J. Hilgard and Morgan, 1965). The study was unpublished but provided a background for much of the later work with children. Many of the observations made at that time are referred to in this chapter.

Clinical measurement scales for children aged 4 to 8 were completed in 1975 and provided a further opportunity to supplement quantitative results with qualitative findings (Morgan and J. Hilgard, 1978/79). Differences between the child's fantasy life at the two ends of the 4 to 8 age span led to the concept of "protohypnosis" as transitional to the more usual hypnosis (J. Hilgard and Morgan, 1976; 1978).

A developmental perspective calls for tracing the life of fantasy and imaginative involvement through the course of its development in everyday life, independent of anything identified as hypnosis. We will explore how the development of fantasy life from the time of early childhood nurtures the capacity for the absorbing experiences that characterize the hypnotizable individual. We will first direct attention to the stimulus-aroused experiences that start very early in life, then continue on to the development of independent fantasy in the preschool and school years. The development of hypnotic ability tends to parallel changes in fantasy until, by the time of later childhood and the adolescent years, hypnotic performance is little different from that of the adult.

Stimulus-Aroused Experiences

We find it useful to distinguish between experiences in early life that are aroused by sensory-affective nonverbal stimuli, such as rocking or caressing, and those that are aroused by verbally communicated imaginative elements such as stories.

Sensory-Affective Arousal. Sensory-affective experiences in early life bring simple, primitive, nonverbalized pleasure to the infant and child. A friendly smiling face (vision), humming, crooning, singing (audition), a pleasant warm breeze (temperature), stroking, the feel of soft fabrics (touch), rocking or being gently moved (kinesthetic), mildly perfumed powders and oil (smell), and food (taste) combine to create a deeply satisfying milieu for the child. These pleasures continue as children attain greater intellectual competency and are able to broaden their sources of stimulation. With age, for example, they develop an appreciation of more sophisticated sensory experiences such as viewing a sunset, a field of colorful wild flowers, a panorama from a mountain top; hearing the songs of birds in the stillness of the forest or the crash of ocean waves endlessly rushing across the shore; smelling aromas typical of a pine forest or of favorite garden flowers; feeling the warmth of the sun while lying in warm sand or the coolness of dew on the grass under bare feet; swaying with the breeze or soft music. All are gentle, mild, pleasurable, and often sensuous experiences characterized by high involvement in the experience itself. They are also essentially passive; that is, conscious direction is abdicated as the individual briefly surrenders to it. In psychoanalysis, a distinction is made between the primitive nonlogical thinking known as "primary process" and the more orderly, rational thinking known as "secondary process." In the experiences we are describing, primary process predominates. Communication in this mode is essentially nonverbal.

The mother of Blanche, age 7, described her daughter's involvement in such sensuous experiences: "She likes to feel things like fur and silk. She will wear a bikini into the rain and wind in order to enjoy the way these feel on her body. She sits with me in a redwood forest while we both listen to the sounds and movements around us." Blanche's quiet absorption in these feelings is not expressed in words.

In the large sample of college students described in Chapter 8, many reported the prominence of sensory-affective experiences in childhood and the continuation of such experiences into the present. Those for whom these experiences were rated as "intense" proved to be hypnotizable (J. Hilgard, 1970/79). When hypnotically responsive children, adolescents, or adults receive a suggestion that they will find themselves in the midst of a restful experience of their own choosing, they frequently transport themselves in imagination to relaxed scenes in their gardens, at lakes, ocean beaches, and forests. Hypnotherapists realize that the sensory affective experiences are readily available, and they use them frequently with their patients.

Stimulus-Aroused Imaginative Experiences. The early perceptual processes are stimulus-bound to colors, movements, natural sounds, space. Early games like peek-a-boo, songs, and simple rhymes serve as the initial bases for incorporating sensory experiences into the child's imagination. How much the child is exposed to imaginative materials depends largely on the attitudes of parents who are in a position to encourage imagination through sharing their own imaginative experiences. As cognitive processes develop, the experiences become enriched, and a wide range of more complex spoken, recorded, and enacted experiences of others soon will serve as the basis of imaginative experiences. Myths, novels, biography, autobiography, history, tales of adventure, plays, musical performances, television, all serve to arouse imaginative activity.

When specific imaginative experiences, with their affective components, become stored in memory, they become available for imaginative recall. One concomitant development at these early stages is the ability to sustain attention, provided the stimulus materials are sequentially organized, as in stories or TV programs.

TV viewing. We have selected TV viewing as representative of stimulus-aroused imaginative experiences because it is almost universally present in the American home, and children are exposed to it from their earliest years. Because of its prevalence throughout childhood and adolescence, TV viewing offers a unique opportunity to study age-related changes in children's ability to sustain absorbed attention, so important in the development of hypnotic talent.

Studies of age-related changes begin with the preschool child (Alwitt, Anderson, Lorch, and Levin, 1980). Between the ages of 1 and 4 years, for example, children studied by Anderson and Levin (1976) showed a dramatic increase in attention to a Sesame Street program on television. Surrounded by toys and with their mothers present, children younger than 2 1/2 years did not systematically watch the TV screen, though their attention might be "captured" by it for perhaps a minute or less. On the other hand, children between the ages of 2 1/2 and 4 years deliberately and frequently glanced at the screen. Some 4-year-olds looked at it for periods as long as seven minutes at a time.

It has also been shown that children do not stare passively at the screen—they are not zombies, and TV is no plug-in drug. Their attention includes active cognitive involvement. Children begin to appreciate the meaning of the dynamic flow of images and sounds on television when they are approximately 2 1/2 years old (Anderson, 1979). A study of 5-year-old children bore this out by showing that variations in the comprehensibility of the TV program accounted for much of the variability in children's attention span (Lorch, Anderson, and Levin, 1979).

The relationship between the kinds of attentive involvement that take place in television viewing and the development of hypnotic abilities became evident from interviews with children and parents who took part in the investigation in which the two generations participated (J. Hilgard and Morgan, 1965). The reactions of two of the children in this study serve to illustrate the extent and type of their involvement in television.

Enid, who was 6 1/2, said that while watching TV she feels she is in the midst of everything happening on the screen. Her mother confirmed this. "She often talks to the characters on TV. If the hero is about to be hurt, she'll warn him that 'so-and-so is behind a tree' . . . She gets completely absorbed, she is oblivious to everything else, she can't hear you when you speak to her." Thus, in the short span of four years, Enid's experience contrasts markedly with the briefly sustained attention characteristic of a 2 1/2-year-old.

Jim's reactions to TV programs illustrate the intensity of attention and concentration in someone 11 years old. Both Jim and his mother were separately interviewed about his interests. While watching slapstick comedy or amusing movies on TV, Jim said simply, "They are real to me." Jim's mother described how he became completely "wrapped up" in them, his whole body participating in the fun as he doubled up in laughter. He was equally involved in adventures or in dramatic productions. If he watched a serious mystery story that became scary, he would begin backing out of the room. The scarier it became, the further he backed out, but always with his eyes glued to the screen. If it was too upsetting, he put more and more distance between himself and the screen until he had backed out of the room completely, to return only after the emergency had passed. Jim's remarks indicated that he was not just watching, he was caught in the action. "It gives me the creeps." Because of the desire to escape the scenes that frightened him, Jim separated himself physically from the screen but could not escape the fascination of the program.

Knowing Enid's and Jim's degree of involvement, we expected them to be highly hypnotizable. On the 12-point children's hypnotizability scale used for testing, Enid scored 11 and Jim scored 12. Immersion in the early experiences of TV viewing illustrates the type of imaginative involvement so important in the development of hypnotic talent. Equally deserving of notice is the degree to which the capacity for sustained and absorbed attention, also vital in hypnotic talent, may already be present by the age of 6, and intense in later childhood.

The sequence of events in a TV program is determined by the writer; the child does not have to provide much in the way of imaginative supplement. To be sure, the events on the screen become personalized as a child lives the experiences, but the fascinating detail of the story is in other hands. We turn now to the spontaneous initiation of imagination which, although not too sharply distinguished from the stimulus-aroused experiences, does have distinctive features of its own.

The Development of Spontaneous Fantasy in Childhood

When a child self-determines the content of the fantasy and the sequence of action, something has been altered from the stimulus-aroused imaginative experiences. Spontaneous fantasies as they develop in the young child begin as fantasy portrayed in action (pretend play and sociodramatic play) and are followed somewhat later by fantasied action, which can take place while the child is sitting quietly, as in daydreaming where imaginative activity is internalized.

Pretend Play: Fantasy Portrayed in Action. The development of pretend play, or make-believe play as it is alternatively called, is the forerunner of developed imagination. It is preceded, according to Piaget (1962), by learned imitation. When children reach the age of 2, they are imitative par excellence. They actively seek repetition of an adult modeled action. They want it to be exactly the same with nothing added, no embellishments—a pure, uncluttered replica. This holds true for simple stories and rhythms which children of this age like to have repeated and which they will soon try to repeat themselves:

> *Teddy bear, teddy bear, turn around.*
> *Teddy bear, teddy bear, touch the ground.*
> *Teddy bear, teddy bear, look at your shoe.*
> *Teddy bear, teddy bear, 23 skiddoo.*

Piaget believes that as development proceeds, imitation is represented in imagery. The images can be manipulated in constructive imagination or in pretend play. The someone or something that is personified in pretend play usually exists in the real world. A child adopts and acts out a role that is supported by environmental objects. The 3-year-old son of one of the authors (S. L.) was running around the house making the sound of a fire engine. "Are you pretending to be a fire engine?" asked his father. Michael stopped abruptly and replied with conviction, "I *am* the fire engine." Michael's response, typical of children of this age, makes quite clear that the term "pretend play" was formulated by adults, not by children.

In the 1920s and 1930s, pretend play became a basic technique in child therapy. Young children who found it difficult to put their worries into words were encouraged to express them indirectly in their play with miniature figures. A child would be provided with small figures designed to represent himself and others involved in his problems, for example, dolls resembling a young boy, a sister (if he had a sister), a mother and a father. Often there was a miniature house with a few furnishings in the various rooms. Through play with these figures, the theory held that a child would recapitulate a home situation that was troubling him, could express his feelings, and with the therapist's help, could work out a solution.

Sometimes children will talk through the medium of their favorite toys. Four-year-old Shirley, ill with cancer, was unhappy but unable to talk about it. One day, as she was playing with her teddy bear and clown in the presence of the therapist, she had the teddy bear say, "I'm frightened, very frightened." Since she was also holding the clown, the therapist asked, "What does the clown say?" Shirley replied, "The clown says 'I know . . . so am I very frightened.' " At this point she turned to the therapist and said, "The clown is very frightened." After specific fears of both creatures were discussed, reassurance helped Shirley to feel better.

Pretend play continued to be used in therapy during the 1940s and 1950s when it became a research tool as well. Sears and his collaborators viewed pretend play as a projective test through which an observer could see the "inner person" of the child (1957). By the late 1960s and early 1970s, research was directed toward the nature of pretend play itself—its prevalence, sex differences, age relationships, and so forth. For an excellent review of this constantly expanding area, the reader is referred to Fein (1981).

Sociodramatic Play: Fantasy Portrayed in Action. A development in pretend play termed sociodramatic play gradually evolves by 3 years of age when isolated play begins to incorporate others. In sociodramatic play, the child includes one or more persons in the fantasy, assigning them various roles.

Gigi's mother described how Gigi, at age 3 1/2, began to incorporate other people into her playlets. "She pretends she's the mother and I'm the child. I hear myself, just the way I sound. She'll pick up the phone and have a long phone conversation. She'll go to the door as though the door bell has rung and she'll have another long conversation. Sometimes she pretends that her brother is her husband, only she has changed both of their names. He becomes John and she becomes Sandra. She prepares meals for them. . . . "

Her mother added that sometimes Gigi pretends that she is Gigi's friend, Deedee, who has come to the house to play while Gigi is away on a trip. She then, appropriately, speaks to her mother in the third person. "Mrs. Grant, may I play with Gigi's toys?" As Deedee, Gigi plays the usual games, occasionally interacting with her mother. When her mother finally says that it is time for all this to be over, Gigi will say a couple of magic words and announce "Gigi is back now."

Gigi's pretend play began a year or more earlier in response to the imaginative games of her sisters. Her mother described Gigi's personality: "She was a delightful baby. I enjoyed her tremendously. She is engaging, happy, terribly independent—won't allow you to do anything for her. She is very affectionate."

Sociodramatic play as represented by Gigi clearly represents fantasy portrayed in action, an advanced form of pretend play. During the preschool years, rapid growth takes place in skills related to sociodramatic play: in mimicry, in the ability to take initiative for one's own dramas or to participate in someone else's, in the capacity to sustain imaginative sequences, and in the expansion of interpersonal relationships. Estimates of its prevalence vary considerably according to place of observation, age of child, and type of measurement. In one study, all 4-year-olds engaged in role-playing activities (Iwanaga, 1973).

The fantasies in sociodramatic play are complex and characterized by the involvement of other people, by extensive conversations, and by varied settings. While still a part of fantasy portrayed in action, sociodramatic play is intermediate between pretend play and fantasied action.

Fantasied Action: Internalized Imagination.   In both pretend play and sociodramatic play, the imagined events are accompanied by overt action visible to an onlooker. On other occasions, even though the action itself is not visible to an external observer, rich fantasies occur in which the person is involved in active events. For example, college subjects reducing the pain of ice water through hypnosis gave varying accounts of how they had reduced pain. One reported swimming in the warm water of a tropical river and while involved in that fantasy was unaware of the cold water. Such action, taking place in fantasy, represents internalized imagination.

The differences between fantasy portrayed in action and fantasied action are readily demonstrated in adults. The stage hypnotist relies primarily upon fantasy portrayed in action, so that the audience may be entertained. A hypnotized volunteer will flap his arms as wings and crow like a rooster, or cast his line off the stage in the belief he is fishing for bass. The hypnotherapist is much more likely to invite fantasied action: the subject or patient usually reclines in an easy chair, relaxed with eyes closed, involved in an elaborate fantasy of trips to seashore, mountains, or distant lands. Some individuals become so involved that the fantasy seems to acquire an autonomous existence of its own. In one instance, a hypnotized woman took a magic carpet ride to Hawaii, but when she touched down on Waikiki Beach, the strangeness of the sight caused a large crowd to gather; in genuine embarrassment, she took off immediately for home! We have previously alluded to these spontaneous and creative fantasies as characteristic of highly hypnotizable subjects.

Sociodramatic play reaches its peak between 5 and 6 years and then declines. The decline is particularly evident between 6 and 8 years. After an earlier start, internalized imagination progresses rapidly between the ages of 6 and 9 years (Singer, 1973). In other words, ages 6 to 8 or 9 represent a period of overlap, with early pretend play skills less in evidence and the advanced imaginative skills increasingly prominent. In our experience with children in hypnotherapy, marked individual differences characterize this age range. A few children at age 6 are willing to close their eyes during hypnosis, and the actions that are experienced take place in their private fantasies. Conversely, some children at ages 8 or 9 still prefer to experience hypnosis with eyes open, and fantasy portrayed in action. Although pretend play, sociodramatic play, and fantasied action generally develop in sequence, it is not clear how much one level displaces or enriches the other.

The Measurement of Fantasy. The investigation of age differences, sex differences, and changes in the duration and quality of fantasy life, independent of hypnotic fantasy, is of increasing interest to developmental psychologists. This interest has led to the construction of several self-report instruments for studying these changes in the early years. We shall give two illustrations: the first, a guided interview about fantasy called the Imaginative Play Predisposition Interview (IPPI), and the second, an inventory of fantasy items termed the Children's Fantasy Inventory (CFI). The Imaginative Play Predisposition Interview was developed by Singer (1973) and uses four questions that can be amplified in an open-ended interview:

1. What is your favorite game? What do you like to play the most?
2. What game do you like to play best when you are all alone? What do you like to do best when you are all alone?
3. Do you ever have pictures in your head? Do you ever see make-believe things with pictures in your mind or think about them? What sort of things?
4. Do you have a make-believe friend? Do you have an animal or toy or make-believe person you talk to or take along with you? Did you ever have one, even though you don't anymore?

Scoring of this interview questionnaire, based on a 5-point scale (0–4), is done by psychologists familiar with the scale who act as judges. Usually children who score below 2 are considered low-fantasy subjects and those who score 2 and above are high-fantasy subjects.

The major emphasis of the instrument is on make-believe or pretend play. The first two questions attempt to clarify play preferences with respect to make-believe elements. Playing hopscotch or jump rope would not involve as much fantasy as "cops and robbers," "house," or "school." The third question appears to be transitional to later stages. The imaginary companion, in the fourth question, represents a continuation of make-believe play. Singer's discussion contains many pertinent observations, but there is little emphasis on normative data.

The Children's Fantasy Inventory, or CFI, developed by Rosenfeld, Huesmann, Eron, and Torney-Purta (1982), includes 45 questions. This instrument was tested on a large sample of children approximately 6- and 8- or 9-years-of-age in the first and third grades. A factor analysis yielded three styles of fantasy which the authors describe as fanciful fantasy, intellectual fantasy, and aggressive/dysphoric fantasy. Fanciful fantasy refers to pretend play and happy daydreaming. Intellectual fantasy covers curiosity about how things work, daydreams about people in distant lands, and magic. Aggressive/dysphoric fantasy includes daydreams about aggressive acts towards others, daydreams of running away from unjust punishment, and embarrassing daydreams (dysphoric). Included in the scale, but not yielding separate factors, were questions designed to measure absorption and vividness of imagery, both related to our interests in hypnotizability.

The scales that discriminate best between subjects in the first and third grades are fanciful fantasy and intellectual fantasy, on which the younger, 6-year-old children score higher. Fanciful fantasy and intellectual fantasy appear to represent the most childlike and conflict-free type of behavior. Intellectual fantasy is indicative of the simple curiosity younger children show. (This happy, conflict-free fantasy life of younger children also corresponds well with the typical features of children's fantasies as they appear in hypnotic age regression.) Six-year-olds report more scary fantasies of the exciting, monster type, but to them such fantasies are appparently not dysphoric. The 8- and 9-year-old third graders engage in more aggressive fantasy. They also score higher in absorption, which can be interpreted as lessened distractibility and in increasing capacity for internalizing imagination.

Boys score higher than girls on active heroic fantasies, a finding which is not unexpected. Girls score higher on fanciful fantasies that stress happy affect and that include more references to fairy tales and playing pretend games when younger. Girls appeared to express more affect of both a positive and a negative quality than boys. There were no sex differences on the aggressive fantasy scale, but girls scored higher than boys on the dysphoric fantasy scale which contains items about fear of harm and punishment.

The Essential Role of Affect

Affect occupies a central position in hypnotherapy just as it does in all psychotherapy. Children and adults with long-term illnesses suffer feelings of frustration, discouragement, conflict, and worry, and, understandably, may dwell upon their unhappiness to the exclusion of all else. Sometimes, of course, the realities of an illness are bleak. Even in the midst of an uncertain future, however, it is often possible to rekindle pleasant thoughts. Richard, whose metastatic terminal cancer caused him persistent pain that could be relieved only by frequent morphine injections, found relief from pain through pleasant, ego-syntonic fantasies (Chapter 5). The sense of mastery he achieved over pain, even though limited, was sufficient to permit him to take short trips away from the hospital to his home where he enjoyed some of his former pleasures. Jennie, the young patient who had lost her appetite during radiation therapy, was able to appreciate food again after she had experienced happy fantasies within hypnosis of her horse's successful performance at the races and of her picnic lunch at his side (Chapter 2). With Jennie, as with Richard, this shift into positive affect during the relatively brief experience of hypnosis carried with it an aftermath of pleasant feeling for a day or days, in any case quite out of proportion to the time spent in hypnosis. Related observations with other children support the finding that when pleasant affect within hypnosis has overcome discouragement, the pleasant feelings tend to persist.

Affect has so many aspects that the measurement of age-related changes presents difficulties. Fortunately, one measurable aspect of the development of positive affect is the expression of humor, which appears frequently as a feature in the fantasies preferred by children.

Humor and Its Development with Age. Recent research on humor has dealt specifically with its age-related development during the childhood years. Just as TV provided a vehicle for studying the development of sustained and absorbed attention to fantasies, so humor provides an exceptional opportunity to study the development of positive affect with age.

Before turning to its developmental aspects, we wish to call attention to the role of humor, generally, in the therapeutic process. We found in our investigations, for example, that a number of children (including some who did not require or want hypnotherapy) spontaneously hit upon humor as a coping device (Chapter 6). Cynthia, Herbert, and Dan who conversed, Kent and Martha who screamed, Ed who liked to imagine past TV programs, Randy who concentrated on feelings in his hands as they gripped the table, all combined humor with their major coping methods.

A child's humor often involves playful distortions and exaggerations of events, or incongruities, or just nonsense. During the preschool years, humor is closely related to topics that reflect the strong perceptual orientation of this period when children learn about the appearance of objects and events. Piaget reports the presence of humor in children as early as their second year (1962). As mastery over the correct meaning of words increases, a child in a playful mood may endlessly amuse himself by calling a well-known object any name but the right one. Amidst gales of laughter, a dog becomes a cat or a boy or a spoon. Language itself may attract the child, as reflected in playful manipulations of sound changes. Young children find it very funny to rhyme real words with nonsense words, for example, "happy, dappy, sappy," etc. Between the ages of 3 and 6, after they have become thoroughly familiar with the distinctive characteristics that define various objects, they like to distort them, laughing as they imagine a dog that has two heads, says meow, or rides a bicycle.

A major change in children's perception of the incongruous occurs at around 6 or 7 years of age, when their humor begins to resemble that of adults. For example, as they begin to understand that two meanings can be applied to the same word, they realize that a particular word in a given situation will produce a factual answer, while the same word, with a second meaning, will create an incongruous impression and therefore be humorous. In an experimental setting, a situation required children to choose between a factual answer appropriate to the occasion and a joking answer, based on a double meaning such as that used in riddles. The were asked, "Which is funnier?" "Why did the old man tiptoe past the medicine cabinet?" Serious answer: "Because he dropped a glass and didn't want to cut his foot." Joking answer: "Because he didn't want to wake up the sleeping pills" (McGhee, 1974). The results showed that kindergarten and first-grade children chose either answer equally often. By the second grade, however, the ability to grasp this dual interpretation of words began, and it improved progressively through the sixth grade. By the seventh grade, children were apt to become bored by riddles.

We witnessed a variation of the story about the sleeping pills in the clinic. Chris, the 8-year-old boy who previously had required three people to restrain him because of his needle phobia, learned a magical way to make his hand numb in order to remain calm during the "needle sticks" to his finger (Chapter 2). He expressed pride in his achievement and called the attention of various nurses to it. When the director of the Oncology Unit passed him, Chris showed him how his hand had "fallen asleep." The director acknowledged his feat by joking, "That's good, but don't talk too loud or you might wake it up." Chris loved it.

Up to this point humor has been viewed primarily as a combination of playfulness, fantasy, and cognitive mastery, for the most part conflict-free. As we move into the grade-school years, humor takes on new complexities that reflect both the developing cognitive abilities of the child and the background of the culture. Psychodynamic determinants now become more prominent. As examples, consider the following jokes:

> Roses are red
> Violets are blue
> I copied your paper
> And I flunked too.

This joke looks deceptively simple. Its humorous interpretation requires both familiarity with the usual "Roses are red" ditty to make its ending a surprise, an awareness that copying a test is taboo behavior, and the final shock that the paper copied was not worth cheating for.

Another example:

"Did you hear about the woman who got married four times? Her first husband was a millionaire; her second was a famous actor; her third was a well-known minister; and her fourth was an undertaker."

"So?"

"One for the money, two for the show, three to get ready, and four to go."

In a class of fourth-graders, 80 percent of the class thought this story was very funny (Brodzinsky, 1977). The conclusion is similar to the "Roses are red" joke because it draws on a familiar rhyming jingle but with a surprise ending. In his *Jokes and Their Relation to the Unconscious* (1905; reprinted 1960), Freud emphasized the way jokes could serve to disguise and provide an outlet for forbidden impulses. As psychoanalytic theory developed, attention focused primarily on sexual and aggressive drives. A sexual motivation for humor, generally subdued during the grade school years, of course rises sharply during adolescence. Wolfenstein (1954), in her book on children's humor, felt that other psychodynamic processes at work in adolescence were those related to the child's intellectual mastery over the environment. Psychologists whose basic approach to the study of childhood humor arises from an experimental orientation find both psychodynamic and cognitive determinants in humor, but with particular emphasis on the innate pleasure afforded by felt competency (McGhee, 1979; Pinderhughes and Zigler, 1983; Zigler, Levine, and Gould, 1967).

Humor in Hypnotherapy.   Where does humor fit in with the use of hypnotherapy for pain? Because heterohypnosis involves an interpersonal relationship, the contagiousness of humor can be used to good advantage. Contagion is a frequently observed but rarely examined aspect of children's humor (Edward Zigler, personal communication, September, 1982). Zigler noted that "glee" can move through a group of preschool children like a wave and that it appears to be almost totally involuntary.

Dr. G. W. Fairfull Smith, a dentist in Glasgow, Scotland, makes wide use of laughter in his practice with children. He explains his successful method for keeping child patients happy and pain-free while they are undergoing various dental procedures (personal communication, 1976). The method employs liberal doses of laughter, magic games, and sometimes hypnosis. "I always try to create a 'laughter-happy' mind-set before starting to work." Dr. Smith, who possesses a very hearty laugh, says that the more *he* laughs, the more the child laughs, because laughter is infectious. He inquires of the child, "Can you laugh with me?" After both laugh, he continues, "Come on, you can do better." So both laugh again more enthusiastically. And again, if need be.

If the procedure is a tooth extraction, the magic game begins with this question: "Do you know any magic words? . . . I've got one . . . Abracadabra. . . . I'm going to rub your gums with my *magic finger* and we will both say it." Dr. Smith rubs the gum with 2 percent Xylotox while he and the child repeat together "Abracadabra." Just before he injects Xylocaine, he announces, "I'm going to touch your teeth with my *magic wand* and we'll both say the magic word." They do, the child is intrigued, and he injects. The actual extraction is next. "Now you'll notice that your lip feels cotton-wooly and your tooth has gone to sleep . . . Sleep! . . . Have you heard anybody snore?" Dr. Smith, the child, and the nurse all practice snoring. "The tooth is going to snore just the same way . . . Now I'm going to test it." So saying, he extracts the tooth. "Now . . . I want you to blow your tooth out . . . rub my hand . . . say the magic word . . . blow into my hand . . . let's have a look and see if you've blown your tooth out." The tooth appears and both patient and doctor gaze admiringly at it. Dr. Smith estimates that in the course of many extractions, almost all children have responded favorably.

For children ages 3 to 5 1/2, Dr. Smith drills a cavity without using an analgesic. After the usual prologue when laughter is induced, he tells the child, "I'm going to *tickle* your tooth . . . Later on your *nose will become itchy*, and when your nose becomes itchy, I want you to laugh, just as you did."

Dr. Smith says that he keeps reinforcing laughter throughout the dental work because laughter is "an antithetical mood to pain." Certainly it is antithetical to the apprehension that accompanies the expectation of pain. By the time a possibly painful dental procedure is under way, the pretend game of magic has also captured the child's attention and counteracted the pain.

Describing how he goes about filling a tooth in a school-age child using hypnosis as the sole anesthetic, Dr. Smith told us about his patient Jane, who had a deeply decayed tooth to be drilled and filled. In front of Jane is a long cord belt (now seldom seen in North American dentists' offices) that rolls around and around on small pulleys to activate the drill. After he has established a lighthearted mood, Dr. Smith places two bits of white cotton on the belt as it moves in its course, and then introduces an imaginative story: "Watch the two bunnies going round and round. Do you see them?" Jane's eyes fixate on the rabbits. "Pretty soon you will see a naughty fox chasing them [this is entirely hallucinated, with no cotton as a prop] . . . When you see a naughty fox chasing them, your hand and arm will get very light like a feather and your mouth will open." After a few complete runs of the belt, the hand and arm rise, the mouth opens. "Now I'm going to use the vacuum on your tooth. It's a tickly machine. I'm going to tickle your tooth . . . It will make your nose very itchy and you'll laugh." By this time, Dr. Smith is drilling and he says the children never notice, even though a nerve has been touched. Once the tooth was sufficiently drilled, the hole in the tooth was incorporated in the story as the hiding place for the bunnies after they had escaped from the fox—a hiding place whose entrance Dr. Smith then closed with the filling. The procedure ended, Jane hopped out of the chair, still smiling.

The hypnotic procedures are introduced so subtly and informally that the reader may miss the extent to which some of the familiar features of hypnosis have been used. First, a compatible relationship with the hypnotist was established as a shared jovial mood. The attentive focus on bits of cotton moving with the belt serves to accomplish eye fixation, which is followed by suggestions of arm levitation and mouth opening. The bunnies are hallucinated by using the cotton as a prop, and the fox is hallucinated without props. Jane's eyes fixated but never closed, a familiar feature of hypnosis in young children. With the mood always pleasant and attention focused outward, any pain Jane might have felt was dissociated or converted by suggestion to tickling in the tooth or itching in the nose.

A variation of the foregoing procedure was pictured on a 1982 British Broadcasting Corporation television program on hypnosis.[1] The actual course of events, where facial expressions can be scrutinized carefully, conveys the reality far better than a description in words. The prevalence of humor throughout is impressive.

Because all hypnotherapy has an element of learning in it, maximum results may take some time and repetition. Anything that aids one's concentration can be turned to advantage. Humor, as we have noted, seems to serve as a focus while learning how to counteract pain. In another context, research indicates that inserting bits of humor into children's educational programs increases the children's visual attentiveness and facilitates the acquisition of information. This enhanced learning occurs in children as young as 5 and 6 years old and continues throughout the school years (Bryant, Zillman, and Brown, 1983).

We did not plan the introduction of humor in our therapy protocol, but we reviewed our records to see to what extent it had occurred spontaneously. We found that when it occurred, it was usually the patients who had initiated it through the choice of their own satisfying fantasies. In the end, humor turned out to be a powerful resource.

Parental Influences on Fantasy

In our discussions on the development of imagination in the child, we have thus far implied a role for parents and siblings, who clearly comprise the major part of the child's social environment and are responsible also for the physical environment of play and other influential experiences. We wish now to turn more directly to these family influences, particularly those of the parents, who are the primary identification figures.

The life of imagination has its roots in both stimulus-arousal and pretend play that starts during the preschool years when the child is in the home. Parental characteristics and styles of life affect the child in a number of ways. The parents are not only models, but they can also directly encourage or discourage the development of imagination by providing materials that stimulate imaginative projects and ideas. Play materials or construction toys that promote more than one possible outcome or answer (divergent thinking) rather than those that permit only one possible answer (convergent thinking) appear to be most likely to enhance a child's imagination. In this respect, imagination is probably stimulated by modeling clay more than already prepared objects, and by white sheets of paper with washable paints or crayons more than coloring books with outlined figures in place. Similarly, puppets or dolls the child can manipulate give more imaginative leeway than dolls dressed for one role. Obviously, parents differ in their ability to provide a support system for imaginative development, the differences largely attributable to their own childhood experiences and potential for free play.

Parents not only encourage or fail to encourage imagination in their children, but they also use fantasy in their informal "cures" of children's aches and pains. This was indicated in a pilot study by LeBaron and Zeltzer (1983) in which 30 child and adolescent patients varying widely in age gave retrospective accounts of the extent to which their parents had used fantasy with them when they were 4 to 6 years old. In addition to the first three questions in Singer's interview, there were two more questions: (1) Did your parents tell or read stories to you; if so, how often? (2) Did you believe in magic; if so, did you believe magic could help relieve pain or illness? On the basis of responses in the interview, the patients were divided into high- and low-fantasy patients. Most of the high-fantasy patients had believed in magic, and had believed it could help them. Many of these patients described how their parents would perform imaginary magical "cures" on childhood aches and scrapes; these parental treatments included kisses, rubbing, direct suggestions for pain relief, and in one case, a father's declaration that his "magic hand" would make the child feel better. By contrast, parents of the low-fantasy patients tended to rely more on either medicine or a realistic type of distraction ("Think of something else," or "Run outside and play now"). These results are consistent with other kinds of evidence regarding the relationship between family environment and fantasy development.

Parent-Child Relationships in Two Families. To illustrate a parental background that provides optimal support for the child's development of imaginative involvement, we turn again to Gigi whose imaginative abilities we previously described, and to George, her older brother whom we have not met. At age 9, George proved to be highly imaginative, with marked involvement in a number of areas. When observed watching television, he was described as "very engrossed" . . . "gone" . . . "totally absorbed." His mother spontaneously mentioned that he was even more absorbed in his reading this year than he was the previous year, and, although quite sociable, now will forego friends for reading. He loves science fiction. On field trips, he notices the beauty of nature; he calls attention to a sunset or to leaves, blossoms, lines, and shadows. Many things around him stimulate his imagination, and he tends to make up stories about them.

George was tested at age 6 and again at age 9 on a 12-point children's scale of hypnotic responsiveness. Each time he scored 11, indicating high hypnotizability, which is consistent with his level of imaginative involvement.

Mr. Grant, the children's father, when asked about the extent to which he had been imaginative as a child answered, "And how! Definitely. As an only child, I had to be. I developed games by myself. I used to build Indian huts . . . I played war games." With the encouragement of his parents, he became deeply involved in reading. He read several books from the public library every week, books like *Swiss Family Robinson,* books about pioneers. "I would become part of the whole scene. I still do, both in reading and in TV. I'm *in* the story. I'm part of the main character." Both of his parents were avid readers, his mother in particular read and reread many books from the public library.

"I always liked going to the movies and still do. I'm so involved, I won't even try to anticipate what's going to happen next." (Do you ever analyze what's happening?) "I never analyze as I go along. I'm deeply into it."

"Music, too, always meant a lot to me. I can listen to Handel's "Messiah" and my hair will rise right up in goose bumps."

The mother of the children recalled that as a child, "when I read of other countries, I would transport myself to other lands . . . I liked to act out characters that I read about. Even today when I start to read, I forget everything else. I get lost in the book and it becomes real. I'm not identified with the character, though, I'm more in the situation." The theater had long interested her. "I become completely absorbed in plays. When people are sad, I cry. I can't bear to see anyone dying—I come too close to feeling it myself." The mood of the entire production affects her, not a single characterization.

Her love of nature went back to early experiences with her own mother. "Every spring mom and I would inspect the new flowers, the rebirth after the winter. I enjoy a sunset and looking at a big cactus . . . anything beautiful . . . a waterfall, a picture, a cloud, the stars. They represent God and beauty and peace." (Do you analyze sometimes?) "I am not the dissecting type, that upsets me. I appreciate serenity in nature."

The references to the grandparents of Gigi and George underscore the continuity of a capacity for imaginative involvement from one generation to the next. The reading habits of the father's parents encouraged his own reading habits, and in their appreciation of nature, reading, and humor, Gigi's mother and grandmother were much alike.

As parents of hypnotizable children, this mother and father were themselves above average in hypnotizability on the Stanford Hypnotic Susceptibility Scale. Their influence on the children was evident. George's involvements were similar to those of his parents. Like them, he became deeply involved in imaginative reading, drama, and independent fantasy. When asked who George was like, the mother said he was like both of them. "He is so much the way I was when I was little, his interest in the out-of-doors, his made-up stories, and his determination to complete a job even when it is unpleasant." She said that in his bubbling enthusiasm he was more like his father. When Gigi engaged in pretend play, her mother was reminded of her own childhood. She enjoyed listening to Gigi's make-believe, and on occasion was willingly drawn into it. The contagion of imaginative experiences through three generations does not often come to attention so clearly.

Anita, age 6 1/2, our second illustration of parental support for imaginative experiences, derived her abilities from her father. She scored 11 on a 12-point children's scale of hypnotic susceptibility, something very unusual for a child so young. Anita's parents are at opposite poles in hypnotizability and imaginative involvement. Mr. Anderson scored at the top of the 12-point Stanford Hypnotic Susceptibility Scale, and Mrs. Anderson scored 1. The correspondence between their hypnotic scores and their imaginative involvements is impressive. The father had been highly imaginative since early childhood. The mother had had no involvement in imaginative pursuits at any time in her life. She was very competent in managing the house and in community work, and she was warmly interested in Anita. Anita's father was a college English professor. In reading novels or biographies, he commented, "I become involved . . . I become the main character and for a time afterwards, too. In the theater, I really live the situation . . . In listening to music I become part of it and I'm not aware of my surroundings . . . I enjoy singing, too." He belongs to a singing group and often becomes the leader. Anita's father thought he had picked up his interest in singing because as a boy he had joined his father in Salvation Army "sings." When his own father participated enthusiastically either in singing or in playing his harmonica, the son took part with equal zest. These sings constituted his father's main recreation; he did not become involved in reading, drama, or storytelling. Anita's father described his own father as giving him and his sister "a simple, warm love."

He also described his mother and his identification with her. "My mother became so involved in reading that she ate the apple and all of the pits in it. We had to shake her to get her attention." His mother told stories, myths, Greek fairy tales, and supernatural things to him and his sister. "I was quite carried away. She had a wonderful, smooth voice, knew how to involve me personally in her stories. I do this with Anita. We take imaginary trips of fantasy to make-believe lands." The father said of his mother, "she was warm and involved with us. She was curious and wanted to know about everything."

From the age of 2, Anita enjoyed listening to her father's stories, particularly fairy tales. One might have expected Anita's mother to have read some of the stories to her daughter, but in this case, it was the English professor father who read them. At the age of 6 1/2 when he read stories to her, she sat "as if entranced by the experience; she really lives the characters." She will often make up her own imaginative stories. When watching science fiction on TV, she becomes as involved as when listening to stories.

The fact that Anita could become absorbed in imaginative experiences did not interfere with her social development. Her father described her as active with a strong need for other children, among whom she was apt to be the leader.

Besides illustrating the "climate" some parents produce for their child's imaginative involvement, the Grants and the Andersons illustrate that the child's imaginative involvement may derive from one parent or both. The sex of the parent does not override the influence on imagination. That is, identification with the imaginative parent of either sex is likely to produce an imaginative child, and identification with an unimaginative parent of either sex is likely to produce a less imaginative child. These influences are asserted with caution, because parents are not the sole influences upon a child's imagination: there are other important persons in their environment —grandparents, siblings, friends, teachers. Sometimes when a child spends much time alone, fantasy will fill the empty hours. In addition to these environmental factors, the child's temperament may also exert an important role on the development of imagination.

American Indian Story Tellers: A Native's Experience. The reason for including the following story is that it tells how powerful the imaginative and affective experience can be for a child who develops in an environment where stories are handed down from generation to generation by skilled storytellers.

An 18-year-old college student with an American Indian family background gave a vivid description of the effect which oft-told tales by parents and grandparents had exerted upon her. Mae spoke of the wondrous tales she had heard, not once but many times, from her grandparents and parents throughout her childhood. Her grandfather, who was a highly placed medicine man, and her grandmother, in particular, related stories that retained a special magic for her. The story is condensed here:

The Man, the Bird, the Squirrel, and the Witch

A man was on the peak of a high rock. He could not move forward or backward without falling off. A bird overhead saw his plight. They talked together and the bird agreed to seek aid. The bird, meeting a squirrel, enlisted its help. (Much conversation is interspersed among man, bird, and squirrel.) The squirrel planted a nut by the rock, then made the tree that sprouted grow faster by running up and down it. When it had grown to such a point that it reached the man, he climbed down. At the bottom, the squirrel gave the man a bow and arrow, telling him that if he were ever in trouble to shoot the arrow. The man met a witch who wanted to wash his hair for him in the creek, so they went there together and she began. The man realized, however, that as she washed, she was casting a spell over him. He quickly shot the arrow into the air, it curved groundward, hit and killed the witch. . . .

In answer to questions, Mae said that she sees both the details of the story and herself in it very vividly. "I can see myself standing there by the river while the witch is washing the man's hair. I'll feel a breeze because it's late in the day. Then I feel it's cold because it's twilight." Worthy of attention is Mae's visualization of the scene by the river bank where she is experiencing the dissociation of watching and reliving (experiencing) at the same time as she tells the story. This is itself a practiced dissociation. She said of her grandparents as storytellers, *"They feel it so much that you feel it too; they create an atmosphere."* When asked about hearing the voices of the storytellers, she replied that she could still hear the voices as clearly today as at the time the stories were told.

Mae has given us a clear picture of empathic identification when she says, "They feel it so much that you feel it too; they create an atmosphere."

Succeeding generations become the storytellers who communicate the fantasies and create this compelling affect. As might be expected, Mae proved highly hypnotizable and enjoyed the hypnotic experience.

The imaginative parents whom we described did much more than encourage or promote imaginative adventures in their children. They not only shared a part of themselves and communicated a delight in fanciful play; they modeled and set the rules that governed such fantasy. Gigi's mother, after participating in Gigi's pretend play, told her when it was time to stop, whereupon Gigi responded with a couple of magic words and terminated it. Exercise of this type of shared fantasy is constructive and time-limited.

Inhibitors of Childhood Fantasy

Not all children develop their potential for imaginative involvement. It appears that unless the foundation for fantasy is established early in childhood, it may never develop. Parents or other important persons in the early environment may or may not be able to maintain an environment that is conducive to the nurturance of imagination. In addition, some personality and temperamental characteristics of the child may interfere with the development of a capacity for fantasy. We have considered primarily parental influences favorable to fantasy, and now we will consider conditions that inhibit fantasy.

Activity as an Inhibitor. Those who have studied make-believe play in young children have noted that the more imaginative children display less motor activity. Among preschool boys, vigorous physical play was accompanied by less make-believe play (Singer, 1973; Pulaski, 1973). Korner (1982), on the basis of her own investigations and a review of the literature, pointed out that typical energy levels were quite persistent throughout childhood and were related significantly to the development of a number of characteristics and temperamental differences. Children in the same family could be unlike in their activity levels at birth and these levels proved to be quite stable over time (Buss, Block, and Block, 1980).

In order to give a concrete illustration of the contrasts between two children in their activity levels, and how the differences affected their imaginative involvements, we turn to Eric, who was 9 years old and his sister Peggy, who was a year younger. He had an inherently high activity level while she was quiet, contemplative, and leisurely in action. The differences were reflected in their hypnotic susceptibility scores. Eric scored 6, while Peggy scored 12 on the 12-point Stanford Susceptibility Scale, modified for children. The parents were highly imaginative and would have been expected to produce hypnotizable children. The mother was perceptive about the children as she noted that while both were imaginative, they differed markedly in their degree of physical activity.

According to his mother, Eric had been active from the time of birth. "Every action and emotion was highly intense. He nursed ferociously, cried, chuckled intensely, could not be calmed down. He climbed out of the crib very early, he has been climbing and falling off stairs since he was 7 months old, he rides a unicycle, loves to swim and has learned rugby. He is adventurous, willing and champing at the bit to try almost anything, but he does not always understand the dangers. While viewing TV attentively, he will be working on a project with his hands, such as making a sail for his sailboat. Eric dislikes the restraint of the routine 15 minutes of silence in his church, and he is restless during silent grace at dinner. Though he can appreciate nature, he likes sports much better."

Eric combines imagination with activity in a manner that permits creative imagination to function in the midst of energetic behavior. According to his mother, "He creates stories and poetry, matches words and makes puns. He takes off from a TV ad and makes up a funny story about it." After studying books on the art treasures of Japan, he sketched from memory drawings of pagodas with rocks behind them.

Although imaginative parents stimulated Eric's creative imagination, his energetic nature which interfered with quiet periods at home and at church, prevented the development of a contemplative orientation to fantasy, the type of imaginative activity that relies on an easygoing receptivity, i.e., involvement in imaginative books, TV programs, and nature. He had difficulty *letting* things happen; rather he used his imagination to *make* them happen. His imaginative involvements were dependent upon his own overt activity in words and actions. As such, Eric's active imagination appeared to be an advanced development of the pretend play in which the child is master of what happens. The binding of activity and imagination with little receptivity was probably responsible for the average score he achieved when tested for hypnotizability.

Peggy had been a placid baby, according to her mother, and at 8 years of age, she remained a quiet child. Her mother said, "She is perceptive, curious, concentrates well . . . she is not afraid of doing things in a way that is unlike other people. She has many friends, is gentle and forthright . . . has a delightful sense of humor and just twinkles." At church Peggy sits quietly during the 15 minutes of silence. When the family has silent grace at the table, Peggy will often begin it, holding out her hand to quiet things.

Peggy liked quiet times by herself and used them to make up stories, songs, and ditties. Her imagination proceeded at a leisurely pace, interlaced with humor. Some of her new verses were quite funny. She built a house with a bamboo pole and a blanket to produce a tentlike structure where she could sing and talk to herself. She seemed to need the privacy she created for herself about twice a week. Although she would put off her friends at these times, she would include her cats.

Peggy's perceptiveness in social situations was striking. It was as though she responded to feeling as much or more than to words. At bedtime, she used to sense which songs her mother particularly liked and would ask her to sing them. She had always loved being read to. From the time she started reading for herself, she had become greatly involved. She also became involved in TV programs.

Peggy's involvements were typical of the hypnotizable person because they included both the receptive areas (quiet contemplation, being read to, reading to herself) and the independent imaginative areas (making up stories, songs, etc.). Her experiences in daily living gave evidence of this dual range of imaginative involvements. In the midst of the same imaginative atmosphere as Peggy, Eric was also imaginative, but with a difference—he read well, he watched television, but he was impatient while engaged in these quiet pursuits. When confronted with a contemplative period before dinner or at school, he exhibited an urgent need to be active. It appears that instead of the usual receptive *and* active imaginative backgrounds on which the hypnotizability that we measure is built, Eric possessed only the active part of that equation. Eric's hypnotic score of 6 on the 12-point scale can be interpreted in terms of the particular gifts which he brought to hypnosis. As therapists, if we understand average-level scores on hypnotizability scales according to the strengths of the patient, therapy can be adjusted to building on such strengths. Note that to understand Eric's type of hypnotizability, we had to take into account the activity level which lay outside the hypnotic testing.

At this point it is informative to refer briefly to Jeff, whom we met in Chapter 4. He was the activity-oriented child of 6 years who liked only to engage in strenuous play. Neither he nor his mother reported any imaginative interests. He scored 3 on the Children's Hypnotic Susceptibility Scale (a 6-point scale). He could not reduce pain in the bone marrow aspiration until the therapist abandoned hypnotic methods that emphasized fantasy and relied entirely on a distraction method that stressed quick activity changes.

Other Inhibitors of Fantasy.   A high activity level is not the only factor that can inhibit the normal development or emergence of fantasy life in a child. Another inhibitor is a particular kind of close emotional dependence of a child upon a parent. In our clinical cases, we found instances where clinging to the mother was the major coping strategy. Such clinging, mentioned in Chapter 4, is part of an earlier, normal attachment, but is expected to be outgrown by the time the children reach the age of those in our sample. This pattern of clinging was observed not just during medical procedures; rather, it was a pervasive aspect of the mother-child relationship and it prevented the use of independent fantasy in hypnotherapy.

Even in children who have been provided with a successful foundation for nurturing their hypnotic talent, subsequent life experiences sometimes inhibit its continued expression or result in a diminution of what was available at an earlier stage in their lives. As the child matures, there are increasing demands for reality-oriented tasks, whether homework for school, sports, music lessons, or social activities with peers. When one is required to read texts in preparation for an examination, there is necessarily less time available to read for pleasure. All of these pursuits may reduce the time available for the free play of fantasy.

Stages in the Development of Hypnosis

The greatest changes in the nature of hypnosis take place in two stages: The first stage, or protohypnosis, develops during the preschool years, and the second stage develops during the early school years when the scores on scales of hypnotizability are beginning to rise rapidly and to approach peak hypnotic performance.

Protohypnosis.   The earliest manifestations of hypnoticlike behavior are in the pretend play of the child which takes form between the ages of 2 and 3 years when language is well enough developed to guide behavior with words. Protohypnosis is like hypnosis in that it is both an imitation of reality and a distortion of it. The pretend or make-believe play has temporary reality for the child but, like hypnotic fantasies, it is time-limited and recognizable as different from ordinary reality. This distinction between involvement in the imagined world and in the real world is one of the beginnings of dissociated experience. There is a similarity between the language of pretend play and that of self-hypnosis; for example, when Gigi was ready to terminate her pretend play, she said magic words just as a self-hypnotized person might do to cancel the hypnotic condition.

The limitations of protohypnosis rest primarily upon the limited cognitive ability of the child; that is, typical hypnotic suggestions and tasks that are beyond the capacity of the child to experience will not be effective. Similarly, a child who has not yet learned to report night dreams cannot be expected to report a dream in hypnosis. Most important is the fact that during this age range, children have little or no capacity for internalized fantasy.

In making use of protohypnosis in therapy with children, it is essential to capitalize upon the child's own make-believe world and to respect the initiative the child is accustomed to having in that domain. During the pilot stages of our research, 5-year-old Timmy, who always screamed piercingly during bone marrow aspirations and needed restraint, was told how he could turn off the pain switches in his head that led to the bone marrow area. During rehearsal Timmy liked the switches, but he failed to use them and continued to scream during the actual bone marrow aspiration. He told us, however, that he now used the "switches" to keep his hand from hitting people at kindergarten. Up to that point he had experienced a great deal of trouble because of his tendency to hit other children. His capacity for utilizing this new instrument of self-control also showed up in a wider use of the switches technique; according to his report, he no longer cried when he cut or bruised himself because he had learned how to "turn off" his switches. At the same time he had not matured enough to exert self-control through the fantasied switches when confronted with the more intrusive pain of the bone marrow aspiration. This points to the transitional nature of protohypnosis.

Protohypnotic capability tends to show itself in fantasy portrayed in action. The little girl talks to her dolls and the little boy shuffles around and choo-choos as a locomotive. Hypnosis commonly continues to call for movement response to suggestion so that the enacted imaginative experience of protohypnosis continues and joins the mature form of hypnosis in later childhood.

From Protohypnosis to Peak Hypnosis. Peak hypnosis refers to the available responses to hypnotic suggestion at the age range (roughly 9 to 12) when the average number of test items passed on hypnotic scales is at a maximum. This is merely a quantitative statement of the fact that hypnosis, through its close ties to highly developed modes of fantasy, is now capable of heightened responsiveness to suggestions calling for intense concentration of attention, acceptance of reality distortions, and tolerance of logical inconsistencies. One illustration of the gradual change that occurs with age as the child moves from protohypnosis to "peak" hypnosis is the ability to internalize fantasy experiences with eyes closed. The child's persistence in keeping the eyes open in pretend play and in protohypnosis has gradually given way to a preference for fantasied action within hypnosis with eyes closed.

As noted earlier in this chapter, LeBaron and Zeltzer (1983) described a pilot study of 30 child and adolescent patients who gave retrospective accounts of their fantasy life between the ages of 4 to 6; those who scored high in fantasy were responsive to parental suggestions of "cures" based on imagination. All of the patients were also administered the age-appropriate form of the Stanford Clinical Hypnotic Scale. When scores were divided at the median into high and lows, a significant relationship ($p < .02$) was found between the degree of fantasy involvement and hypnotic susceptibility. Twelve of 16 high-fantasy patients scored high on hypnotic susceptibility, whereas 10 of 14 low-fantasy patients scored low on susceptibility.

Some of the demands made upon the older child who is being hypnotized for the first time are more complex than they seem. For example, in a typical eye-closure induction, the subject is told to keep the eyes open while concentrating on a target, and as the procedure continues, to notice that the eyes will close by themselves. Responding to this suggestion requires grasping the distinction between "making it happen" and "letting it happen," which is not easy until the child has a concept of voluntary and involuntary action. Other complex demands are involved in the suggestion of posthypnotic amnesia. The plausibility has to be conveyed that something can be "forgotten now" and "remembered later." For the adult, the concept of "temporary forgetting"—that something stored in the memory may be difficult to retrieve at one time but available at another—is familiar. By the age of 9, when the peak has been reached, there is usually no conceptual barrier to the use of the already developed hypnotic potential.

The Maintenance of Hypnotic Talent

Beginning in adolescence, after peak hypnosis, average scores on hypnotic tests show a general decline throughout the adult years. These represent the norm, but they do not tell us why the general decline occurs or why some persons remain highly hypnotizable until late in life. We shall start with the decline and then turn to reasons why some maintain their talent throughout life.

In a study based on individual administration of the 12-point Stanford Hypnotic Susceptibility Scale, Form A, hypnosis reached an average score of 7.6 between the ages of 9 and 12 years. This was the peak of hypnotic potential. The hypnotic scores then declined gradually until they reached 6.6 among people in their mid-30s. After this, they dropped more rapidly to 5.2 among those over the age of 40 (Morgan and E. Hilgard, 1973). Even so, the total average drop from the peak to the later score was less than one-third of the score at the peak, so that two-thirds of the hypnotic talent persisted into the later years.

Although average hypnotic scores tend to decline slowly during the adolescent and adult years, for those who do retain their imaginative involvements, their level of fantasy within hypnosis can become much deeper and more pervasive. They have had time to take advantage of the greater opportunities for enrichment that exist beyond childhood.

To explain the loss of hypnotic talent that begins in adolescence, we have several possibilities to consider. One is that in the course of maturation, some of the relevant abilities—particularly those which are imagery-related—may be lost because of neuropsychological changes in the developing child. A second possibility is that the requirements of life in society demand a reality orientation, especially in the work life, which interferes with the freer use of the mind and feelings as they are expressed in hypnosis. A third possibility is that the specific culture in which we live is oriented against the exercise by adults of the potentials inherent in hypnosis. Obviously, those interpretations are not mutually exclusive, but they can be separately explored.

One explanation favors the maturational interpretation, with a hint provided by the literature on eidetic imagery. An eidetic individual, after having been asked to look attentively at an object, can immediately, or after a certain lapse of time, with eyes open or closed, "see" this object again with images that tend to be of hallucinatory intensity. The specific nature of eidetic images has been a source of controversy. For our purposes, whatever their nature, the early investigators all agreed that capacity for such vivid images was at its height in childhood, with 12 years often suggested as the period of maximum frequency, followed by a decline during or after puberty (Klüver, 1933; Haber, 1979). Because these years correspond so closely to the years of maximum hypnotic responsiveness and its decline, there is the possibility that forms of imagery and imaginative involvement related to hypnosis may follow the same course.

The second possibility, that pressure for reality orientation interferes with time and opportunity for the exercise of previously developed imaginative involvements, is illustrated by a medical student who scored low in hypnotizability. In an interview subsequent to his hypnotic test, he recalled how he had been carefree in the years prior to high school, enjoying a deep involvement in reading science fiction and other nonscientific books. His father explained to him as he entered high school that from now on he would have to devote his time to school subjects in order to compete for entry into university and medical school. At that point, he began to drop his interest in science fiction, and he had not read any for a number of years. When the interviewer encouraged him to attempt to recapture this former involvement, he found that he was unable to do so.

Of the third possibility, that the broader culture in the West discourages adult fantasy, we have little evidence one way or the other. There is evidence that hypnotic abilities tend to involve capacities which are associated with right cortical brain function (Chen, Dworkin, and Bloomquist, 1981;

E. Hilgard and J. Hilgard, 1975/83). Our culture has been described by some as a "left-hemisphere culture" because of its emphasis on rational consecutive thinking and problem-solving to the neglect of the right-hemisphere functions of aesthetic sensitivity and fantasy (Kinsbourne and Hiscock, 1978). To relate these hemispheric preferences to changes in hypnotizability with age would be highly conjectural at this time.

The Stanford Scales of Hypnotic Susceptibility have been translated into a number of languages in many parts of the world, but age comparisons between children and adults are not available. We are on firmer ground in noting conditions under which hypnotic talent, once achieved, can be maintained beyond the age when normative data suggest that it is usually declining.

One of the most hypnotizable adults we tested at the Stanford laboratory was a man in his 50s. Not only was he a scientist whose work demanded continuous attention to detail, but he was also a high-level administrator with extensive responsibilities. In his spare time he often read novels and biographies with deep involvement, immersed himself in listening to classical music, imagined scripts of interesting stories, and enjoyed adventurous involvements such as skiing. His imaginative and adventuresome involvements were continuous from childhood as he successfully pursued a demanding work schedule in addition to full participation in imaginative and adventuresome activities during his leisure hours.

He represents how reality demands of adult life can be met while at the same time the imaginative involvements from early years are sustained by continued use. In other words, in a well-rounded life which allows room for recreational activities as well as for work, reality-orientation is fully compatible with time-limited fantasy.

We have noted age changes in the growth of hypnotic behavior during childhood—changes related particularly to imagination, attention, and affect—and have coordinated them with findings in developmental psychology. The contribution of hypnotic studies and general developmental studies to each other could well enrich both.

Notes

1. BBC, London, Michael Barnes, Editor, Science and Features. Released in September, 1982.

10 Opportunities for Research

Many clinicians who have used hypnotherapy for treating pain have found innovative ways of adapting their techniques to individual patient needs, and their published case studies are valuable to other professionals working in the field. At the present time, however, in order to produce generalizations from a myriad of findings, it is incumbent on clinicians to report research in a scientific framework. Clinical researchers need to provide adequate documentation in respect to the type and degree of pain, the exact hypnotherapeutic techniques used, and the various outcomes. Next, individual cases need to be grouped in coherent ways so that assumptions and hypotheses can be assessed beyond anecdotal and idiosyncratic experiences. Artistry and inventiveness must join hands with scientific discipline. Only then will contributions to the growing body of knowledge in hypnotherapy be consonant with the dynamic contributions of the human beings—patients, colleagues, family members, and institutional staff members—who provide the opportunity for conducting eloquent research.

Based on summaries of research topics pursued in 1970 and research publications related to hypnosis which appeared between 1971 through 1977, Fromm (1979) predicted future trends in hypnotic research. She noted that child hypnotherapy was missing in the 1970 listing and only a few publications on this topic appeared each year among the 1000 studies on hypnotic research classified by topic in the survey of publications. This upward trend has continued, though slowly.

In the course of our investigation, we identified several new questions related to hypnosis with children which could be answered by further research. These areas of inquiry offer exciting research opportunities for those who share an interest in the emotional, cognitive, and social development of children. The following topics will be discussed briefly: the

195

development of hypnotic ability, especially during early childhood; the measurement of hypnotic ability in children; heredity and environmental influences on the development of hypnotic ability; and variations in the clinical use of hypnosis for children.

The Nature and Development of Hypnosis

The bulk of the research on hypnosis has been done with college students and other adults. Greater knowledge of the sequence of development from earliest childhood would add immeasurably to the understanding not only of hypnosis in children but of hypnosis at all ages. Our research and that of other investigators have already uncovered leads to be followed, enough to show that further investigation of hypnosis in childhood could contribute substantially to the science of human development.

Pretend Play and Protohypnosis.   A preschool child who becomes involved in pretend play already shows signs of readiness to respond to suggestions without a hypnotic induction; that is, to "waking" suggestion, either self-initiated or coming from someone else. We found a number of young children who could, through waking suggestion, use their pretend play to obtain relief from minor pain and the anxiety component of pain. One instance is the mother who put the "powerful" lotion on her son's finger so that he would no longer feel the finger stick. The power of the lotion was ascribed to the authority of the hypnotherapist who proposed its use. In childhood, the distinctions are blurred among such influences as the authority of a hypnotist, the direct effect of suggestion, and the concentration of attention on pretend play. To unravel these relationships through research will require subtle and imaginative approaches. The question arises whether the early stage that we have called protohypnosis is equivalent to hypnosis in the older child. The answer to the question may be that they are essentially alike, quite different, or alike for some children and different for others.

Fantasy and Attention.   Further research is needed to understand how fantasy changes with age, and its relation to attentive processes.

The changes in fantasy with age were discussed in Chapter 9, where it was noted that the scales available at present for testing fantasy are not fully adapted to the needs of hypnosis. It would be desirable to have scales reflecting stimulus-aroused sensory-affective experiences, stimulus-aroused imagination, absorbed attention, imagination portrayed in action (pretend play), and fantasied action (internalized imagination). Certain aspects of affect should also be included in revised scales. By including appropriate subscales, such instruments could span a wide range of ages and indicate quantitatively those functions that persist, those that tend to decline with age, and those that begin at somewhat older ages.

Modifications of attention have long been considered a prominent feature of hypnosis. We have already noted that the hypnotized person pays close attention to the words of the hypnotist, with whom special rapport has been established, and ignores remarks by others present or any background noises. We have also indicated the intensity of the attention that develops in a fantasy situation, whether sustained by TV or by an interesting story. Indeed, the complementary relationship between fantasy and attention provides an excellent opportunity for research on the specific interactions that bind them.

The transition between the period when the child's hypnotic ability is at its peak, and adolescence when it begins to decline, may be related to a reduction in imagery or a lessening of interest in imaginative involvement. It is convenient to assume that the greater demands for reality-oriented competence begin to encroach on the younger child's freedom to be playful and to fantasize. Although a sensible hypothesis, studies directed towards illuminating this concept remain to be done.

Self-Hypnosis and Heterohypnosis in Children. For the child, irrational suggestions offered in hypnosis such as using magic medicine as part of a playful fantasy is legitimized by the hypnotist's participation in the "game." Because children participate so fully in this play world, and find the experience so congenial, it is not surprising that some of them are able to initiate and maintain the experience by themselves. They do this by instructing themselves to perform the dissociated activity, a step toward self-hypnosis.

When a child is able to respond to heterohypnosis but is unable to make effective use of self-hypnosis, it is probable that self-hypnosis places too much of a demand upon the child's initiative. In contrast, we have had glimpses of children who prefer to create their own fantasies rather than respond to the suggestions of a hypnotist. Children who successfully create their own fantasies may be continuing a trend set by those who become most absorbed in their own pretend play. We have proposed that pretend play has much in common with self-hypnosis and may be transitional to it. This interpretation is based on observations which make it plausible, but it deserves critical examination. There may be other personality differences that produce the relative effectiveness of heterohypnosis and self-hypnosis.

Dissociation and Hypnotic Age Regression in Children. In Chapter 8, we reported on a concealed awareness of pain revealed by a few adults in the midst of their conscious reduction of pain through suggested hypnotic analgesia. The report of this concealed awareness was described as indicating a "hidden observer," a metaphor for a cognitive system processing information at a level outside of the subject's awareness during hypnotic analgesia. We noted that this phenomenon had not been investigated in children. We are not proposing at this point that it be investigated, because in the therapeutic setting it might be confusing to the young patient. However, hypnotic age regression, to which the hidden observer is related, could be studied more carefully.

An important finding, recounted by Nogrady, McConkey, Laurence, and Perry (1983), was that the presence of a hidden observer was related to a duality of experience during hypnotic age regression. That is, subjects with a hidden observer reported the reality of an experience during regression of being a child again at the same time as they preserved the adult self who was observing the child self. Those who failed to report a hidden observer connected with the hypnotic pain experience, reported in hypnotic-regression the sole experience of being a child again.

The duality in age regression, with the adult and child experiences present simultaneously, raises questions regarding the development of such a split in childhood. One question is whether progressive changes occur between early age regression in the young child and age regression in the adult. Until the child is old enough to perceive the age regression as being substantial—contrasting the child at present and the "younger one" of a year or more earlier—age regression for the child cannot be expected to be fully developed. The question can be studied by conducting such observations at successive ages. It is possible that the capacity will already have begun in make-believe play where regression is not clearly involved. Perhaps at a given early age, one child will be completely immersed in the imagined role, while another at the same age may be familiar with an observing part which is not participating in the make-believe. That child might grow up to reveal a hidden observer.

If the first steps yield convincing evidence of a duality in consciousness, later studies might eventually be directed to detecting the hidden observer phenomenon in children. Such investigations could be done by using something less threatening than concealed pain. Instead of concealed pain, it would be possible to use other negative hallucinations such as the inability to hear someone's voice or the inability to see a person who is sitting nearby. The hidden observer, if present, should be able to report having heard the voice or having seen the person. It will be recalled that 16-year-old Gwen (Chapter 8) reported a duality in age regression and a hidden observer in experiments both on reduced pain and reduced hearing.

Measurement of Hypnotic Talent

The present scales for the measurement of hypnotic potential have proven their worth in studies of both children and adults. They are limited, however, and can be improved in two respects: 1) in the assessment of differences among those whose scores at any one age fall within the same level, and 2) in understanding qualitative differences that take place with age. New information is especially needed about the qualitative changes that are taking place as various aspects of hypnotic talent begin to emerge.

The Construction of Clinical Measurement Scales. Based on scales designed for adults (Weitzenhoffer and Hilgard, 1959, 1962), London (1962) developed an extensive Children's Hypnotic Susceptibility Scale (CHSS) in two parts. The first part used the same 12 items as in the Stanford Hypnotic Susceptibility Scale, Form A (SHSS:A), reworded appropriately for children. This scale emphasizes motor control, with only two items of a cognitive type (auditory hallucination and amnesia). The second part used 10 items and is based largely on items in the Stanford Hypnotic Susceptibility Scale, Form C (SHSS:C). Except for the response to eye closure in the induction, it consists exclusively of items rich in cognitive content, primarily positive and negative hallucinations, age-regression, and dreaming within hypnosis. London felt that it was important to record the subjective involvement of the subject along with the behavior measures, and made provision on the scoring form for doing this.

London, with a collaborator, later provided norms that included a detailed summary of age-related changes occuring in children's responses to specific items on the scale (London and Cooper, 1969; see also Cooper and London, 1978/79). Rich as the scale is, it requires at least an hour for its full administration, although for those who do poorly in the first part, it is proposed that the second part not be given.

With other demands upon the clinician's time, shorter scales which included cognitive items like hallucinations, dreams, and age regression, appeared desirable. Such an abbreviated scale was designed first for adult use (Morgan and J. Hilgard, 1978/79), and adapted for use in clinical work with children (SHCS:Child). This is the scale that was used in our Stanford study, to which reference has been made throughout this book. The scale proved successful in our research except for one problem: because it was too easy at the high end, discrimination between the moderately hypnotizable and the highly hypnotizable child was less precise, although for the same reason it was quite successful at detecting the very low hypnotizable child. For clinical use, a scale less detailed than that of London CHSS but more discriminatory than the Stanford SHCS: Child needs to be developed.

The long experience of psychologists in the construction of measurement scales has served to define criteria for scale construction—typically a long, somewhat tedious, time-consuming and expensive set of operations —criteria which few working in the field of hypnosis have been prepared to meet. The criteria include item selections according to purpose intended, item scoring to achieve objectivity while still reflecting the essential purposes, and various developmental steps to determine the interrelationship of the item scores with revisions based on adequate pretesting until a final test is "packaged" and norms obtained on a representative sample.

For a satisfactory hypnotic clinical scale, no matter how brief, the desirable items appear to be: motor responses (enacted as a response to direct suggestion); motor inhibition (enacted); positive and negative hallucinations; dreaming within hypnosis; age regression; posthypnotic suggestion, and amnesia.

To produce a very short scale, selection has to be made, but at some sacrifice, so that modifications can be made for convenience. There are adult single-item scales, for example, which give rough measures of hypnotizability, two of which depend primarily upon arm levitation, the Hypnotic Induction Profile (HIP) (Spiegel and Spiegel, 1978) and the Stanford Hypnotic Arm Levitation Induction and Test (SHALIT) (Hilgard, Crawford, and Wert, 1979). In the HIP, there are advanced items that can test the upper range of hypnotizability, but they are poorly standardized and seldom used. The authors of the SHALIT recommend the use of more detailed scales after a preliminary sorting on the short test. The same considerations apply to designing tests for children. One approach in improving a children's scale might be to develop a scale with two levels of difficulty: The first level would contain items appropriate to those of low to moderate hypnotizability, and all items would have to be successfully passed before the patient would be tested on the more difficult items comprising the second scale. This two-level configuration might provide greater differentiation at the upper levels of hypnotic talent—important if the research is to bear on the reduction of severe pain. The present SHCS would suffice for those able to score only 0 to 3; those who scored 4 to 5 would continue with additional items to provide greater differentiation among the more responsive.

It has been shown in many contexts that only the highly hypnotizable reduce severe pain to any significant degree. More refined measures are desirable in order to demonstrate, in greater detail, the relationship between hypnotizability and clinical outcome.

Qualitative Studies of Age-Related Changes in Hypnotic Talent. The age-related changes in hypnotizability have already been well documented by use of scales exhibiting score changes with age. Along with these score changes there are, however, qualitative changes in the nature of the hypnotic experience when the young child first begins to show signs of hypnotic responsiveness, when peak hypnosis is reached, and when an average decline in hypnotic ability starts. We have already discussed the qualitative age changes in eye closure. We have mentioned, too, possibilities for research on the dissociative aspects of age regression. Now we turn to two illustrative areas that are included in the scales: dreams and posthypnotic amnesia.

Dreams within hypnosis. The ability to produce a dream within hypnosis proved to be an easy-to-pass item on the London and Cooper Scale—58 percent passing at ages 5 to 6 and 90 percent by ages 9 through 12. Subjects who passed hallucinations in sensory modalities such as audition, vision, taste, and smell, reached their highest percentages at the same age level of 9 through 12. The dreams of children within hypnosis differ at the young ages from those produced by adults. For children, differences are blurred between images of remembered or fantasied experiences and dreams within hypnosis similar to night dreams. For adults, not all suggested dreams within hypnosis seem like night dreams, but the distinctions between them can be made through subsequent inquiry.

Recent data on night dreams reported by young children, with many of the same 44 children studied over a period of years, showed that 3- to 5-year-olds dream little, or offer simple statements such as "I was asleep in the bathtub" (Foulkes, 1982). The reported dream content showed little evidence of fantastic characters and little representation of impulse in this age group. The 5- to 7-year-olds began to report brief stories of dream happenings, and the 7- to 9-year-olds were often characters in their own dreams. Not until adolescense did the adult quality of dreams become evident, that is, narrative events no longer reflected specific memories but instead indicated symbolic distortions. Foulkes interpreted his findings as evidence that the capacity for dreaming followed developmental stages rather like those of waking thought. We would expect hypnotic dreams in children and adolescents to correspond to the same pattern of cognitive development as expressed in night dreams, but nothing can be asserted with confidence without a more intensive collection of dreams within hypnosis and their subsequent analysis.

Posthypnotic amnesia. Recoverable amnesia is so important in the history of hypnosis that the word for a highly hypnotizable person—somnambulist—at first referred to one who spontaneously exhibited amnesia after awakening from hypnosis. It is therefore important in any thorough study of age-related changes in hypnosis to investigate the phenomenon of amnesia. To do so in children, however, poses difficulties. Cooper (1979) has estimated that 30 percent of the children capable of passing the usual "forgetting" tests of posthypnotic amnesia would be unable to recover the forgotten material. In other words, the amnesia would not classify as "reversible," which is of most interest in the study of hypnosis. In the London and Cooper study, for example, Cooper's assertion would mean that instead of the 80 percent who "passed" amnesia at ages 11 to 12, only 56 percent would have passed by reversibility standards; this latter figure is more in line with findings for adults. Cooper estimates that of the adults who pass the "forgetting" criteria for amnesia, 96 percent will also pass the "reversibility" criteria. Cooper did not analyze the children's scores on amnesia by age, so we do not know how soon the adult pattern is reached. Further studies to establish norms for reversible amnesia at successive ages would make a valuable contribution.

On the qualitative side, it would be helpful to relate *how* the reversible amnesia was accomplished at different development levels in childhood. When amnesia was suggested to college students, for some who were successful, the experiences to be forgotten were hidden behind a barrier such as a heavy curtain. For other students, their minds simply became blank until the suggestion was reversed. One subject reported, "It was just like being on a merry-go-round and reaching for the ring. It's gone before you get a chance to grab it, and on the next time around you almost get it but not quite. It's always just out of reach." Suggested amnesia is often partial so that some of the experienced items are recalled.

Hereditary and Environmental Origins of Hypnotic Talent

Hypnotic behavior is a form of social response and, as such, is inevitably conditioned by the experiences of early childhood within the context of home and family, community, and school. In the development of all personal-social behavior, however, both hereditary and environmental influences are at work.

Hereditary Influences. Regardless of the human performance area under consideration, a determination of the relative influence of inborn factors versus those due to experience has always proved extremely difficult. The nature-nurture controversy in human intelligence began in the 19th century and continues today. The favored method for obtaining evidence on hereditary factors is by studying resemblances between identical and fraternal twins, and particularly identical twins who have been reared apart in diverse environments. To our knowledge there are no studies of hypnotizability in identical twins reared apart, but there are studies comparing hypnotic responsiveness scores between identical and fraternal twins. In one such study conducted in Australia, Rawlings (1972) examined

121 pairs of twins, of whom 47 were identical (monozygotic) and 74 were fraternal (dizygotic), with 46 of the same sex and 28 of unlike sex. Although the majority ranged in age from 16 to 40, about 20 percent were children below the age of 16. The scale used to test hypnotic talent consisted of 15 tasks of increasing difficulty. Results indicated a significantly higher correlation of hypnotizability ($r = .67$, $p < .001$) among the identical twins than among the fraternal ($r = .18$, nonsignificant).

These results agree with data obtained in Morgan's study of twins in which subjects were tested on the Stanford Hypnotic Susceptibility Scale, Form A (SHSS:A) (Morgan, 1973). Specifically, a significant correlation ($r = .52$, $p < .001$), was found for 58 pairs of identical twins, in contrast to an insignificant correlation ($r = .18$), for the 53 pairs of fraternal twins of the same sex. The difference between these two correlations was statistically significant. From a hereditary point of view, the higher correlation for identical twins is to be expected because identical twins have the same genes, whereas fraternal twins are no more alike genetically than ordinary nontwin siblings. The higher correlation for identical twins may not be due entirely to hereditary factors, however, because their environments—even in the same home—may be more alike than for the fraternal twins, i.e., if twins look alike, their parents may treat them alike.

The congenital differences noted in activity levels at birth may have a hereditary base. If activity levels affect hypnotizability, as they appear to do, the inheritance of hypnotic talent could be related to this factor, among others. That is, there need not be a specific "gene for hypnotizability" in order for hypnotic potential to be influenced by heredity.

Environmental Influences. Parental influences upon the development of fantasy—as components of hypnotizability—have been treated in some detail in Chapter 9. These observations indicate inherent difficulties in interpreting the relative contributions of heredity and environment, for we noted that imaginative parents encouraged imaginative children. The transmission could have been both biological and social—some temperamental characteristics inherited, some practices taught.

Another approach to the influence of environmental factors on hypnotizability is to study fluctuations of scores on repeated tests which deviate from the expected changes with age. These changes can then be interpreted according to events in the specific experiences of the child. Studies of this kind have proved useful, for example, in studying modifications in IQ on repeated testing (Sontag, Baker, and Nelson, 1958). The use of this method in hypnosis can be illustrated by the data from Ross, one of the young subjects in the family study (J. Hilgard and Morgan, 1965).

Ross showed a decline in hypnotizability between the ages of 6 and 9, when increasing scores are generally found. At the time of the first testing, Ross, age 6, and his brother, age 8, were tested on a 12-point scale. Ross scored 6 and his brother scored 8. The score of 6 at the age of 6 is a satisfactory indication of potential hypnotizability, and the higher score of the older brother is to be expected even if their potentials are alike. Both parents scored in the medium range of hypnotizability. In other words, Ross grew up in the context of a moderately hypnotizable family. Reports of Ross's earliest years already suggested the likelihood of his hypnotizability. Since the age of 3 he had greatly enjoyed make-believe activities, such as pretending to be a record player or filling a box with make-believe rabbits. By the age of 6, an interest in puppetry had started.

When both children were retested three years later, the brother scored 9, but Ross had dropped from 6 to 2. The question is why Ross had decreased in his hypnotic score.

It appeared that developing fears might account for the decline. In Ross's dramatic play shortly after the first testing, he had introduced the theme of a bully puppet frightening a helpless little puppet, and he identified with the little puppet. Fears, as he watched television programs like "Star Wars" were so overwhelming to him that he was no longer permitted to watch science-fiction programs. His mother reported that he was not at all adventurous in real life for fear of making mistakes. It is not surprising that in the face of such fears, Ross found it important to be in control—an attitude that conflicted with being hypnotized. If the opportunity had been available, it would have been valuable, both to him and to us, to deal therapeutically with his fearfulness, and to discover whether the decline in hypnotizability was reversible.

The research implications of this case suggest that we need developmental studies of individuals to contrast with the study of the average trends revealed by group studies. On a clinical level, diagnosing and understanding emotional blocks to hypnotizability may restore latent hypnotizability.

The Effect of Motivation on Hypnotizability

Many clinicians believe that the intense motivation of patients to be rid of pain contributes significantly to their success in reducing pain. Believing that such motivation cannot be duplicated in the laboratory, they regard the results of laboratory experiments as not sufficiently comparable to constitute a reliable basis for guiding clinical practice. Unfortunately, there have not been any studies carried out on differences between the motivation of the patient who comes for the hypnotic relief of pain and the subject who volunteers for a pain experiment in a university laboratory, because clinicians who treat patients and laboratory researchers who study subjects (generally college students) tend to inhabit different professional worlds.

Further investigations which extend and improve on our own are needed in order to determine whether measurement instruments used in laboratory experiments are indeed applicable to the clinic. Our results led to affirmative conclusions, but these need to be replicated and elaborated in the kind of detail that can only come from a much larger sample of patients than we were able to deal with in the Stanford study. If larger samples are gathered, there are some important types of studies to be made. For example, within each level of measured hypnotic responsiveness, there are those who profit more and those who profit less from hypnotherapy for pain. If these could be studied more extensively according to, say, three levels of hypnotizability—low, medium, and high—present data would suggest that the amount of pain reduction would vary by level. But that is not what would be most informative. Within each level, some would be more successful and some less successful in pain reduction, and these could be studied individually over the years in an established clinical program. Then the controversial issues could be settled on the basis of evidence.

For example, better norms of hypnotizability for random samples of well subjects could be compared with the norms for patients of the same age on the same scale. This comparison would throw light on the question of whether increased motivation due to the desire to get well among the patient group would indeed result in higher responsiveness scores. Care would have to be exercised to take into account other confounding influences, such as debilitation in the patient population, but with some ingenuity the hypnotic scores might be obtained when the patient was in remission.

Another issue to be faced is the role of resistance in reducing manifested hypnosis below the actual hypnotic potential. The research problem is to ascertain whether a low hypnotizability score is due to resistance and not to low talent for hypnosis, rather than to assign resistance as an excuse for failure. From the standpoint of research, the best way to do this is to find a number of patients whose low scores appear to be due to resistance, then to direct the initial therapy to the causes of the resistance rather than to attempt direct training in hypnotic skills. If, following such therapy, hypnotic responsiveness scores rise, there will be evidence that the full extent of hypnotic potential was not indicated in the original hypnotic testing. It is easy to demonstrate that deliberate resistance can reduce hypnotic scores just as it can reduce scores on intelligence tests. In many instances, hypnotic scores rise on a second test after the person taking the test feels more comfortable about it. This fact has given rise to the concept of plateau hypnotizability in laboratory studies; that is, the level achieved when hypnotizability stabilizes after a second testing (Shor, Orne, and O'Connell, 1966). Studies of plateau hypnosis indicate that some subjects continue to score low on the standard tests even under the most favorable of attitudinal conditions and practices. The presumption is that they lack the talent. In our own study, there were five patients who tested low in hypnotizability for whom pain was little changed by hypnotherapy. On the other hand, there were four patients who tested high in hypnotizability who also did not respond to hypnotherapy for their pain. With larger samples, efforts could be made to overcome possible resistance in those scoring low in order to determine whether or not some latent talent could become available to them, at which point, conceivably, they might also benefit from hypnotherapy. Similarly, in those scoring high, there may well be inhibiting factors that make their hypnotic talents less available for pain reduction. If this is interpreted as resistance, it is not a resistance to hypnosis *per se*, but as resistance to therapy, which is a second type of resistance. Only larger samples with careful studies of individual patients will serve both the purpose of establishing the underlying processes in hypnotherapy and of providing suggestions for improvement in hypnotherapeutic practices.

The Hypnotic Therapy of Pain

Among the desiderata for clinical research are a limited and specifiable set of symptoms that occur with sufficient frequency to be important in the history of human problems. Pain is so ubiquitous as to meet the requirement. The importance of specificity of symptoms is that they may be measured so that their change in intensity can be appraised. This also applies to pain. Furthermore, there must be some evidence through earlier experience that there are methods which appear to be effective in treatment; in other words, it is seldom that precision in therapy comes before there is evidence that benefit is likely to arise. As a psychological method, the history of successes with hypnotherapy has been great enough for years to justify further quantitative clinical studies.

Another requirement for clinical research on the therapy of pain is that the therapeutic practice must itself be subject to parametric study. For example, in studying the effectiveness of drugs as painkillers, one criterion could be a demonstration of dose-specificity, i.e., the greater the quantity of drug, the greater the effect. Such a demonstrated relationship would provide strong evidence that the drug is the effective agent. In the case of hypnosis, the criterion of a parametric relationship is met by the tests of hypnotizability; and if relief is proportional to measured hypnotic talent, this is equivalent in its own way to the dose-specific calibration of drugs.

Considerations such as these call attention to the feasibility of further research on the hypnotherapy of pain.

What topics of research, then, would broaden and enrich knowledge beyond the direction that our study took? Several problems appear to be representative of the many open for further research. The first concerns variations in hypnotherapeutic practice, such as use of direct or indirect suggestions, the pacing of therapeutic contacts, and the degree to which the patient takes initiative. Another pertains to problems related to pains of varying duration which require treatment over different lengths of time. Finally, research should be directed to a comparison of hypnotherapy with other behavioral therapies, such as biofeedback and behavior therapy.

Variations in Hypnotherapeutic Practice. Within methods that have the same general orientation, there are individual variants. This is certainly true of hypnotherapy where a range of practices exist. The best way to find out about the validity of the claims for one practice over another is to make a comparison between them by operators who are experienced in the methods under consideration. If the comparison indicated no general advantages of one method over another, the choice of method would be left to the preference of the hypnotherapist.

Direct and indirect suggestions in reference to hypnotizability. Milton Erickson (1952) proposed a distinction between direct and indirect suggestion. Joseph Barber gives an example of the difference. He notes that instead of the direct suggestion, "Your eyes are going to close," one might use an indirect suggestion: "I wonder if you will enjoy watching your eyelids begin to close, and if you do, I hope you'll notice how very comfortable it can be to let them remain closed." An indirect suggestion carries no implication of prior or special knowledge on the part of the clinician, since any response (including no reponse) is usually permitted. However, an invitation is offered for the subject to close his or her eyes and to enjoy the associated comfort (Barber, 1982, p. 45).

Barber is not averse to the use of direct suggestions—those which clearly indicate what the patient is supposed to do—if the indirect suggestions do not produce compliance. For example, he reports the case of a 66-year-old woman who had suffered for three years with severe pain related to metastatic cancer (Barber,1980). She had scored 0 on the SHCS: Adults (Morgan and J. Hilgard, 1978/79). After his indirect suggestion failed to prompt the patient to lift her arm to midair and leave it there, he resorted to a direct method. Barber lifted the arm and in order to keep it there, he said,*"And just leave it right there."* Later, after the patient failed to close her eyes following the indirect suggestion of "just watch your eyelids close," the hypnotist said,*"Just close them."* He now proposed to determine whether the arm would resist pressure to lower it, i.e., to exhibit what is known as arm catalepsy. As earlier commanded, the patient was still holding her arm up, and now the hypnotist suggested that she imagine a piece of wood floating in water . . . "You know that if you pressed down on the wood, it would just bounce back up, *right where it belongs."* The clinician pressed down lightly on the hand to assess the degree to which the pressure was counteracted, and the hand resisted "only slightly." Thus Barber's indirect suggestion had exerted little influence, for the patient already had been told to hold the arm up. These occasions for responding were the only points in which indirect suggestions were supposed to lead to observable responses. Since all failed, there was no clear evidence of involuntary response indicative of the dissociations which would identify the condition as hypnosis.

According to Barber, the use of indirect suggestion is much more effective with low hypnotizable patients than a direct approach, enabling such patients to experience various hypnotic phenomena. Barber states that:

> This must tell us that a susceptibility score reflects only responsiveness to a particular hypnotic approach and is not a predictor of general responsivity to hypnosis . . . (1982, p. 44).

In view of failure in the above case to show that the indirect methods yielded hypnotic responsiveness beyond that shown in the low susceptibility score, more evidence is needed to substantiate or refute Barber's claims.

There have been some studies designed to test the relative effectiveness of direct and indirect suggestions on hypnotic response. Three studies in a nonclinical setting indicate that the situation is still uncertain. Reyher and Wilson (1973) and Angelos (1978) found no overall differences in the effectiveness of the two methods of induction upon scores in hypnotic susceptibility. However, Alman and Carney (1980) conducted a study in which indirect suggestions proved more successful than direct suggestions in producing a response to the posthypnotic suggestion of itching on the neck, especially for females. Because the samples were small and the results marginally significant, the authors interpreted the results with caution. These studies bear on hypnotic response but not on therapeutic outcome.

Indirect suggestions, hypnotizability, and therapeutic outcome. Even if indirect suggestions prove to have no advantage over direct ones in their effect on hypnotic response, they may be advantageous in producing desired clinical outcomes such as pain reduction. In subsequent sessions with the woman patient described above, Barber gave indirect suggestions for increased comfort and decreased suffering. The first report of any improvement came after four sessions at weekly intervals when she explained that she slept better and awakened less often with the pain. "It's still there; I know it, but doesn't bother me so much now." This report is quite different from that expected of a highly hypnotizable patient. Barber's treatment was helpful to the patient and indicates why hypnotherapists, regardless of their position on measurement, do not reject patients who happen to score low on the tests. Nonspecific therapeutic factors such as the relationship to an understanding therapist are capable of producing a generally more cheerful, active, relaxed patient, which in the absence of any hypnotic dissociation, may lead to a significant diminution of suffering and perhaps some reduction in pain sensations. Treatment by a professional trained in hypnotherapy, however, does not imply that a successful psychological treatment has involved hypnosis.

A well-controlled test of the relevance of Barber's indirect method of pain control to measured hypnotizability has been provided in an investigation of the management of severe pain in 28 adult patients during hyperthermia treatment for advanced cancer (Reeves, Redd, Storm, and Menagawa, 1983). The patients were given the SHCS:Adult and subsequently were stratified into two groups—the low and the high hypnotizables. The therapeutic method for controlling pain followed Barber's (1977) practice of an indirect induction and posthypnotic suggestions for analgesia on the treatment days. The results were clearcut: The no-hypnosis controls group showed little change in their reported pain over four sessions, whether they were high or low in hypnotizability. The low hypnotizables in two days of attempted hypnosis reacted to hypnosis like the control patients. Only the high hypnotizables showed marked pain reduction on the two treatment days. These results are the clearest evidence that with severe pain, the benefits of hynotic treatment by Barber's methods are available to the high hypnotizables and are of little value to the low hypnotizables when there is measurement of hypnotic potential and a careful estimation of pain reduction.

Evidence for hypnotic dissociation arises within therapy as well as within hypnotic testing, even though it is more difficult to quantify. However, an experienced hypnotherapist seldom has difficulty in deciding whether a patient has been slightly, moderately, or highly responsive to hypnosis. This usually shows not only in objective behavior, but in the subjective reports upon questioning. If hypnosis is to be assigned a significant role in pain reduction, it is important to have some evidence of hypnotic dissociation beyond the fact that the patient becomes more comfortable. Others have noted that it is essential not to confuse hypnotic responsivity with treatment responsivity (Frischholz, Spiegel, and Spiegel, 1981).

Sharp contrasts between direct and indirect suggestions are somewhat artificial unless considered within a specific clinical and interpersonal context. There are other variables which play a role in defining how directive or permissive the therapist is perceived to be. In our work with children, the therapeutic methods placed great emphasis upon the child's own interests and experiences by inviting the child to initiate the fantasy. Whether or not our procedures were "indirect," they were clearly permissive. Yet there were situations in which brief instructions and commands were more effective. In fact, indirect suggestions themselves cover a number of different practices. Lankton and Lankton (1983) have pointed to ten different forms of indirect suggestions. The underlying issues can be better clarified by research taking into account all that is happening in the clinical encounter, rather than advocating one method and assigning a stereotyped definition to the other.

Research makes possible more accurate inferences of cause and effect relationships. Unless the patient's hypnotizability has been assessed, the only defensible statement is that something within the therapeutic interaction was associated with pain reduction. If hypnotic responsiveness was assessed and those scoring high in hypnotizability had greater pain reduction than those scoring low, then one can state with some confidence that hypnosis played an effective part in the pain reduction. If there was no relationship to assessed hypnotizability, it may be inferred that therapeutic variables not specific to hypnosis were responsible for the outcome. Research so designed bears upon the indirect versus direct methods only if the two methods show, in a carefully designed research comparison, that hypnotic factors are more effective in one method than in another.

The pacing of therapeutic contacts. Psychological treatment practices tend to divide, in the extreme, between brief therapies (as in behavior therapy) generally directed toward specific symptoms, and long-term therapies (as in psychoanalysis) directed toward insight and depth of understanding. Hypnotherapy sessions also range along this dimension from single-session treatments to the much longer hypnoanalysis. For some symptoms, such as the reduction of smoking, Spiegel (1970) recommended a single-session treatment, while Hall and Crasilneck (1970) proposed a four-session treatment. Hypnoanalytic sessions may occur several times a week for months or years (Fromm, 1983; Gill and Brenman, 1959; Wolberg, 1964).

In relieving the pain of bone marrow aspirations, our young patients showed that some could make their major gains in the first hypnotic session, some required two sessions, and in one instance, pain reduction was moderate until it became very substantial at the end of the fourth session. Cedercreutz and Uusitalo (1967) used hypnotherapy to treat 37 patients with phantom limb pain following amputation. For 20, the symptoms disappeared completely, while for an additional 10, there was some symptomatic improvement. In following patients up to eight years after treatment, only 8 of the 20 remained symptom-free, although 10 more of the total group reported they were still unimproved. This outcome suggests there was a need for refresher therapy in the interim.

Subsequent to hypnotherapy, Olness (1976) found it desirable to continue to talk with children who had been treated for habit problems. During telephone conversations on a regular basis, the patient reviewed self-hypnosis exercises and the therapist reinforced hypnotic suggestions. Orne (1983) showed that one patient whom he was treating hypnotherapeutically for pain from lesions of the spine profited immediately from her initial hypnotic session in which she also learned self-hypnosis. When she returned a week later, she reported that she had been pain-free for five days, but during the sixth day was no longer able to control the pain adequately. Her ability to control pain tended to wear off repeatedly, but the ability could be restored by the hypnotist's suggestions over the telephone—gradually needed only at longer intervals. On the basis of these and similar experiences, it would appear that the duration of therapeutic benefits from hypnosis is highly variable among patients, and that self-hypnosis in many instances is dependent upon a continuing relationship with the hypnotist.

The implication for research is that initial gains through hypnotherapy do not guarantee the endurance of an effect, and a therapist bears the responsibility for assisting in the maintenance of gains already made. Greater specificity about the amount of time to be devoted—both initially and subsequently—are subject to research.

Degree of patient initiative. Although hypnotherapeutic procedures can be described according to their stylistic character—direct vs indirect, authoritarian vs permissive—the significance of the content of the suggestions is important because the content to be emphasized in therapy can be selected in areas appropriate to the resources of the patient. Very little has been done about this in research with children, although many clinical practices are described.

A distinction can be made in the use of fantasies suggested on the basis of the hypnotist's experience of "what works" with children in general, versus those built upon the actual experiences of an individual child. One illustration of a therapist-initiated deepening technique is the image of a staircase and the fantasy of walking down the steps one at a time, while the clinician counts and adds verbal suggestions of comfort and relaxation. A common method of producing analgesia in children is that of fantasied (or hallucinated) "switches" in the brain that can be turned off by the patient to interrupt pain eliminating the passage of impulses through nerves represented in fantasy by wires (Olness and Gardner, 1978). We made extensive use of blowing out candles on a birthday cake to provide an experience that would counter pain through the vigorous blowing and the pleasant affect associated with the imagery. We also recognized that children responded readily to magic, as illustrated by the use of a "magic lotion." In all instances, the content is that which the *clinician* proposes. Another type of content, which we have used widely, is that which the *patient* proposes out of recalled or imagined experiences.

Our method of adapting fantasies to the resources of the patient began with the initial interview in which each individual's experiences and interests were explored. Next, in the course of rehearsal and treatment, the fantasy experiences to be employed were chosen. Instead of a conventional deepening experience, such as going down the stairs, deeper involvement in the hypnotic fantasy was created by assimilating into the fantasy the rich sensory accompaniment of the fantasied experience: the smell of roses, the wind on the face, the excitement of the race, and so on. Throughout the hypnotic fantasies, we encouraged a two-way communication with the patient who reported on the progress of the fantasy and listened to some appreciative comments or questions from the clinician, which helped to stimulate a continued development of the fantasy. At the same time, the ongoing report of the patient's thoughts provided a significant monitoring of the experience.

One role of research is to assess the efficacy of alternative approaches, each of which has already shown some measure of success. For example, while we have indicated our preference for a two-way process during the therapeutic intervention, we recognize the reported successes that appear to follow a hypnotist's monologue, with little monitoring of the patient's thought processes.

Our only experience with the phenomenon of continuous talking came in the course of observing a mother who successfully helped her daughter reduce pain in this way during a bone marrow aspiration. The mother captured the child's attention by embarking upon a fascinating monologue, thereby diverting attention from the pain (Chapter 6). Exactly what goes on in the patient during a long monologue by a hypnotherapist requires further investigation.

Pain in Childhood and Adolescence

Although children and adolescents belong to an age group with demonstrated ability to learn hypnotic methods for handling pain, relatively little research has been directed toward alleviating their feelings of pain. Many problems need to be addressed: among them are the psychological effects of inhibiting the overt signs of pain as children grow older, the treatment of different types of pain that vary in intensity and duration, and the comparative effectiveness of alternative therapies in relieving pain.

Felt Pain and Its Expression.   On the basis of data discussed earlier, it was evident that important changes with age were taking place in the overt expression of pain at about 10 years of age (Chapter 3). The greater self-control shown by the older patients reflected a general developmental shift toward inhibition of emotional behavior, as children tended to identify with acceptable adult standards (Huston, 1983).

The internal conflict that accompanies this shift in children from 9 to 11 years, an age range considered transitional in terms of pain expression, has been described by Schultz (1971). Boys of this age were asked how they felt when something happened to make them feel pain. Of 38 boys questioned, 28 stated that they were "nervous or afraid" and "wanted to cry but didn't," and 21 reported that they thought of themselves as "brave" in facing their pain. The changed attitudes of the older boys were indicated by the remarks they made: "Only babies cry, big boys don't cry." The responses of the girls were not too different from those of the boys, except that all 36 girls acknowledged that they were "nervous or afraid," and 19 said they "wanted to cry but didn't." Six girls , in contrast to two boys, admitted "wanting to cry and doing so." Probably because of the cultural differences in permissible expression, only 4 of the girls attributed their responses to bravery.

These questions illustrate the type that need to be asked of young patients who are actually facing painful periodic procedures. Rather than depend upon retrospective accounts, the research health specialist would be better able to integrate the patient's discussion of attitudes, inner feelings, and coping strategies if the discussion took place immediately after such a procedure. Due to regularly scheduled appointments, it would be possible to follow the course of anxieties, possibly expressed in symptoms of irritability, sleeplessness, headaches, nausea, or vomiting prior to the next procedure. These data could be correlated with age changes in an effort to understand what happens as the overt expressions of pain become inhibited.

The small differences in pain expression between older boys and girls can be accounted for by the differential treatment given boys and girls by their parents. Block (1978) compared reports of parent practices by parents of children between ages 3 and 18, with reports of young adults recalling their own parent's practices during their childhood. Samples from several northern European countries as well as from the United States were included. Differences in treatment of sons and daughters were consistently reported by four groups: mothers, fathers, adult sons, and adult daughters who reported that males more often than females were taught not to cry or express feelings.

The development of self-control, evidenced in control over the expression of pain, has been approached in other ways. Mischel and Mischel (1983) studied self-control through delay of gratification and reported that toward the end of their fifth year, children showed a growing preference for the kind of strategies that facilitate delay. A marked acceleration of this trend occurred between the third and sixth grades, a time that approximates the age span of 9 to 11, seen as transitional in the self-regulation of pain.

The more we know about felt pain—its developmental aspects, its expression, perhaps the emotional cost as expression is inhibited, types of coping strategies at different ages—the better we will be able to plan treatment programs that take into account the total context in which pain and anxiety occur.

Pain of Varying Duration. Pains are commonly classified into two major groups: *acute* pains, meaning those of recent onset and short duration, and *chronic* pains, meaning those that have persisted for a considerable length of time, often for months or years. In recent years, the concept of chronic pain has been expanded to include what is termed the *chronic pain syndrome.* Implied in this description is that the etiology of the pain is somewhat ambiguous. The symptoms of the patient's distress include not only the consequences of possible organic causes, but consequences of functional factors that serve other motivational or emotional needs. Because some chronic pains are clearly due to organic processes that make the pain persist, Orne (1983) has proposed that this variety of chronic pain be renamed *persistent pain* to distinguish it from the chronic pain syndrome.

Acute pain. For purposes of research on pain, brief painful procedures that are routinely repeated in the clinic are comparable to those produced by various forms of stimulation in the laboratory. For readers who are not familiar with the ways in which pain is commonly studied in the laboratory, we offer a brief summary. In *cold pressor pain,* the hand and arm are dipped in circulating ice water near 0° centigrade. Pain mounts rapidly and is severe within a minute. *Ischemic pain* is produced by a tourniquet to the upper arm in order to cut off the circulation of forearm and hand while the occluded muscles are exercised. This pain mounts gradually and becomes very severe within a few minutes. The Stanford Laboratory generally utilized the cold pressor and ischemic methods. In *electric shock,* a stimulator delivers a shock to a sensitive area. As used in the Stanford Profile Scales, the shock is delivered to an area between the thumb and forefinger; while the right hand is made analgesic through hypnotic suggestion, the left hand serves as its control. *Intense pressure on bone* is occasionally used as a pain stimulus, and other methods may be employed (E. Hilgard, 1978).

Bone marrow aspirations can produce acute pain, as can some lumbar punctures, intramuscular injections and some venipunctures. What the clinically induced pain has in common with the experimentally induced pain is that both are produced by a deliberate act of an outsider. The important difference is that the patient cannot control either the intensity or the duration of the pain, whereas the laboratory subject, whose commitment is voluntary, is free to terminate the pain at any time. For the patient, outside forces have determined and will continue to determine the course of treatment, and each painful procedure acts as a reminder of illness, even for the patient in remission. Furthermore, not only is it unclear how far into the future the painful procedures will be repeated, but the effect of repeating these short, painful procedures, as in bone marrow aspirations, is to some extent cumulative. That is, if a single experience has been distressful and anxiety-provoking, the anticipation of subsequent experiences may be increasingly anxiety-provoking for some patients unless successful pain relief can be instituted. Obviously, the emotional impact on the clinical patient differs from that on the laboratory volunteer.

Persistent pain. Thus far we have described brief pains commonly called "acute" because they rise to a maximum quickly and then are soon over. In Chapter 5, we discussed two patients suffering from persistent pain: Richard, whose large abdominal tumor exerted pressure on sensitive nerve endings, and Tom, who suffered from phantom limb pain after amputation of a leg. These cases are not common among young patients, but it is imperative that they be studied systematically when they do arise because the relief of persistent pain through psychological methods presents special difficulties not found in the treatment of brief episodic pains typical of bone marrow aspirations, bandage changes in burn patients, or drilling in dental patients.

Turner and Chapman (1982), after reviewing reports in the literature, noted the sparseness of scientific work in the hypnotic relief of persistent pain. Although hypnosis had been used longer than any other psychological method of analgesia, there were few clinical investigations that included quantitative data. There were a number of anecdotal reports during the 1950s, 1960s, and 1970s that attested to the relief of clinical pain. Sacerdote, for example, described treatments of eight patients with cancer or arthritis (1962), and four patients with diverse pain syndromes (1970), all of whom showed elimination of pain or considerable relief. For children and adolescents, clinicians such as Crasilneck and Hall (1976) and Gardner and Olness (1981) contributed valuable observations on the use of hypnosis in treating persistent pain.

Social and ethical considerations preclude subjecting well persons to long-enduring pain in the laboratory. Therefore, designing a research project on the use of hypnotherapy for persistent pain calls for the collaboration of clinical professionals, whether the researcher is a therapist working alone or a therapist working in a setting with access to a larger number of patients. In both situations, appropriate clinical cases arise sporadically but need to be systematically followed and reported. It is desirable for clinical research in persistent pain to be broadly designed. The kind of data required to make case reports—whether single or multiple—comparable with case reports by other clinicians, can be specified. They include the diagnosis and prior treatment history, the usual narrative material with respect to the patient and family, a baseline estimate of pain prior to therapy, a measure of the hypnotizability of the patient, a description of the actual procedures used, self-reports of pain in the course of treatment, and appropriate follow-up after termination of regular treatment. If there were advance agreements among therapists on the scales for pain and for measures of hypnotic responsiveness, then a statistical summary from diverse sources would be facilitated.

Because persistent pains differ widely in their origins and history, and in the extent to which they interfere with normal activities, useful generalizations can be made only if pains with similar diagnoses and similar consequences are grouped together. In clinical research it is not possible to reach ideal comparability, but it is important to achieve as much comparability as possible.

The researcher desiring to improve the research base in this field will carefully plan ways that clinical experiences can be reported in a disciplined way, assuring that essential and agreed upon data are collected and pooled, without doing violence to the therapist-patient relationship or disrupting the individual practices of the therapist. Case material based on less frequent diagnoses, and including patients of different ages could be accumulated to provide a data pool for analysis beyond the experience of any one practitioner. The single practitioner who reports each individual case in this way can make a firm contribution to research. Considerations with respect to single-case research designs have been discussed in detail by Kazdin and Tuma (1982).

The opportunities for research on persistent pain exist. To illustrate one research opportunity in this area, we have selected phantom limb pain.

Phantom limb pain: a persistent pain. Phantom limb pain was the prominent symptom in an 18-year-old patient whom we treated (Chapter 5). In a continuing program on an oncology unit, such cases arise because of amputations in connection with solid tumors. It would make sense to collaborate with orthopedic surgeons in a systematic study of young cancer patients who must undergo amputation. Some patients would develop phantom limb pain and some would not. Physical and psychological characteristics of both groups could be checked periodically to understand the natural course of events. Some phantom limb pain would clear spontaneously.

Although phantom pain results from an organic insult, that is, the severance of a portion of the body, and organic roots of the severed body part may persist, they are insufficient to explain the qualitative nature of the experience. The source of the qualitative differences in phantom pain is, at this time, not well understood. Often there has been pain felt in the limb before it is amputated. One suggestion to explain the pain in the phantom limb is that it reflects the pain felt in the limb prior to amputation. Melzack (1973) reports the striking case of a man who, enroute to emergency treatment for the removal of a wood sliver jammed under a fingernail, was in an accident that required the arm be removed. The phantom pain he later felt was a pain under the fingernail of his phantom limb.

Another suggestion to explain the nature of the pain depends upon fantasies about the condition of the amputated bodily member. After surgery, a woman, who was not informed about how her limbs would be disposed of after amputation, revealed in hypnotherapy that fantasies of incineration of the limbs had arisen (Solomon and Schmidt, 1978). The phantom pains she had experienced, and for which she had been referred, were of burning sensations in the lower extremities. This account calls attention to the importance of adequate discussion prior to surgery, discussion designed to elicit the individual patient's fears and specific attitudes about the disposition of amputated limbs.

Phantom pain may occur at any age. The patient we studied was 18 years old, but the sensation of a phantom limb has been reported in a child as young as 4 years old (Eland, 1974). The child told an interviewer that his right foot (the amputated one) had hurt earlier in the day. At this point his mother interrupted to tell the child that his foot could not hurt anymore because it was gone. In private, the interviewer explained to the mother that her son might be experiencing phantom limb pain, and asked her to record any further comments that the child might make about the amputated foot. On numerous occasions over the next few days the child commented on how the amputated foot hurt, itched, and felt as though a shoe were on too tight. This boy's description resembles that of phantom limb pain experienced by adults, with whom most of the studies of hypnotherapy in phantom limb pain have been done. This field of inquiry could begin early and extend as far into the life cycle as desired.

Our illustrations of phantom limb pain, the so-called "sensory-ghosts," have suggested some of the dimensions that research on the subject might take. These include:

1. The frequency and duration of the phantom as related to age, reason for the amputation, and location of it.

2. The specificity of the phantom in relation to the individual case history. Such specificity is suggested by references to the finger-sliver prior to its amputation, and to the fantasy of incineration of the limbs. It would be important to know the relative frequencies

of symptoms falling in various classes, of which those based on memories and on fantasies are but two of the possibilities.

3. Research on phantom limb pain should be part of a more general study of physical and psychological adjustments following the loss of a limb, such as changes in body image.

4. Treatment practices and their consequences. Orthopedic and psychological treatment could be coordinated, with orthopedic intervention directed to physical problems such as the neuromas which develop on the stump at the site of the amputation, and psychological treatment taking various forms such as hypnotherapy. A comprehensive treatment program would be directed not only to the phantom limb pain, but would take into account the reactions of the total individual reacting to a very traumatic experience.

The chronic pain syndrome. It is hoped that a study of persistent pain among young patients will contribute to a better understanding of the chronic pain syndrome that is so prevalent among adults. Close to onset, less established in patterns of reaction, and less complicated by considerations of secondary gain, persistent pain offers greater possibilities for the development of successful coping strategies than does chronic pain, as found in the chronic pain syndrome. Sometimes, however, continuing pain as it endures may lead to a chronic pain syndrome, a shift that can be studied within a broad framework of variables, such as the nature of the disease process, involvement of neurological structures, reactions of family members, and the personality of the patient. Hypnotherapy may be the treatment of choice, or it may serve an auxiliary function.

The proliferation of pain centers for adults over the past twenty years attests to the incidence of chronic pain in this age group, and the absence of such centers for children suggests that the chronic pain syndrome may be infrequent among individuals under age 20. From the two adult pain centers established in 1960, the pain-center concept exploded: There are now well over 1,000 adult pain clinics and pain centers in the United States. In contrast, only one center, associated with the Pediatrics Department at the Johns Hopkins Medical School, has been set up specifically for the problem of pain in childhood (B.L. Crue, personal communication, 1982).

It is probable that most of the persistent or recurrent pains in childhood are associated with a relatively small number of conditions, such as rheumatoid arthritis, sickle-cell disease, hemophilia, and cancer, which continue to be under active treatment by the family physician, with the patient also under parental care. Under these circumstances, few patients would qualify for a diagnosis of chronic pain syndrome, and centralized pain centers would not be needed.

Comparative Effectiveness of Alternative Psychological Therapies. If symptoms are responsive to psychological treatment, they can be treated by a number of methods, regardless of their organic or functional origin, and pain is no exception. Comparative studies which attempt to determine which of two or more methods are the most effective, are difficult to perform; but if well done, they provide information of great value. We have mentioned several such studies (Elton, Burrows, and Stanley, 1979; Stern, Brown, Ulett, and Sletten, 1977; Zeltzer and LeBaron, 1982). More are needed.

There are several difficulties which beset such studies. One of the favorite designs, which is to use an untreated control group, cannot answer the comparative question, for an untreated control group can simply demonstrate whether something in the way of treatment is better than nothing. We know from other types of therapy that a satisfied patient is no basis on which to judge the relative effectiveness of treatment, because any kind of care often is better than no care at all. Another control is the use of a placebo instead of a more active intervention. A placebo as a control has been standard in double-blind studies of drug action, double-blind in the sense that neither the patient or the physician knows whether the capsule administered is the active agent or the chemically inactive placebo. However, the use of placebos in the study of psychologically effective procedures is more difficult when the "effective" procedure is psychological, because placebos may also be psychologically "effective" when the physician believes in their effectiveness (Evans, 1984). In the one significant study of placebos compared with hypnotic analgesia, for the hypnotizable subjects, hypnosis was far superior (McGlashan, Evans and Orne, 1969).

The ideal program is to compare methods which are known to be effective, and then determine which works best. This is the most difficult research design under which to produce positive results because it is harder to prove that one satisfactory method is better than another satisfactory method than to prove that it is better than no treatment or a placebo. Why, then should a comparison be attempted? The answer is that one method may not be universally better than another, but it may be demonstrably better than another for some patients or in the treatment of some complaints, including pains of different origin or of different intensity.

Where We Now Stand

Because this chapter describes work ahead of us in the form of research, we do not wish to lose sight of advances already achieved. An understanding of hypnosis, based on laboratory research and clinical investigation, has provided a firm foundation for what lies ahead.

Hypnosis stands alone as a psychological method in which the degree of talent for it and for profiting from treatment have been measured.

Investigations to date suggest that the degree of pain relief to be anticipated in hypnotherapy is related to the degree of talent that the patient possesses. Fortunately, children are highly talented in their hypnotic skills. It is increasingly evident that the amount of measurable hypnotic ability needed to relieve pain varies with the degree of pain that is experienced. The pain of bone marrow aspirations requires a high degree of talent, that in lumbar punctures somewhat less, while most venipunctures and "finger sticks" qualify as minor pains. None of these statements can be regarded as a firm conclusion, but the directional arrows are clear.

The measurement of hypnotic talent becomes useful not only in relation to pain reduction in hypnotherapy but also in relation to pain reduction by psychological methods thought to be nonhypnotic, such as acupuncture, relaxation, or guided imagery. When these techniques show outcomes positively correlated with measured hypnotizability, similar underlying mechanisms for the control of pain can be inferred.

While there is still much to be learned about the components of hypnotic talent, the major conponent in childhood hypnosis, and probably in adult hypnosis as well, is the utilization of fantasy. It is possible to unravel types of fantasy that feed into the hypnotic process, i.e., capacities for receptive imagination and for self-initiated imagination. Fantasied involvements permit the acceptance of temporary reality distortion and tolerance of logical inconsistencies. We can understand better the rapt attention of the hypnotized person as we observe the extent to which it has been bound since earliest childhood to immersion in fantasied experiences outside of hypnosis and is now available for use within hypnosis.

Throughout the history of hypnosis, many have repeatedly noted the heightened suggestibility of the hypnotized person. We believe that our experience provides an explanation for this by way of enhanced fantasy. Once a child has become involved in a fantasied experience which has only loose ties to reality, what the hypnotist suggests can readily be incorporated in the child's fantasy—more readily than if the fantasy had not already been activated.

The effective use of hypnosis requires a theoretical framework that is broad enough to encompass the range of experiences of the hypnotizable person while specific enough to demarcate hypnosis from other domains of psychology. The concept of dissociation serves very well to explain the phenomena of hypnosis, while avoiding the persistent controversies over state-nonstate theories.

Because of our concentration on the problem of pain and other distress connected with cancer, we have not dealt with the many other conditions for which hypnotherapy is used. It has been shown to be successful in systematic studies of asthma, warts, and phobic reactions. It has frequently been successful in tension and migraine headaches, sleep disturbances, tics, and functional disorders of many types. However, because pain poses the most severe test for any psychological method of treatment, the demonstrated utility of hypnotherapy in this connection has offered unusual opportunities for evaluating the preferred clinical methods of the hypnotherapist.

We know that hypnotherapy flourishes best in an atmosphere where physicians, parents, patients, nurses, social workers, psychologists, and psychiatrists, all participate in a broad-based and coordinated treatment plan. The medical model of the past, where the authority and full responsibility for all decisions rested with the physician, is giving way to a team approach responsive to the needs of the young patient and the family.

Continuing programs are needed to help children and adolescents in pain, whether the pain is related to cancer or to other conditions in which pain is a problem. The more soundly these programs are associated with research, the greater their chances for increased effectiveness.

APPENDIX A. *Accreditation of Hypnotic Services*

For 25 years the disciplines of medicine and psychology have recognized the scientific status of hypnosis: the British Medical Association in 1955, the American Medical Association in 1958, and the American Psychological Association in 1960.

The establishment of scientific societies with high standards of membership represented a step toward greater protection of the public. In the United States, two professional societies and a division of the American Psychological Association devote their efforts to promoting the scientific understanding of clinical and experimental hypnosis. Qualifications for membership include competence in hypnosis as well as appropriate standing within one of the following professions: medicine, dentistry, or psychology. Thus the societies are composed of specialists who possess proper credentials in hypnosis and they can provide information about members practicing in a local area. It is best for those who desire hypnotic therapy to seek professional advice before selecting self-advertised hypnotherapists; some may be adequately trained but many are not.

Inquiries can be addressed to:

> The American Society of Clinical Hypnosis
> 2250 East Devon Avenue, Suite 218
> Des Plaines, Illinois   60018

> The Society for Clinical and Experimental Hypnosis
> 129-A Kings Park Drive
> Liverpool, New York   13088

> The American Psychological Association
> Division 30, Psychological Hypnosis
> 1200 Seventeenth Street, N.W.
> Washington, D.C.   20036

Outside the United States the hypnotic societies which correspond most closely to those listed above are affiliated with the International Society of Hypnosis. A directory of affiliated societies and its current members is available from:

> The International Society for Hypnosis
> c/o Unit for Experimental Psychiatry
> 111 North 49th Street
> Philadelphia, Pennsylvania   19139

APPENDIX B. *Acupuncture, Behavior Therapy, and Biofeedback*

Acupuncture

The Chinese practice of acupuncture for the relief of pain dramatically came to the attention of the American public in 1971 when James Reston, a *New York Times* columnist, described his emergency appendectomy in China under normal anesthesia, with postoperative pain relieved by acupuncture. For Reston's postappendectomy pain, the needles were positioned into the outer part of his right elbow and below each knee. In other words, the proper meridian points for insertion may be located some distance from the area of pain. Once the needles are correctly placed, the acupuncturist manipulates them either by mechanical means or by electrical stimulation to activate the sensitive points. Bonica (1974) reported that when acupuncture analgesia was used in China, after careful screening of potential patients, only 10 percent of surgical patients were selected to receive it.

At present the efficacy of acupuncture in the relief of pain is unclear. The findings of Knox and associates (1977, 1979, 1981) are representative of a number of laboratory studies. They found that acupuncture was a weak analgesic in the relief of cold pressor pain, but even this slight effect depended in part on procedures designed to enhance a subject's expectations of success. In their 1981 study, the stimulation of true acupuncture points was no more effective than the stimulation of placebo or false acupuncture points (Knox and associates, 1981). On the other hand, another group of investigators showed that subjects could reduce experimentally produced mild dental pain through properly placed needles, in contrast to subjects who were unable to reduce the same degree of pain when needles were improperly placed (Chapman and associates, 1976). In a clinical study, the success of acupuncture analgesia varied with the *kind* of pain: better in

225

headaches, tennis elbow, and shoulder pain than in the persistent pains in the lower back and neck (Katz and associates, 1974).

In some studies where hypnotizability was evaluated, successful responses to acupuncture were related to higher levels of hypnotizability (Knox, 1981).

Behavior Therapy

In behavior therapy, a therapist rewards (thereby "reinforces") changes in a desired direction and ignores (thereby "extinguishes") repetitions of undesired behavior. For example, if a patient is spending too much time in bed, the patient is rewarded when walking and ignored when in bed. The success of therapy can be judged by the increased amount of "up time."

Early in the 1970s, Fordyce stimulated interest in applying the learning principles exemplified in operant conditioning methods to the treatment of chronic pain (Fordyce, 1978). Working with an inpatient hospital population, he demonstrated a decrease in the patients' tendency to grimace, moan, and make pain-related statements when hospital staff withdrew attention from them, and a subsequent increase when staff renewed their attention. Health care providers and the patient's family were advised to pay as little attention as possible to complaints of pain and, instead, praise behavior leading to greater participation in activities and responsibilities. This therapeutic method is now widely used in pain clinics designed to treat adults, many of whom have suffered chronic pain for years. Through participation in activities, patients are expected to live more normally in the presence of their pain and perhaps to be less aware of it.

In addition to Fordyce, investigators such as Cairns and Pasino (1977), who treated chronic low back pain, have reported a considerable degree of success with patients who were carefully selected for the programs.

In behavior therapy as traditionally conceived, the patient assumes less responsibility than the therapist; much of what is accomplished by the patient depends upon manipulation of the social environment by the therapist, who arranges for the presence or absence of reinforcements. However, with the addition of cognitive strategies, such as expectation, the proposed therapies give the patient more responsibility (Turner and Chapman, 1982).

Biofeedback

In biofeedback training, individuals receive direct information (feed-back) about their own physiological responses to pain, such as increases in muscle tension, heart rate, or blood pressure, which they are normally unaware of and which, with the help of the feedback information, they learn to control. As an example, in tension headaches the muscles of the head and neck may be tight or contracted. If these muscles can be relaxed, the headache will lessen or disappear. With tension in the frontalis, or forehead muscle, as an indicator, electrodes are attached to the forehead so that any movement of the muscle is electrically recorded, amplified, and fed back to the individual as an auditory signal. The signal or tone increases in pitch when the muscle contracts and decreases when it relaxes. Through their own voluntary monitoring, patients learn how to prolong the muscular relaxation that relieves the tension. When this happens, the headache diminishes or disappears.

An alternative method used in feedback training is finger temperature, measured by a thermistor attached to one finger. Anxiety can lead to peripheral vasoconstriction, as represented by the cold hands of the frightened person. Studies have shown that finger temperature and forehead temperature have an inverse relationship, so that increasing finger temperature will be associated with decreasing forehead temperature. Such a combination leads to increased relaxation and decreased anxiety. This method of biofeedback has often been used successfully in the relief of migraine headache pain where vasodilation of the cerebral blood vessels underlies the symptomatology. Two major areas of pain reduction for which biofeedback has been used, in fact, are tension and migraine headaches (Orne, 1980).

The goal of biofeedback—in which the patient attempts to reduce heart rate and blood pressure—has characteristics of voluntary selection; because of this forward goal direction, it has sometimes been referred to as a "feedforward" technique (Pribram, 1976). The specificity of biofeedback training is still unclear, since in some instances the same results that biofeedback produces can be achieved through relaxation. Yates (1980) remarks on the fact that the literature on biofeedback contains almost no empirical studies relating to chronic pain.

One of the clearest ways in which biofeedback differs from hypnosis is that the biofeedback patient becomes increasingly sensitive to the physiological processes that are being monitored and uses that heightened awareness to exercise control. In hypnosis, the patient shifts attention away from physiological indicators, as in the hypnotic denial of pain even when the organic source of the pain persists.

References and Index to Authors of Works Cited

The boldface numerals following each reference indicate the pages in the text on which the reference provides a background for the discussions.

ABU-SAAD, H., and HOLZEMER, W. L. (1981) Measuring children's self-assessment of pain. *Issues in Comprehensive Pediatric Nursing, 5:* 337–349. **19, 135**

ALMAN, B. M., and CARNEY, R. E. (1980) Consequences of direct and indirect suggestions on success of posthypnotic behavior. *The American Journal of Clinical Hypnosis, 23:* 112–118. **208**

ALTMAN, A. J. and SCHWARTZ, A. D. (1978) Malignant diseases of infancy, childhood, and adolescence. vol. 18 in the series: *Major problems in clinical pediatrics.* Philadelphia: W. B. Saunders Co. **14**

ALWITT, L. F., ANDERSON, D. R., LORCH, E. P., and LEVIN, S. R. (1980) Preschool children's visual-attention to attributes of television. *Human Communication Research, 7:* 52–67. **170**

ANDERSON, D. R. (1979) Active and passive processes in children's television viewing. Paper presented at the American Psychological Association annual meeting, New York, September, 1979. **170**

ANDERSON, D. R., and LEVIN, S. R. (1976) Young children's attention to "Sesame Street." *Child Development, 47:* 806–811. **170**

ANDREOPOULOS, S. (1982) Hodgkin's success story: How they did it. *Campus Report,* Stanford University, May 12, 1982, 9–12. **15**

ANGELOS, J. A. (1978) "A comparison of the effect of direct and indirect methods of hypnotic induction on the perception of pain." Doctoral dissertation, California School of Professional Psychology, San Diego, California, 1978. **208**

BANYAI, E. I., and HILGARD, E. R. (1976) A comparison of active-alert hypnotic induction with traditional relaxation induction. *Journal of Abnormal Psychology, 85:* 218–224. **7, 149**

BARABASZ, A. F. (1982) Restricted environmental stimulation and the enhancement of hypnotizability: Pain, EEG, alpha, skin conductance and temperature responses. *International Journal of Clinical and Experimental Hypnosis, 30:* 147–166. **32**

BARBER, J. (1977) Rapid induction analgesia: A clinical report. *American Journal of Clinical Hypnosis, 19:* 138–147. **166, 209**

BARBER, J. (1980) Hypnosis and the unhypnotizable. *American Journal of Clinical Hypnosis, 23:* 4–9. **207**

BARBER, J. (1982) Incorporating hypnosis in the management of chronic pain. In J. Barber and C. Adrian (eds.) *Psychological approaches to the management of pain.* New York: Brunner/Mazel. **207, 208**

BARBER, T. X. (1979) Suggested ("hypnotic") behavior: The trance paradigm versus an alternative paradigm. In E. Fromm and R. E. Shor (eds.) *Hypnosis: Developments in research and new perspectives.* New York: Aldine Publishing Company. **159**

BARBER, T. X., and WILSON, S. C. (1978/79) The Barber Suggestibility Scale and the Creative Imagination Scale: Experimental and Clinical Applications. *American Journal of Clinical Hypnosis, 21:* 84–108. **148, 150**

BARNETT, M. A., KING, L. M., HOWARD, J. A. and DINO, G. A. (1980) Empathy in young children: Relation to parents' empathy, affection, and emphasis on the feelings of others. *Developmental Psychology, 16:* 243–244. **127**

BARTLETT, F. C. (1920) Psychology in relation to the popular story. *Folklore, 30:* 264–293. **140**

BEECHER, H. K. (1956) Relationship of significance of wound to pain experienced. *Journal of the American Medical Association: 161,* 1609–1613. **123**

BENSON, H., BERRY, J. F., and CAROL, M. P. (1974) The relaxation response. *Psychiatry, 37:* 37–46. **149**

BERNICK, S. M. (1972) Relaxation, suggestion, and hypnosis in dentistry. *Pediatric Dentistry, 11:* 72–75. **21**

BERNSTEIN, N. R. (1963) Management of burned children with the aid of hypnosis. *Journal of Child Psychology and Psychiatry, 4:* 93–98. **21**

BERNSTEIN, N. R. (1965) Observations on the use of hypnosis with burned children on a pediatric ward. *International Journal of Clinical and Experimental Hypnosis, 13:* 1–10. **21**

BLOCK, J. H. (1978) Another look at sex differentiation in the socialization behaviors of mothers and fathers. In J. Sherman and F. L. Denmark (eds.) *The psychology of women: Further directions of research.* New York: Psychological Dimensions. **213**

BONICA, J. J. (1974) Acupuncture anesthesia in the People's Republic of China. *Journal of the American Medical Association, 229:* 1317–1325. **225**

BRODZINSKY, D. M. (1977) Conceptual tempo as an individual difference variable in children's humour development. In A. J. Chapman and H. C. Foot (eds.) *It's a funny thing, humour.* Oxford, England: Pergamon Press. **179**

BRYANT, J., ZILLMAN, D., and BROWN, D. (1983) Entertainment features in children's educational television: Effects on attention and information acquisition. In J. Bryant and D. R. Anderson (eds.) *Children's understanding of television: Research on attention and comprehension.* New York: Academic Press. **181**

BUSS, D. M., BLOCK, J. H., and BLOCK, J. (1980) Preschool activity level: Personality correlates and developmental implications. *Child Development, 51:* 401–408. **187**

CAIRNS, D., and PASINO, J. (1977) Comparison of verbal reinforcement and feedback in the operant treatment of disability due to chronic pain. *Behavior Therapy, 8:* 621–630. **226**

CEDERCREUTZ, C., and UUSITALO, E. (1967) Hypnotic treatment of phantom sensations in 37 amputees. In J. Lassner (ed.) *Hypnosis and psychosomatic medicine.* New York: Springer-Verlag. **90, 210**

CHAPMAN, C. R., WILSON, M. E., and GEHRIG, J. D. (1976) Comparative effects of acupuncture and transcutaneous stimulation on the perception of painful dental stimuli. *Pain, 2:* 265–283. **225**

CHEN, A. C. N., DWORKIN, S. F., and BLOOMQUIST, D. S. (1981) Cortical power spectrum analysis of hypnotic pain control in surgery. *International Journal of Neuroscience, 13:* 127–136. **193**

COOPER, L. M. (1979) Hypnotic amnesia. In E. Fromm and R. E. Shor (eds.) *Hypnosis: Developments in research and new perspectives.* New York: Aldine Publishing Company. **201**

COOPER, L. M., and LONDON, P. (1978/79) The Children's Hypnotic Susceptibility Scale. *American Journal of Clinical Hypnosis, 21:* 170–185. **199**

COWHERD, M. (1977) One child's reaction to acute pain: Nursing intervention. *Nursing Clinics of North America, 12:* 639–643. **129, 135**

CRASILNECK, H. B., and HALL, J. A. (1975) *Clinical hypnosis: Principles and applications.* New York: Grune and Stratton. **22, 23, 215**

DEUTSCH, F. and MADLE, R. A. (1975) Empathy: Historic and current conceptualizations, measurement, and a cognitive theoretical perspective. *Human Development, 18:* 267–287. **127**

EDMONSTON, W. E., Jr. (1981) *Hypnosis and relaxation: Modern verification of an old equation.* New York: John Wiley and Sons, Inc. **149**

ELAND, J. M. (1974) "Children's communication of pain." Unpublished master's thesis, University of Iowa. Reported in A. K. Jacox (1977) *Pain: A source book for nurses and other health professionals.* Boston: Little, Brown and Company. **217**

ELAND, J. M. and ANDERSON, J. E. (1977) The experience of pain in children. In A. K. Jacox (ed.) *Pain: A source book for nurses and other health professionals.* Boston: Little, Brown and Company. **18, 125, 135, 137**

ELLENBERG, L., KELLERMAN, J., DASH, J., HIGGINS, G., and ZELTZER, L. (1980) Use of hypnosis for multiple symptoms in an adolescent girl with leukemia. *Journal of Adolescent Health Care, 1:* 132–136. **24**

ELLSWORTH, P. C., and ROSS, L. (1976) Intimacy in response to direct gaze. *Journal of Experimental and Social Psychology, 11:* 592–613. **139**

ELTON, D., BURROWS, G. D., and STANLEY, G. V. (1979) Hypnosis in the management of chronic pain. In G. D. Burrows, D. R. Collison, L. Dennerstein (eds.) *Hypnosis 1979: Proceedings of the Eighth International Congress of Hypnosis and Psychosomatic Medicine,* Melbourne, Australia, August 19–24, 1979. Amsterdam, New York, Oxford: Elsevier/North Holland Biomedical Press. **20, 219**

ERICKSON, M. H. (1952) Deep hypnosis and its induction. In L. LeCron (ed.) *Experimental hypnosis.* New York: Macmillan. **150**

ERICKSON, M. H. (1967) An introduction to the study and application of hypnosis for pain control. In J. Lassner (ed.) *Hypnosis and psychosomatic medicine.* New York: Springer-Verlag. **207**

ERICKSON, M. H. (1980) *The collected papers of Milton H. Erickson on hypnosis.* Edited by Ernest L. Rossi, 4 vols. New York: Irvington Publishers, Inc. **160**

ESTABROOKS, G. H. (1957) *Hypnotism.* New York: Dutton. **162**

EVANS, F. J. (1984) Expectancy, therapeutic instructions, and the placebo response. in L. White, B. Tursky, and G. F. Schwartz (eds.) *Placebo: Clinical phenomena and new insights.* New York: Guilford Press. **219**

EVANS, F. J., and ORNE, M. T. (1971) The disappearing hypnotist: The use of simulating subjects to see how subjects perceive the experimental procedures. *International Journal of Clinical and Experimental Hypnosis, 19:* 277–296. **33**

EVANS, M. B., and PAUL, G. L. (1970) Effects of hypnotically suggested analgesia on physiological and subjective responses to cold stress. *Journal of Consulting and Clinical Psychology, 35:* 362–371. **153**

FEIN, G. G. (1981) Pretend play in childhood: An integrative review. *Child Development, 52:* 1095–1118. **173**

FORDYCE, W. E. (1978) Learning processes in pain. In R. A. Sternbach (ed.) *The psychology of pain.* New York: Raven Press. **226**

FOULKES, D. (1982) *Children's dreams: Longitudinal studies.* New York: Wiley. **201**

FREUD, S. (1905) *Der Witz und seine Beziehung zum Unbewussten.* Leipzig and Vienna: Deutiche. Translated and reprinted as *Jokes and their relation to the unconscious.* New York: Norton, 1960. **179**

FRISCHHOLTZ, E. J., SPIEGEL, H., and SPIEGEL, D. (1981) Hypnosis and the unhypnotizable: A reply to Barber. *The American Journal of Clinical Hypnosis, 24:* 55–58. **209**

FROMM, E. (1979) Quo vadis hypnosis? Predictions of future trends in hypnosis research. In E. Fromm and R. E. Shor (eds.) *Hypnosis: Developments in research and new perspectives,* 2nd ed. New York: Aldine Publishing Company. **195**

FROMM, E. (1983) Theory and practice of hypnoanalysis. Invited address delivered at the American Psychological Association Meeting, August 28, 1983, Anaheim, California. **210**

GARDNER, G. G. (1976) Childhood, death, and human dignity: Hypnotherapy for David. *International Journal of Clinical and Experimental Hypnosis, 24:* 122–139. **23, 96**

Gardner, G. G., and Olness, K. (1981) *Hypnosis and hypnotherapy with children.* New York: Grune and Stratton. **21, 23, 24, 96, 215**

Gill, M. M., and Brenman, M. (1959) *Hypnosis and related states.* New York: International Universities Press, Inc. **150, 158, 210**

Gilot, F., and Lake, C. (1964) *Life with Picasso.* New York: McGraw-Hill. **155**

Groos, K. (1901) *The play of man.* Translation with the author's cooperation by Elizabeth L. Baldwin, with a preface by J. Mark Baldwin. New York: D. Appleton and Company. **1**

Gruenewald, D., Fromm, E., and Oberlander, M. I. (1979) Hypnosis and adaptive regression: An ego-psychological inquiry. In E. Fromm and R. E. Shor (eds.) *Developments in research and new perspectives.* New York: Aldine Publishing Company. **159**

Haber, R. N. (1979) Twenty years of haunting eidetic imagery: Where's the ghost? *The Behavioral and Brain Sciences, 2:* 583–594. **193**

Haley, J. (1958) An interactional explanation of hypnosis. *American Journal of Clinical Hypnosis, 1:* 41–57. **148**

Hall, J. A., and Crasilneck, H. B. (1970) Development of a hypnotic technique for treating chronic cigarette smoking. *International Journal of Clinical and Experimental Hypnosis, 18:* 283–289. **210**

Haslam, D. R. (1969) Age and the perception of pain. *Psychonomic Science, 15:* 86–87. **137**

Henning, J., and Fritz, G. K. (1983) School reentry in childhood cancer. *Psychosomatics, 24:* 261–269. **136**

Hilgard, E. R. (1965) *Hypnotic susceptibility.* New York: Harcourt, Brace, and World, Inc. **10, 160**

Hilgard, E. R. (1973) A neodissociation interpretation of pain reduction in hypnosis. *Psychological Review, 80:* 396–411. **161**

Hilgard, E. R. (1977a) *Divided consciousness: Multiple controls in human thought and action.* New York: John Wiley and Sons, Inc. **3, 150, 161, 162**

Hilgard, E. R. (1977b) The problem of divided consciousness. A neodissociation interpretation. *Annals of the New York Academy of Sciences, 296:* 48–59. **161**

Hilgard, E. R. (1978) Pain perception in man. In R. Held, H. W. Leibowitz, and H. L. Teuber (eds.) *Perception (Handbook of sensory physiology),* vol. 3. New York: Springer-Verlag. **214**

Hilgard, E. R. (1984) Book review of the collected papers of Milton H. Erickson on hypnosis, 4 vols. Edited by E. L. Rossi. *Journal of Clinical and Experimental Hypnosis,* in press. **160**

Hilgard, E. R., Crawford, H. J., and Wert, A. (1979) The Stanford Hypnotic Arm Levitation Test (SHALIT): A six-minute induction and measurement scale. *International Journal of Clinical and Experimental Hypnosis, 27:* 111–124. **8, 200**

Hilgard, E. R., and Hilgard, J. R. (1975/83) *Hypnosis in the relief of pain.* Los Altos, California: William Kaufmann, Inc. **19, 194**

HILGARD, E. R., MORGAN, A. H., and MACDONALD, H. (1975) Pain and dissociation in the cold pressor test: A study of hypnotic analgesia with "hidden reports" through automatic key pressing and automatic talking. *Journal of Abnormal Psychology, 84:* 280–289. **162**

HILGARD, J. R. (1970/79) *Personality and hypnosis: A study of imaginative involvement.* Chicago and London: The University of Chicago Press. **11**

HILGARD, J. R. (1974) Imaginative involvement: Some characteristics of the highly hypnotizable and the non-hypnotizable. *International Journal of Clinical and Experimental Hypnosis, 22:* 138–156. **155**

HILGARD, J. R., and HILGARD, E. R. (1962) Developmental-interactive aspects of hypnosis: Some illustrative cases. *Genetic Psychology Monographs, 66:* 143–178. **167**

HILGARD, J. R., and LEBARON, S. (1982) Relief of anxiety and pain in children and adolescents with cancer: Quantitative measures and clinical observations. *International Journal of Clinical and Experimental Hypnosis, 30:* 417–442. **51, 56**

HILGARD, J. R., and MORGAN, A. H. (1965) Interviews and hypnotic testing of six families. Stanford Laboratory of Research in Hypnosis. Unpublished. **168, 170, 203**

HILGARD, J. R., and MORGAN, A. H. (1976; 1978) Treatment of anxiety and pain in childhood cancer through hypnosis. Paper presented at the 7th International Congress of Hypnosis and Psychosomatic Medicine in Philadelphia, 1976. In F. H. Frankel and H. S. Zamansky (eds.) (1978) *Hypnosis at its bicentennial.* New York: Plenum Press. **43, 168**

HULL, C. L. (1933) *Hypnosis and suggestibility: An experimental approach.* New York: Appleton-Century-Crofts. **160**

HUNTER, I. M. L. (1981) Imagery and imagination in American psychology. *Journal of Mental Imagery, 5:* 40–42. **140**

HUSTON, A. C. (1983) Sex-typing. In P. H. Mussen (ed.) *Handbook of child psychology,* vol. 4. New York: Wiley. **213**

ISEN, A. M. (1970) Success, failure, attention, and reaction to others: The warm glow of success. *Journal of Personality and Social Psychology, 15:* 294–301. **131**

ISEN, A. M., and LEVIN, P. F. (1972) Effect of feeling good on helping: Cookies and kindness. *Journal of Personality and Social Psychology, 21:* 384–388. **143**

IWANAGA, M. (1973) Development of interpersonal play structures in 3, 4, and 5 year old children. *Journal of Research and Development in Education, 6:* 71–82. **174**

IZZARD, R. (1955) *The Abominable Snowman.* New York: Doubleday. **141**

JANET, P. (1889) *L'Automatisme psychologique.* Paris: Felix Alcan. **3**

JOHNSON, J. E., KIRCHHOFF, K. T., and ENDRESS, M. P. (1975) Altering children's distress behavior during orthopedic cast removal. *Nursing Research, 24:* 404–410. **126, 135**

KATZ, R. L., KAO, C. Y., SPEIGEL, H., and KATZ, G. L. (1974) Pain, acupuncture, hypnosis. In J. J. Bonica (ed.) *Advances in neurology,* vol. 4. New York: Raven Press. **226**

KATZ, E. R., KELLERMAN, J., and SIEGEL, S. E. (1980) Behavioral distress in children with cancer undergoing medical procedures: Developmental considerations. *Journal of Consulting and Clinical Psychology, 47:* 356–365. **45, 54**

KAZDIN, A. E., and TUMA, A. H. (eds.) (1982) *Single-case research designs.* San Francisco, Washington, London: Jossey-Bass, Inc. **216**

KELLERMAN, J., ZELTZER, L., ELLENBERG, L., and DASH, J. (1983) Adolescents with cancer: Hypnosis for the reduction of the acute pain and anxiety associated with medical procedures. *Journal of Adolescent Health Care, 4:* 76–81. **25**

KINSBOURNE, M., and HISCOCK, M. (1978) Cerebral lateralization and cognitive development. In J. S. Chall and A. F. Mirsky (eds.) *Education and the brain.* Chicago, Illinois: University of Chicago Press. **194**

KLÜVER, H. (1933) Eidetic imagery. In C. Murchison (ed.) *Handbook of child psychology.* Worcester, Massachusetts: Clark University Press. **193**

KNOX, V. J., and GEKOSKI, W. L. (1981) Analgesic effect of acupuncture in high and low hypnotizables. Paper presented at the Society for Clinical and Experimental Hypnosis, October, 1981, Portland, Oregon. **225, 226**

KNOX, V. J., GEKOSKI, W. L., SHUM, K., and McLAUGHLIN, D. M. (1981) Analgesia for experimentally induced pain: Multiple sessions of acupuncture compared to hypnosis in high- and low-susceptible subjects. *Journal of Abnormal Psychology, 90:* 28–34. **225, 226**

KNOX, V. J., HANDFIELD-JONES, C. E., and SHUM, K. (1979) Subject expectancy and the reduction of cold pressor pain with acupuncture and placebo acupuncture. *Psychosomatic Medicine, 41:* 477–486. **225**

KNOX, V. J., SHUM, K., and McLAUGHLIN, D. M. (1977) Response to cold pressor pain and to acupuncture analgesia in Oriental and Occidental subjects. *Pain, 4:* 49–57. **225**

KOOCHER, G. P. and O'MALLEY, J. E. (1981) *The Damocles Syndrome.* New York: McGraw-Hill. **16**

KORNER, A. F. (1982) Individual differences at birth: Implications for later development. Paper presented on November 13, 1982, at the Second Annual Interdisciplinary Symposium on Development, Stanford University, Palo Alto, California. **187**

KROGER, W. S. (1977) *Clinical and experimental hypnosis in medicine, dentistry, and psychology,* 2nd ed. Philadelphia: Lippincott. **56**

KUPST, M. J., SCHULMAN, J. L., MAWRER, H., HONIG, G., MORGAN, E., and FOCHTMAN, D. (in press, 1984) Family coping with pediatric leukemia: A two-year follow-up. *Journal of Pediatric Psychology.* **32**

LaBAW, W. C. (1973) Adjunctive trance therapy with severely burned children. *International Journal of Child Psychotherapy, 2:* 80–92. **21**

LaBAW, W. C., HOLTON, C., LOWELL, K., and ECCLES, D. (1975) The use of selfhypnosis by children with cancer. *American Journal of Clinical Hypnosis, 17:* 233–238. **24**

LANKTON, S., and LANKTON, C. (1983) *The answer within: A clinical framework to Ericksonian hypnotherapy.* New York: Bruner/Mazel. **210**

LAURENCE, J. R., and PERRY, C. (1981) The "hidden observer" phenomenon in hypnosis: Some additional findings. *Journal of Abnormal Psychology, 90:* 334–344. **163**

LEBARON, S., and ZELTZER, L. (1983) "Developmental factors in the use of fantasy for relief of pain and anxiety in children with cancer." Paper presented at the annual scientific meeting of the American Society of Clinical Hypnosis, Dallas, Texas, November, 1983. **191**

LEBARON, S., and ZELTZER, L. (in press) Assessment of acute pain and anxiety in children and adolescents by self-reports, observer reports, and a behavior checklist. *Journal of Consulting and Clinical Psychology.* **19, 54, 56**

LEBARON, S., and ZELTZER, L. (in press) Behavioral intervention for reducing chemotherapy-related nausea and vomiting in adolescents with cancer. *Journal of Adolescent Health Care.* **96**

LONDON, P. (1962) *The Children's Hypnotic Susceptibility Scale.* Palo Alto, California: Consulting Psychologists Press. **199**

LONDON, P., and COOPER, L. M. (1969) Norms of hypnotic susceptibility in children. *Developmental Psychology, 1:* 113–124. **199**

LORCH, E. P., ANDERSON, D. R., and LEVIN, S. R. (1979) The relationship between visual attention and children's comprehension of television. *Child Development, 50:* 722–727. **170**

MCGHEE, P. E. (1974) Development of children's ability to create the joking relationship. *Child Development, 45:* 552–556. **178**

MCGHEE, P. E. (1979) *Humor: Its origin and development.* San Francisco: W. H. Freeman and Company. **179**

MCGLASHAN, T. H., EVANS, F. J., and ORNE, M. T. (1969) The nature of hypnotic analgesia and placebo response to experimental pain. *Psychosomatic Medicine, 31:* 227–246. **219**

MCGUIRE, L., and DIZARD, S. (1982) Managing pain in the young patient. *Nursing, 82:* 52–55. **137**

MCILWRAITH, R. D., and SCHALLOW, J. R. (1983) Television viewing and styles of children's fantasy. *Imagination Cognition and Personality, 2:* 323–331. **142**

MEAD, G. H. (1934) *Mind, self, and society.* Edited by C. W. Morris. Chicago: University of Chicago Press. **159**

MELZACK, R. (1973) *The puzzle of pain.* New York: Basic Books. **217**

MISCHEL, H. N., and MISCHEL, W. (1983) The development of children's knowledge of self-control strategies. *Child Development, 54:* 603–619. **213**

MORGAN, A. H. (1973) The heritability of hypnotic susceptibility in twins. *Journal of Abnormal Psychology, 82:* 55–61. **11, 203**

MORGAN, A. H., and HILGARD, E. R. (1973) Age differences in susceptibility to hypnosis. *International Journal of Clinical and Experimental Hypnosis, 21:* 78–85. **10, 192**

MORGAN, A. H., HILGARD, E. R., and DAVERT, E. C. (1970) The heritability of hypnotic susceptibility of twins: A preliminary report. *Behavior Genetics, 1:* 213–224. **11**

MORGAN, A. H., and HILGARD, J. R. (1978/79) The Stanford Hypnotic Clinical Scale for Adults. *American Journal of Clinical Hypnosis, 21:* 134–147. **49, 88, 199, 207**

MORGAN, A. H., and HILGARD, J. R. (1978/79) The Stanford Hypnotic Clinical Scale for Children. *American Journal of Clinical Hypnosis, 21:* 148–169. **10, 36, 49, 50, 148, 152, 168**

MORGAN, A. H., JOHNSON, D. L., and HILGARD, E. R. (1974) The stability of hypnotic susceptibility: A longitudinal study. *International Journal of Clinical and Experimental Hypnosis, 22:* 249–257. **11**

MYERS, S. A. (1983) The Creative Imagination Scale: Group norms for children and adolescents. *International Journal of Clinical and Experimental Hypnosis, 31:* 28–36. **148**

NEISSER, U., and BECKLEN, R. (1975) Selective looking: Attending to visually-specified events. *Cognitive Psychology, 7:* 480–494. **161**

NOGRADY, H., McCONKEY, K. M., LAURENCE, J. R., and PERRY, C. (1983) Dissociation, duality, and demand characteristics in hypnosis. *Journal of Abnormal Psychology, 92:* 223–235. **163, 198**

OLNESS, K. (1976) Auto-hypnosis in functional megacolon in children. *The American Journal of Clinical Hypnosis, 19:* 28–32. **211**

OLNESS, K. (1981) Imagery (self hypnosis) as adjunct therapy in childhood cancer: Clinical experience with 25 patients. *Journal of Pediatric Hematology/Oncology, 3:* 313–321. **24**

OLNESS, K., and GARDNER, G. G. (1978) Some guidelines for uses of hypnotherapy in pediatrics. *Pediatrics, 62:* 228–233. **211**

ORNE, M. T. (1980) Assessment of biofeedback therapy: Specific versus nonspecific effects. Report of the Task Force on Biofeedback of the American Psychiatric Association. Washington, D.C.: American Psychiatric Association. **227**

ORNE, M. T. (1983) Hypnotic methods for managing pain. In J. J. Bonica and others (eds.) *Advances in pain research and therapy.* New York: Raven Press. **211, 214**

ORNE, M. T., and O'CONNELL, D. N. (1967) Diagnostic ratings of hypnotizability. *International Journal of Clinical and Experimental Hypnosis, 15:* 125–133. **22**

PACKARD, E. (1981) *Who Killed Harlowe Thrombey?* New York: Bantam Books. **141**

PERRY, C., and LAURENCE, J.-R. (1980) Hilgard's "hidden observer" phenomenon: Some confirming data. In M. Pajntar, E. Roskar, and M. Lavric (eds.) *Hypnosis in psychotherapy and psychosomatic medicine.* Ljubjana, Yugoslavia: University Press. **163**

PIAGET, J. (1962) *Play, dreams, and imitation in childhood.* New York: Norton. **172, 177**

PINDERHUGHES, E. E., and ZIGLER, E. (1983) Cognitive and motivational determinants and children's humor responses. Unpublished manuscript. **179**

PRIBRAM, K. H. (1976) Self-consciousness and intentionality. In G. E. Schwartz and D. Shapiro (eds.) *Consciousness and self-regulation: Advances in research,* vol. 1. New York: Plenum Press. **227**

PRINCE, M. (1906) *The dissociation of a personality.* New York: Longmans, Green. **160**

PULAKSI, M. A. (1973) Toys and imaginative play. In J. L. Singer (ed.) *The child's world of make-believe: Experimental studies of imaginative play.* New York: Academic Press. **187**

RAWLINGS, R. M. (1972) The inheritance of hypnotic amnesia. Paper presented at the 44th Congress of the Australian and New Zealand Society for the Advancement of Science (ANZSAS), July, 1972. **202**

REEVES, J. L., REDD, W. H., STORM, F. K., and MINAGAWA, R. Y. (1983) Hypnosis in the control of pain during hyperthermia treatment of cancer. In J. Bonica et al (eds.) *Advances in pain research and therapy.* New York: Raven Press. **209**

REYHER, J., and WILSON, J. G. (1973) The induction of hypnosis: Indirect vs direct methods and the role of anxiety. *American Journal of Clinical Hypnosis, 15:* 229–233. **208**

ROSENFELD, E., HUESMANN, L. R., ERON, L. D., and TORNEY-PURTA, J. V. (1982) Measuring patterns of fantasy behavior in children. *Journal of Personality and Social Psychology, 42:* 347–366. **175**

ROSS, D. M., and ROSS, S. A. (1984) The importance of type of question, psychological climate, and subject set in interviewing children about pain. *Pain, 19:* 71–79. **18**

ROSS, D. M., and ROSS, S. A. (in press, 1984) Teaching the child with leukemia to cope with teasing. *Issues in Comprehensive Nursing.* **136**

ROSSI, E. L. (ed.) (1980) *The collected papers of Milton H. Erickson on Hypnosis. 4 vols.* New York: Irvington Publishers, Inc. Halstead Press Division of John Wiley and Sons, Inc. **160**

RUCH, J. C., and MORGAN, A. H. (1971) Subject posture and hypnotic susceptibility: A comparison of standing, sitting, and lying-down subjects. *International Journal of Clinical and Experimental Hypnosis, 19:* 100–108. **149**

SACERDOTE, P. (1962) The place of hypnosis in the relief of severe protracted pain. *American Journal of Clinical Hypnosis, 4:* 150–157. **215**

SACERDOTE, P. (1970) Theory and practice of pain control in malignancy and other protracted or recurring painful illnesses. *International Journal of Clinical and Experimental Hypnosis, 18:* 160–180. **215**

SARBIN, T. R. (1950) Contributions to role-taking theory: I. Hypnotic behavior. *Psychological Review, 57:* 255–270. **159**

SARBIN, T. R., and ALLEN, V. L. (1968) Role theory. In G. Lindzey and E. Aronson (eds.) *Handbook of social psychology,* 2nd ed., vol. 1. Reading, Massachusetts: Addison-Wesley. **159**

SARBIN, T. R., and COE, W. C. (1972) *Hypnosis: A social psychological analysis of influence communication.* New York: Holt, Rinehart and Winston. **159**

Schafer, D. W. (1975) Hypnosis on a burn unit. *International Journal of Clinical and Experimental Hypnosis, 23:* 1–14. **21**

Schultz, N. V. (1971) How children perceive pain. *Nursing Outlook, 19:* 670–673. **135, 213**

Sears, R. R., Maccoby, E. E., and Levin, H. (1957) *Patterns of child rearing.* Evanston, Illinois: Row, Peterson and Company. **173**

Shor, R. E., Orne, M. T., and O'Connell, D. N. (1966) Psychological correlates of plateau hypnotizability in a special volunteer sample. *Journal of Personality and Social Psychology, 3:* 80–95. **206**

Sidis, B. (ed.) (1902) *Psychopathological researches: Studies in mental dissociation.* New York: Stechert. **160**

Siegel, E. F. (1979) Control of phantom limb pain by hypnosis. *American Journal of Clinical Hypnosis, 21:* 285–286. **90**

Singer, D. G., Singer, J. L., and Zuckerman, D. M. (1981) *Teaching television: How to use TV to your child's advantage.* New York: The Dial Press. **141**

Singer, J. L. (1973) *The child's world of make-believe: Experimental studies of imaginative play.* New York: Academic Press. **174, 175, 187**

Solomon, G. F., and Schmidt, K. M. (1978) A burning issue: Phantom limb pain and psychological preparation of the patient for amputation. *Archives of Surgery, 113:* 185–186. **217**

Sontag, L. W., Baker, C. T., and Nelson, V. L. (1958) Mental growth and development: A longitudinal study. *Monographs of the Society of Research in Child Development, 23:* Serial no. 68. **203**

Spiegel, H. (1970) A single-treatment method to stop smoking using ancillary self-hypnosis. *International Journal of Clinical and Experimental Hypnosis, 18:* 235–250. **210**

Spiegel, H., and Spiegel, D. (1978) *Trance and treatment: Clinical uses of hypnosis.* New York: Basic Books. **200**

Stern, J. A., Brown, M., Ulett, G. A., and Sletten, I. (1977) A comparison of hypnosis, acupuncture, morphine, Valium, aspirin, and placebo in the management of experimentally induced pain. In W. E. Edmonston, Jr. (ed.) *Conceptual and investigative approaches to hypnosis and hypnotic phenomena.* Annals of the New York Academy of Sciences, Vol. 296. New York: The New York Academy of Sciences. **19, 219**

Tellegen, A. (1978/79) On measures and conceptions of hypnosis. *American Journal of Clinical Hypnosis, 21:* 219–237. **153**

Tellegen, A. (1981) Practicing the two disciplines for relaxation and enlightenment: Comment on "Role of the feedback signal in electromyograph biofeedback: The relevance of attention" by Qualls and Sheehan. *Journal of Experimental Psychology: General, 110:* 217–226. **155**

Tesler, M. D., Wegner, C., Savedra, M., Gibbons, P. T., and Ward, J. A. (1981) Coping strategies of children in pain. *Issues in Comprehensive Nursing, 5:* 351–359. **137**

THOMAS, L. (1983) *The youngest science: Notes of a medicine-watcher.* New York: The Viking Press. **134, 138**

TOMKINS, S. S. (1979) Script theory: Differential magnification of affects. *Nebraska Symposium on Motivation,* vol. 26. Lincoln: University of Nebraska Press. **154**

TURNER, J. A. and CHAPMAN, C. R. (1982) Psychological interventions for chronic pain: A critical review: II. Operant conditioning, hypnosis, and cognitive-behavioral therapy. *Pain, 12:* 23–46. **215, 226**

TWYCROSS, R. G. (1983) Narcotic analgesics in clinical practice. In J. J. Bonica, U. Lindblom, and A. Iggo (eds.) *Advances in pain research and therapy,* vol. 5. New York: Raven Press. **138**

WADDEN, T. A., and ANDERTON, C. H. (1982) The clinical use of hypnosis. *Psychological Bulletin, 91:* 215–243. **157**

WAKEMAN, R. J., and KAPLAN, J. Z. (1978) An experimental study of hypnosis in painful burns. *American Journal of Clinical Hypnosis, 21:* 3–12. **22**

WATKINS, J. G., and WATKINS, H. H. (1979/1980) Ego states and hidden observers. *Journal of Altered States of Consciousness, 5:* 3–18. **166**

WEITZENHOFFER, A. M., and HILGARD, E. R. (1959) *Stanford Hypnotic Susceptibility Scale, Forms A and B.* Palo Alto, California: Consulting Psychologists Press. **10, 156, 199**

WEITZENHOFFER, A. M., and HILGARD, E. R. (1962) *Stanford Hypnotic Susceptibility Scale, Form C.* Palo Alto, California: Consulting Psychologists Press. **199**

WEITZENHOFFER, A. M., and HILGARD, E. R. (1963) *Stanford Profile Scales of Hypnotic Susceptibility, Forms I and II.* Palo Alto, California: Consulting Psychologists Press. **148**

WILBUR, J. R., and DUTCHER, J. (1972) Childhood cancer—A philosophy of therapy. *The Cancer Bulletin, 24:* 1–4. **16**

WILSON, S. C., and BARBER, T. X. (1978) The Creative Imagination Scale as a measure of hypnotic responsiveness: Applications to experimental and clinical hypnosis. *American Journal of Clinical Hypnosis, 20:* 235–249. **148, 150, 151**

WILSON, S. C., and BARBER, T. X. (1983) The fantasy-prone personality: Implications for understanding imagery, hypnosis, and parapsychological phenomena. In A. A. Sheikh (ed.) *Imagery, current theory, research, and application.* New York: John Wiley and Sons, Inc. **160**

WOLBERG, L. R. (1964) *Hypnoanalysis.* New York: Grune and Stratton. **210**

WOLFENSTEIN, M. (1954) *Children's humor.* Glencoe, Illinois: Free Press. **179**

YATES, A. J. (1980) *Biofeedback and the modification of behavior.* New York and London: Plenum Press. **227**

ZELTZER, L. (1980) The adolescent with cancer. In J. Kellerman (ed.) *Psychological aspects of childhood cancer.* Springfield, Illinois: Charles Thomas. **24, 96**

ZELTZER, L., DASH, J., and HOLLAND, J. P. (1979) Hypnotically-induced pain control in sickle cell anemia. *Pediatrics, 64:* 533–536. **22**

ZELTZER, L., KELLERMAN, J., ELLENBERG, L., DASH, J., and RIGLER, D. (1980) Psychological effects of illness in adolescence. II. Impact of illness in adolescents—crucial issues and coping styles. *Journal of Pediatrics, 97:*(1), 132–138. **43**

ZELTZER, L., KELLERMAN, J., ELLENBERG, L., and DASH, J. (1983) Hypnosis for reduction of vomiting associated with chemotherapy and disease in adolescents with cancer. *Journal of Adolescent Health Care, 4:* 82–89. **96**

ZELTZER, L., and LeBARON, S. (1982) Hypnotic and nonhypnotic techniques for reduction of pain and anxiety during painful procedures in children and adolescents with cancer. *Journal of Pediatrics, 101:* 1032–1035. **21, 45, 51, 52, 92, 219**

ZELTZER, L., and LeBARON, S. (1984) Effects of the mechanics of administration on Doxorubicin induced side effects: A case report. *American Journal of Pediatric Hematology/Oncology, 6:*(1), 107–110. **97**

ZELTZER, L., and LeBARON, S. (1984) Coping with childhood illness: The adolescent with cancer. In R. W. Blum (ed.) *The disabled and chronically ill adolescent.* New York: Grune and Stratton. **52, 138**

ZELTZER, L., LeBARON, S. and ZELTZER, P. M. (1982) Hypnotic and nonhypnotic techniques for reduction of distress in children with cancer. Paper presented at the Ninth International Congress of Hypnosis and Psychosomatic Medicine, Glasgow, Scotland, August, 1982. **52**

ZELTZER, L., LeBARON, S., and ZELTZER, P. M. (1984) A prospective assessment of chemotherapy-related nausea and vomiting in children with cancer. *American Journal of Pediatric Hematology/Oncology, 6:*(1), 25–37. **97**

ZELTZER, L., LeBARON, S., and ZELTZER, P. M. (in press) The effectiveness of behavioral intervention for reduction of nausea and vomiting in children and adolescents receiving chemotherapy. *Journal of Clinical Oncology.* **97**

ZELTZER, L., ZELTZER, P. M., and LeBARON, S. (1983) Cancer in adolescence In M. S. Smith (ed.) *Chronic disorders in adolescence.* Littleton, Massachusetts: John Wright, PSG, Inc. **103, 134, 138**

ZIGLER, E., LEVINE, J., and GOULD, L. (1967) Cognitive challenge as a factor in children's humor appreciation. *Journal of Personality and Social Psychology, 6:* 332–336. **179**

Subject Index